CW01034197

Bayesian Statistics for the Social Sciences

Methodology in the Social Sciences

David A. Kenny, Founding Editor
Todd D. Little, Series Editor
www.guilford.com/MSS

This series provides applied researchers and students with analysis and research design books that emphasize the use of methods to answer research questions. Rather than emphasizing statistical theory, each volume in the series illustrates when a technique should (and should not) be used and how the output from available software programs should (and should not) be interpreted. Common pitfalls as well as areas of further development are clearly articulated.

RECENT VOLUMES

APPLIED MISSING DATA ANALYSIS
Craig K. Enders

PRINCIPLES AND PRACTICE OF STRUCTURAL EQUATION MODELING, THIRD EDITION
Rex B. Kline

APPLIED META-ANALYSIS FOR SOCIAL SCIENCE RESEARCH
Noel A. Card

DATA ANALYSIS WITH Mplus
Christian Geiser

INTENSIVE LONGITUDINAL METHODS: AN INTRODUCTION TO DIARY AND EXPERIENCE SAMPLING RESEARCH
Niall Bolger and Jean-Philippe Laurenceau

DOING STATISTICAL MEDIATION AND MODERATION
Paul E. Jose

LONGITUDINAL STRUCTURAL EQUATION MODELING
Todd D. Little

INTRODUCTION TO MEDIATION, MODERATION, AND CONDITIONAL PROCESS ANALYSIS: A REGRESSION-BASED APPROACH
Andrew F. Hayes

BAYESIAN STATISTICS FOR THE SOCIAL SCIENCES
David Kaplan

Bayesian Statistics for the Social Sciences

David Kaplan

Series Editor's Note by Todd D. Little

THE GUILFORD PRESS
New York   London

© 2014 The Guilford Press
A Division of Guilford Publications, Inc.
72 Spring Street, New York, NY 10012
www.guilford.com

Printed in the United States of America

This book is printed on acid-free paper.

Last digit is print number: 9   8   7   6   5   4   3   2   1

Library of Congress Cataloging-in-Publication Data

Kaplan, David, 1955–
  Bayesian statistics for the social sciences / David Kaplan.
    pages cm. — (Methodology in the social sciences)
  Includes bibliographical references and index.
  ISBN 978-1-4625-1651-3 (hardback)
  1. Social sciences—Statistical methods. 2. Bayesian statistical decision
theory. I. Title.
  HA29.K344 2014
  519.5'42—dc23   2014017208

To Sam, who taught me that babies are Bayesians

Series Editor's Note

I have known David Kaplan for a number of years now. We are both members of the Society of Multivariate Experimental Psychology and the American Psychological Association; we also served together on an Institute of Education Sciences standing review panel and overlapped as Associate Editors for *Multivariate Behavioral Research.* He and one of his students also contributed a terrific chapter to one of the handbooks that I edited. When I see him at the annual conferences of these societies or at panel meetings, he is regularly engaged in deep intellectual discussions with others in attendance because they seek him out for his guidance and input on their own research. I have benefited from his scholarly acumen in this manner a number of times. Given my admiration and respect for him, when David first mentioned that he would like to contribute a book to the Guilford series Methodology in the Social Sciences, I was elated. When he mentioned that the book would be about Bayesian procedures, I was even happier. When he mentioned that he would use the R software platform for all of his working examples, I reached the peak of elation.

David Kaplan is in a very elite class of scholar. He is a methodological innovator who is guiding and changing the way that researchers conduct their research and analyze their data. He is also a distinguished educational researcher whose work shapes educational policy and practice. I see David's book as a reflection of his sophistication as both a researcher and a statistician; it shows depth of understanding that even dedicated quantitative specialists may not have and, in my view, it will have an enduring impact on research practice. David's research profile and research skills are renowned internationally and his reputation is globally recognized. His profile as a prominent power player in the field brings instant credibility. As a result, when David says Bayesian is the way to go, researchers listen. Now his book brings his voice to you in an engaging and highly serviceable manner.

Why is the Bayesian approach to statistics seeing a resurgence across the social and behavioral sciences? (It's an approach that has been around for some time.) One reason for the delay in adopting Bayes is technological. Bayesian estimation can be computer intensive and until about a score of years ago the computational demands limited its widespread application. Another reason is that the social and behavioral sciences needed an accessible translation of Bayes for these fields so that we could understand not only the benefits of Bayes but also how to apply a Bayesian approach. David is clear and practical in his presentation and shares with us his experiences and helpful and pragmatic recommendations. I think the Bayesian perspective will see a spirited adoption now that David has penned this indispensable resource. In many ways, the zeitgeist for Bayes is favorable—because researchers are asking and attempting to answer complex questions.

The blind empiricism of frequentist thinking is giving way to a modeling perspective. Complex theoretical models abound in social science research. Such models are most informative if the modeler has a strong theory and good data. Some analysts will argue that data should not get in the way of good theory and others will argue to never let theory get in the way of good data. Neither position, however, will yield useful and generalizable findings. An informed dialogue with data—the heart of the Bayesian perspective—is essential for good data models. The theory that drives the modeling endeavor derives from the modeler's intuitions, born from experience and informed by the extant literature. These intuitions are coupled with an informed understanding of the utilized design and the acquired measures. These critical ingredients are carefully mixed to specify a Bayesian statistical model grounded in prior knowledge and insights. The model is then estimated against the data and the conversation thereby begins. As an iterative process, finalizing a statistical model is a process of commensuration. Model modifications must balance improvement in model fit and estimation precision with the verisimilitude of any model changes. Model modifications are statements of theory that emerge when the modeler has carefully balanced errors of the type I and II variety. The modifications must be reconciled in the context of the larger model and the broader literature. Blind allegiance to theory or unequivocal adherence to data—hallmarks of traditionally trained researchers—will not deliver useful knowledge. Optimal gains in knowledge can only occur when we engage in an informed dialogue with data.

TODD D. LITTLE
Atlanta's Hartsfield–Jackson International Airport

Preface

Bayesian statistics has long been overlooked in the quantitative methods training of social scientists. Typically, the only introduction that a student might have to Bayesian ideas is a brief overview of Bayes' theorem while studying probability in an introductory statistics class. This is not surprising. First, until recently, it was not feasible to conduct statistical modeling from a Bayesian perspective owing to its complexity and the lack of available software. Second, Bayesian statistics represents a powerful alternative to frequentist (classical) statistics, and is, therefore, controversial.[1]

Recently, however, there has been a renaissance in the developments and application of Bayesian statistical methods, due mostly to the availability of powerful statistical software tools. As a result, scores of books have been written over the last 10 years and at a variety of levels that lead the reader through Bayesian theory and computation. The goal of this book is to introduce practicing social scientists to the Bayesian perspective via methodologies commonly used in the social sciences. Thus, this book is written for social scientists who are well trained in statistical modeling within the frequentist paradigm and are interested in exploring commonly used methodologies from the Bayesian perspective. In addition, this book is written for graduate students in the social sciences who wish to have an accessible entrée into Bayesian statistics.

---

[1] I use the term *frequentist* to describe the paradigm of statistics commonly used today; it represents the counterpart to the Bayesian paradigm of statistics. Historically, however, Bayesian statistics predates frequentist statistics by about 150 years.

I do not presume that the reader has had any exposure to Bayesian statistics, and I develop the arguments in favor of the Bayesian approach from first principles. That said, it is assumed that the reader does have a good background in applied statistics—including a good command of frequentist hypothesis testing, as well as a background in applied statistical modeling, preferably including courses in regression analysis, analysis of variance, and at least some exposure to multilevel modeling and structural equation modeling. Some background in elementary calculus is useful, but I make every attempt to explain equations thoroughly. Derivations are relegated to appendices unless needed to reinforce conceptual understanding.

The book is organized into three parts. Part I covers the foundations of Bayesian statistics. Chapter 1 provides an introduction to frequentist versus Bayesian probability and introduces Bayes' theorem. Chapter 2 introduces the elements of Bayesian statistical inference, including the concept of exchangeability, likelihood, prior and posterior distributions, and the Bayesian central limit theorem. Chapter 3 introduces some important distributions used in the social sciences. For each distribution, I indicate how it is used in practice and provide its conjugate prior distribution for use in Bayesian analysis. Chapter 4 introduces the method of Markov chain Monte Carlo estimation.

Part II introduces Bayesian model building and Bayesian general and generalized linear modeling. Chapter 5 discusses the topic of Bayesian hypothesis testing and model building, highlighting the fundamental differences between the Bayesian approach and the frequentist approach. Chapter 6 discusses Bayesian linear regression analysis and introduces extensions to Bayesian generalized linear modeling—particularly focusing on Bayesian logistic regression. Chapter 7 ends Part II with a discussion of missing data problems from a Bayesian context.

Part III extends Bayesian statistics to advanced, but popular, methodologies in the social sciences. Chapter 8 discusses Bayesian approaches for multilevel modeling. Chapter 9 examines Bayesian models for continuous and categorical latent variables—focusing on confirmatory factor analysis, structural equation modeling, growth curve modeling, and growth mixture modeling.

As the outline of the book suggests, my aim is to cover Bayesian approaches to the main methodologies that are currently used in the social sciences. Moreover, to support the pedagogical features of this book, the data and software code for each example are available on the book's website (*http://bise.wceruw.org/publications.html*). However, I don't believe that a book on Bayesian statistical inference would be complete without a discussion of the philosophical issues that underlie Bayesian methodologies. Therefore, Chapter 10 covers the main philosophical underpinnings of Bayesian statistical inference, and in particular the theory of subjective probability as a framework for addressing problems of uncertainty and the growth of knowledge in science. I draw on the seminal writings of de Finetti, Lindley, Savage, Jeffreys, Jaynes, Berger, and Bernardo, and I contrast the framework of subjective Bayesian statistics with that of objective Bayesian statistics.

DATA AND SOFTWARE

The examples provided throughout this book utilize data from large-scale educational surveys. Particular focus is on analyses using data from the Program for International Student Assessment sponsored by the Organisation for Economic Co-operation and Development. For analysis of longitudinal data in Chapter 9, I utilize data from the Longitudinal Study of American Youth (Miller, Hoffer, Sucher, Brown, & Nelson, 1992).

This book relies entirely on statistical programs available via the R statistical programming environment (R Development Core Team, 2012). My reason for focusing on R is twofold. First, R is the lingua franca of statistical computing, and thus it is important to demonstrate its power for statistical computing in a Bayesian context. Second, R is an open-source software program, and, as such, the software code is available for inspection, modification, and new dissemination. However, it is not the purpose of this book to introduce the reader to the R programming environment, nor will I provide new R programs specific to the examples in this book. Rather, I draw on a set of programs for Bayesian analysis already available in the Comprehensive R Archive Network (CRAN; R Development Core Team, 2012), which I have found to be particularly flexible and useful. Specifically, many of the examples in this book will rely on programs within the R package "MCMCpack" (A. D. Martin, Quinn, & Park, 2010). Bayesian computation diagnostics make use of the R package "coda" (Plummer, Best, Cowles, & Vines, 2006), and Bayesian model averaging makes use of the R package "BMA" (Raftery, Hoeting, Volinsky, Painter, & Yeung, 2009). Some examples in this book utilize the R interface with the "JAGS" software program (Plummer, 2003) referred to as "rjags" (Plummer, 2011), which closely resembles "WinBUGS" (Spiegelhalter, Thomas, Best, & Lunn, 2003). In this way, the reader does not have to master the R language and can easily adapt the example programs to fit individual needs.

The programs that I have chosen in this book are not exhaustive of the scores of programs available on the CRAN and should not be taken as a specific endorsement of these programs over any others. A perusal of the Bayesian section of the CRAN Task View page (*http://cran. open-source-solution.org/web/views/Bayesian.html*) provides the reader with a detailed list of Bayesian programs available on the CRAN. Finally, all R programs used in this book are made available in chapter appendices and also on the book's website.

Acknowledgments

I am indebted to Jianshen Chen and Soojin Park, my two outstanding doctoral students, for assisting in the data analyses and graphics that appear in this book. Without question, it would have been difficult to complete this book in a reasonable period of time without their assistance. I also wish to especially thank Fabrizzio Sanchez for coming on late to this project but still providing expert R programming support.

I would like to thank my colleagues Daniel Bolt and Jee-Seon Kim, along with the reviewers who were initially anonymous: Feifei Ye, Department of Psychology in Education, University of Pittsburgh; Jay Myung, Department of Psychology, Ohio State University; Jim Albert, Department of Mathematics and Statistics, Bowling Green State University; John J. McArdle, Department of Psychology, University of Southern California; and David Rindskopf, Department of Educational Psychology, City University of New York. All of these scholars' comments have greatly improved the quality and accessibility of the book. Of course, any errors of commission or omission are strictly my responsibility.

I am forever grateful to C. Deborah Laughton, my editor at The Guilford Press, who has been a constant source of encouragement, support, and friendship throughout the development of this book and well beyond. Her professionalism is without peer, and one could not ask for a better editor.

The development of this book was supported in part by a Kellett Mid-Career Award from the University of Wisconsin–Madison and by the Institute of Education Sciences, U.S. Department of Education, through Grant No. R305D110001 to the University of Wisconsin–Madison. The opinions expressed are my own and do not necessarily represent the views of the Institute or the U.S. Department of Education.

Finally, as always, this book would not be possible without the love and support of my family—Allison, Rebekah, Hannah, my son-in-law, Joshua, and my grandson, Sam, to whom this book is dedicated.

Contents

The data and software code for the book's examples
are available on the companion website
http://bise.wceruw.org/publications.html.

Part I

Foundations of Bayesian Statistics

1

Probability Concepts and Bayes' Theorem

1.1 RELEVANT PROBABILITY AXIOMS

Most students in the social sciences were introduced to the axioms of probability by studying the properties of the coin toss or the dice roll. These studies address questions such as (1) What is the probability that the flip of a fair coin will return heads? and (2) What is the probability that the roll of two fair die will return a value of 7? To answer these questions requires enumerating the possible outcomes and then counting the number of times the event could occur. The probabilities of interest are obtained by dividing the number of times the event occurred by the number of possible outcomes.

But what about more complex situations such as the famous "Monty Hall" problem? In this problem, named after the host of a popular old television game show, a contestant is shown three doors, one of which has a desirable prize, while the other two have undesirable prizes. The contestant picks a door, but before Monty opens the door, he shows the contestant another door with an undesirable prize and asks the contestant whether she wants to stay with the chosen door or switch. To address this situation requires an understanding of the axioms of probability. Indeed, many axiomatic systems for probability have relevance to epistemology as well as statistical practice. In this chapter we consider (1) probability as long-run frequency, (2) the Kolmogorov axioms of probability (Kolmogorov, 1956), (3) the Rényi axioms of conditional probability (Rényi, 1970), (4) Bayes' theorem, and (5) epistemic probability. Treating probability as a representation of epistemic knowledge along with the Rényi axioms of conditional probability provides the theoretical foundation for Bayes' theorem. It is not the goal of this chapter to engage the debate between the Bayesian and frequentist schools of statistics directly. More will be said about the epistemological difference between these schools in Chapter 10.

1.1.1 Probability as Long-Run Frequency

Probability is often considered synonymous with long-run frequency. This view of probability underlies what we have been calling the frequentist (or classical) school of statistics. The canonical example of probability *qua* frequency concerns the dice roll. In this case the number of possible outcomes of one roll of a fair die is 6. If we wish to calculate the probability of rolling a 2, then we simply obtain the ratio of the number of favorable outcomes (here there is only one favorable outcome) to the total possible number of outcomes (here 6). Thus, the frequentist probability is $\frac{1}{6} = .17$.

A key characteristic of probability as long-run frequency concerns the conceptual idea of the "long run." That is, the frequentist probability of rolling a 2 is purely theoretical insofar as the die might not be truly fair and the conditions of the toss might vary from trial to trial. Thus, the frequentist probability of .17, in this case, relates to the relative frequency of rolling a 2 in a very large (indeed infinite) number of dice rolls. We will consider the implications of long-run frequency for epistemology and statistical practice in more detail in Chapter 10 when we discuss philosophical issues relevant to Bayesian statistical inference.

1.1.2 The Kolmogorov Axioms of Probability

Before introducing Bayes' theorem, it is useful to remind ourselves of the axioms of probability that have formed the basis of frequentist statistics. These axioms of probability can be attributed to the work of Kolmogorov (1956). This particular set of axioms relates the notion of probability to the frequency of events over a large number of trials and forms the basis of the frequentist paradigm of statistics.

Consider two events denoted A and B. To keep the example simple, consider these both to be the flip of a fair coin. Then the following are the axioms of probability—namely

1. $p(A) \geq 0$

2. The probability of the sample space is 1.0.

3. Countable additivity: If A and B are mutually exclusive, then $p(A \text{ or } B) \equiv p(A \cup B) = p(A) + p(B)$. Or, more generally,

$$p\left\{\bigcup_{j=1}^{\infty} A_j\right\} = \sum_{j=1}^{\infty} p(A_j) \tag{1.1}$$

which states that the probability of the union of mutually exclusive events is simply the sum of their individual probabilities.

A number of other axioms of probability can be derived from these three basic axioms. Nevertheless, these three can be used to deal with the relatively easy case of the coin flipping example mentioned above. For example, if we toss a fair coin an infinite number of times, we expect it to land heads 50% of the time.[1] This probability, and others like it, satisfy the first axiom that probabilities are greater than or equal to 0. The second axiom states that over an infinite number of coin flips, the sum of all possible outcomes (in this case, heads and tails) is equal to 1. Indeed, the number of possible outcomes represents the *sample space*, and the sum of probabilities over the sample space is 1. Finally, with regard to the third axiom, assuming that one outcome precludes the occurrence of another outcome (e.g., the coin landing heads precludes the occurrence of the coin landing tails), then the probability of the joint event $p(A \cup B)$ is the sum of the separate probabilities—that is, $p(A \cup B) = p(A) + p(B)$. We may wish to add to these axioms the notion of *independent events*. If two events are independent, then the occurrence of one event does not influence the probability of another event. For example, with two coins A and B, the probability of A resulting in "heads" does not influence the result of a flip of B. Formally, we define independence as $p(A \text{ and } B) \equiv p(A \cap B) = p(A)p(B)$.

---

[1] Interestingly, this expectation is not based on having actually tossed the coin an infinite number of times. Rather, this expectation is a prior belief. Arguably, this is one example of how Bayesian thinking is automatically embedded in frequentist logic.

1.1.3 The Rényi Axioms of Probability

In the previous paragraph, we discussed quite simple cases—in particular, the case of independent events. However, the Kolmogorov axioms do not take into account how probabilities might be affected by conditioning on the dependency of events. An extension of the Kolmogorov system that accounts for conditioning was put forth by Rényi (1970). As a motivating example, consider the case of observing the presence or absence of lung cancer (C) and the behavior of smoking or not smoking (S). We may be able to argue on the basis of prior experience and medical research that C is not independent of S—that is, the joint probability $p(C \cap S) \neq p(C)p(S)$. To handle this problem, we define the *conditional probability* of C "given" S (i.e., $p(C|S)$) as

$$p(C|S) = \frac{p(C \cap S)}{p(S)} \tag{1.2}$$

The denominator on the right-hand side of Equation 1.2 shows that the sample space associated with $p(C \cap S)$ is reduced by knowing S. Notice that if C and S were independent, then

$$p(C|S) = \frac{p(C \cap S)}{p(S)}$$

$$= \frac{p(C)p(S)}{p(S)}$$

$$= p(C) \tag{1.3}$$

which states that knowing S tells us nothing about C.

Following Press (2003), Rényi's axioms can be defined with respect to our lung cancer example. Let G stand for genetic history of cancer. Then,

1. For any events C, S we have $p(C|S) \geq 0$ and $p(C|C) = 1$.

2. For disjoint events C_j and some event S,

$$p\left\{ \bigcup_{j=1}^{\infty} C_j | S \right\} = \sum_{j=1}^{\infty} p(C_j|S)$$

3. For every collection of events (C, S, G), with S a subset of G (i.e., $S \subseteq G$) and $0 < p(S|G)$, we have

$$p(C|S) = \frac{p(C \cap S|G)}{p(S|G)}$$

Rényi's third axiom allows one to obtain the conditional probability of C given S, while conditioning on yet a third variable G, for obtaining the conditional probability of lung cancer given observed smoking, while in turn conditioning on whether there is a genetic history of cancer.

1.1.4 Bayes' Theorem

An interesting feature of Equation 1.2 sets the axiomatic foundation for Bayes' theorem. Specifically, joint probabilities are symmetric—namely, $p(C \cap S) = p(S \cap C)$. Therefore, we can also express the conditional probability of smoking, S, given the observation of lung cancer, C, as

$$p(S|C) = \frac{p(S \cap C)}{p(C)} \qquad (1.4)$$

Because of the symmetry of the joint probabilities, we obtain

$$p(C|S)p(S) = p(S|C)p(C) \qquad (1.5)$$

Therefore,

$$p(C|S) = \frac{p(S|C)p(C)}{p(S)} \qquad (1.6)$$

Equation 1.6 is *Bayes' theorem*, also referred to as the *inverse probability theorem*.[2] In words, Bayes' theorem states that the conditional probability of an individual having lung cancer given that the individual smokes is equal to the probability that the individual smokes given that he/she has lung cancer times the probability of having lung

---

[2]It is an interesting historical fact that the inverse probability theorem was actually developed by the mathematician Pierre-Simon Laplace (Stigler, 1988). What we now refer to as Bayesian probability should more accurately be referred to as *Laplacian probability*.

cancer. The denominator of Equation 1.6, $p(S)$, is the marginal probability of smoking. This can be considered the probability of smoking across individuals with and without lung cancer, which we write as $p(S) = p(S|C) + p(S|\neg C)$.[3] Because this marginal probability is obtained over all possible outcomes of observing lung cancer, it does not carry information relevant to the conditional probability. In fact, $p(S)$ can be considered a *normalizing factor*, ensuring that the probability sums to one. Thus, it is not uncommon to see Bayes' theorem written as

$$p(C|S) \propto p(S|C)p(C) \qquad (1.7)$$

Equation 1.7 states that the probability of observing lung cancer given smoking is proportional to the probability of smoking given observing lung cancer times the marginal probability of observing lung cancer.[4]

1.1.5 Epistemic Probability

A modification of the Kolmogorov axioms was advanced by de Finetti (1974), who suggested replacing the (infinite) countable additivity axiom with finite additivity and also treating $p(\cdot)$ as a *subjective* probability.[5] For de Finetti (1974), "only *subjective* probabilities exist—i.e. the *degree of belief* in the occurrence of an event attributed by a given person at a given instant with a given set of information" (pp. 4–5, emphasis in original). As noted in Press (2003), the first mention of probability as a degree of subjective belief was made by Ramsey (1926), and it is this notion of probability as subjective belief that led to considerable resistance to Bayesian ideas. A detailed treatment of the axioms of epistemic (subjective) probability can be found in Fishburn (1986).

Use of the term *subjective* is perhaps unfortunate, insofar as it promotes the idea of fuzzy, unscientific, reasoning. Lindley (2007) relates the same concern and prefers the term *personal probability* to *subjec-*

---

[3] The symbol $\neg$ denotes "not."

[4] It is interesting to note that Bayesian reasoning resolves the so-called base-rate fallacy—the tendency to equate $p(C|S)$ with $p(S|C)$. That is, without knowledge of the base-rate $p(C)$ (the prior probability) and the total amount of evidence in the observation $p(S)$, it is a fallacy to believe that $p(C|S) = p(S|C)$.

[5] A much more detailed set of axioms for subjective probability was advanced by Savage (1954)

tive probability. For this book, I prefer to follow Howson and Urbach (2006) in adopting the less controversial term *epistemic probability* to reflect our notion of probability as an individual expression of a greater or lesser degree of uncertainty about our knowledge of a particular problem at hand. More will be said about this issue in Chapter 10.

1.1.6 Coherence

How might we operationalize the notion of epistemic probability? The example most frequently used to illustrate epistemic probability is the bet. If an individual enters into a bet that does not satisfy Rényi's (1970) axioms of probability, then he/she is not being *coherent.* Press (2003) uses the example in which a person bets on two events, *A* and *B*. Let *A* be the person's belief that there is a 70% chance that the Chicago Cubs will go to the National League Championship Series and let *B* be the person's belief that there is a 50% chance that the Green Bay Packers will go to the Super Bowl. Moreover, assume that the same individual knows that these events are independent and further believes that there is a 10% chance of both events *A* and *B* occurring. If this individual has placed money on this bet, he/she is sure to lose regardless of the outcome. This is because

$$p(A \cap B) = p(A)p(B) = .35 \neq .10$$

Thus, placing such a bet is not coherent with the axioms of probability.[6]

EXAMPLE 1.1. THE MONTY HALL PROBLEM

Let's return to the Monty Hall problem in order to demonstrate the complexities of conditional probability and how a Bayesian perspective can be helpful. At the start of the game, it is assumed that there is one desirable prize and that the probability that the desirable prize is behind any of the three doors is $\frac{1}{3}$. Once a door is picked, Monty Hall shows the contestant a door with an undesirable prize and asks the contestant if she would like to switch from the door she originally chose. It is important to note that Monty will not show the contestant the door with

---

[6]This type of bet is referred to as a *Dutch book.*

the desirable prize. Also, we assume that because the remaining doors have undesirable prizes, which door Monty opens is basically random. Given that there are two doors remaining in this three-door problem, the probability is ½. Thus, Monty's knowledge of where the prize is located plays a crucial role in this problem. With the following information in hand, we can obtain the necessary probabilities to apply Bayes' theorem. Assume the contestant picks door A. Then, the necessary conditional probabilities are

1. p(Monty opens door B|prize is behind A) = ½

2. p(Monty opens door B|prize is behind B) = 0

3. p(Monty opens door B|prize is behind C) = 1

The final probability is due to the fact that there is only one door for Monty to choose given that the contestant chose door A and the prize is behind door B.

Let M represent Monty opening door B. Then, the joint probabilities can be obtained as follows.

$$p(M \cap A) = p(M|A)p(A) = \tfrac{1}{2} \times \tfrac{1}{3} = \tfrac{1}{6}$$

$$p(M \cap B) = p(M|B)p(B) = 0 \times \tfrac{1}{3} = 0$$

$$p(M \cap C) = p(M|C)p(C) = 1 \times \tfrac{1}{3} = \tfrac{1}{3}$$

Before applying Bayes' theorem, note that we have to obtain the marginal probability of Monty opening door B. This is

$$p(M) = p(M \cap A) + p(M \cap B) + p(M \cap C)$$

$$= \tfrac{1}{6} + 0 + \tfrac{1}{3} = \tfrac{1}{2}$$

Finally, we can now apply Bayes' theorem to obtain the probabilities of the prize lying behind door A or door C.

$$p(A|M) = \frac{p(M|A)p(A)}{p(M)} = \frac{\tfrac{1}{2} \times \tfrac{1}{3}}{\tfrac{1}{2}} = \tfrac{1}{3}$$

$$p(C|M) = \frac{p(M|C)p(C)}{p(M)} = 1 \times \frac{\tfrac{1}{3}}{\tfrac{1}{2}} = \tfrac{2}{3}$$

Thus, from Bayes' theorem, the contestant's best strategy is to switch doors.

1.2 SUMMARY

This chapter provided a brief historical introduction to probabilistic concepts relevant to Bayesian statistical inference. Although the notion of *epistemic* probability predates the frequentist conception of probability, it had not significantly impacted the practice of applied statistics until computational developments brought Bayesian inference back into the limelight. This chapter also highlighted the conceptual differences between the frequentist and epistemic notions of probability. The importance of understanding the differences between these two conceptions of probability is more than a philosophical exercise. Rather, their differences are manifest in the elements of the statistical machinery needed for advancing a Bayesian perspective for research in the social sciences. We discuss the statistical elements of Bayes' theorem in the following chapter.

1.3 SUGGESTED READINGS

de Finetti, B. (1974). *Theory of probability* (Vols. 1 and 2). New York: Wiley.
Howson, C., & Urbach, P. (2006). *Scientific reasoning: The Bayesian approach*. Chicago: Open Court.
Jeffreys, H. (1961). *Theory of probability* (3rd ed.). New York: Oxford University Press.
Lindley, D. V. (2007). *Understanding uncertainty*. Hoboken, NJ: Wiley.
Savage, L. J. (1954). *The foundations of statistics*. New York: Wiley.

2

Statistical Elements of Bayes' Theorem

The material presented thus far has concerned Bayesian probability. The goal of this chapter is to present the role of Bayes' theorem as it pertains to statistical inference. Setting the foundations of Bayesian statistical inference provides the framework for applications to a variety of substantive problems in the social sciences.

To begin, denote by Y a random variable that takes on a realized value y. For example, a person's socioeconomic status could be considered a random variable Y taking on a very large set of possible values. Once the person identifies his/her socioeconomic status, the random variable Y is now realized as y. Because Y is unobserved and random, we need to specify a probability model to explain how we obtained the actual data values y.

Next, denote by θ a parameter that we believe characterizes the probability model of interest. The parameter θ can be a scalar, such as the mean or the variance of a distribution, or it can be vector-valued, such as a set of regression coefficients in regression analysis or factor loadings in factor analysis. To avoid too much notational complexity, for now we will use θ to represent either scalar- or vector-valued parameters where the difference will be revealed by the context.

We are concerned with determining the probability of observing y given the unknown parameters θ, which we write as $p(y|\theta)$. In statistical inference, the goal is to obtain estimates of the unknown parameters given the data. This is expressed as the likelihood of the parameters given the data, which we denote as $L(\theta|y)$. Often we work with the log-likelihood written as $l(\theta|y)$.

The key difference between Bayesian statistical inference and frequentist statistical inference concerns the nature of the unknown parameters θ. In the frequentist tradition, the assumption is that θ is unknown but has a fixed value that we wish to estimate. In Bayesian statistical inference, θ is considered unknown and should be viewed as a random variable possessing a probability distribution that reflects our uncertainty about the true value of θ. Because both the observed data y and the parameters θ are assumed random, we can model the joint probability of the parameters and the data as a function of the conditional distribution of the data given the parameters and the prior distribution of the parameters. More formally,

$$p(\theta, y) = p(y|\theta)p(\theta) \tag{2.1}$$

where $p(\theta, y)$ is the joint distribution of the parameters and the data. Using Bayes' theorem, we obtain the following:

$$p(\theta|y) = \frac{p(\theta, y)}{p(y)} = \frac{p(y|\theta)p(\theta)}{p(y)} \tag{2.2}$$

where $p(\theta|y)$ is referred to as the *posterior distribution* of the parameters θ given the observed data y. Thus, from Equation 2.2 the posterior distribution of θ given y is equal to the data distribution $p(y|\theta)$ times the prior distribution of the parameters $p(\theta)$ normalized by $p(y)$ so that the posterior distribution sums (or integrates) to 1. For discrete variables,

$$p(y) = \sum_{\theta} p(y|\theta)p(\theta) \tag{2.3}$$

and for continuous variables,

$$p(y) = \int_{\theta} p(y|\theta)p(\theta)d\theta \tag{2.4}$$

In line with Equation 1.7, the denominator of Equation 2.2 does not involve model parameters, so we can omit the term and obtain the *unnormalized posterior distribution*

$$p(\theta|y) \propto p(y|\theta)p(\theta) \tag{2.5}$$

Consider the data density $p(y|\theta)$ on the right-hand side of Equation 2.5. When expressed in terms of the unknown parameters θ for fixed values of y, this term is the *likelihood* $L(\theta|y)$, which we discuss in more detail in Section 2.3. Thus, Equation 2.5 can be rewritten as

$$p(\theta|y) \propto L(\theta|y)p(\theta) \tag{2.6}$$

Equations 2.5 and 2.6 represent the core of Bayesian statistical inference and are what separates Bayesian statistics from frequentist statistics. Specifically, Equation 2.6 states that our uncertainty regarding the parameters of our model, as expressed by the prior distribution $p(\theta)$, is *weighted* by the actual data $p(y|\theta)$ (or, equivalently, $L(\theta|y)$), yielding (up to a constant of proportionality) an updated estimate of our uncertainty, as expressed in the posterior distribution $p(\theta|y)$. Following a brief digression to discuss the assumption of *exchangeability*, we take up each element of Equation 2.6—the prior distribution, the likelihood, and the posterior distribution.

2.1 THE ASSUMPTION OF EXCHANGEABILITY

We saw in Equation 2.6 that Bayes' theorem can be written as the product of the likelihood of the unknown parameters for fixed values of the data and the prior distribution of the model parameters. Before considering the concepts of likelihood and the prior distribution, it is first necessary to discuss the assumption of *exchangeability*.

In most discussions of statistical modeling, it is common to invoke the assumption that the data $y_1, y_2, \ldots, y_n$ are independently and identically distributed—often referred to as the *i.i.d. assumption*. As Lancaster (2004, p. 27) has pointed out, the i.i.d. assumption suggests that probability has an "objective" existence; that there exists a random number generator that produces a sequence of independent random variables. However, such an objectivist view of probability does not accord with the Bayesian notion that probabilities are epistemic. As such, Bayesians invoke the deeper notion of *exchangeability* to produce likelihoods and to address the issue of independence.

Exchangeability arises from de Finetti's representation theorem (de Finetti, 1974) and implies that the subscripts of a vector of data (e.g., $y_1, y_2, \ldots, y_n$) do not carry information that is relevant to describing the probability distribution of the data. In other words, the joint distribution of the data, $p(y_1, y_2, \ldots, y_n)$, is invariant to permutations of the subscripts.[1]

Drawing on a similar example of exchangeability given in Jackman (2009), consider the response that student i ($i = 1, 2, \ldots, 10$) would make to the statement "My teacher is supportive," where

$$y_i = \begin{cases} 1, & \text{if student } i \text{ agrees} \\ 0, & \text{if student } i \text{ disagrees} \end{cases} \tag{2.7}$$

Next, consider three patterns of responses by 10 randomly selected students:

$$p(1, 0, 1, 1, 0, 1, 0, 1, 0, 0) \tag{2.8a}$$

$$p(1, 1, 0, 0, 1, 1, 1, 0, 0, 0) \tag{2.8b}$$

$$p(1, 0, 0, 0, 0, 0, 1, 1, 1, 1) \tag{2.8c}$$

We have just presented three possible patterns, but notice that there are $2^{10} = 1,024$ possible patterns of agreement and disagreement among the 10 students. If our task were to assign probabilities to all possible outcomes, this could become prohibitively difficult. However, suppose we now assume that student responses are independent of one another—which might be reasonable if each student is privately asked to rate the teacher on supportiveness. Then, exchangeability implies that only the

---

[1] Technically, according to de Finetti (1974), this refers to *finite* exchangeability. Infinite exchangeability is obtained by adding the provision that every finite subset of an infinite sequence is exchangeable.

proportion of agreements matter, not the location of those agreements in the vector. In other words, given that the sequences are the same length n, we can exchange the response of student i for student j without changing our belief about the probability model that generated that sequence.

Exchangeability is a subtle assumption insofar as it means that we believe that there is a parameter θ that generates the observed data via a stochastic model and that we can describe that parameter without reference to the particular data at hand (Jackman, 2009). As Jackman points out, the fact that we can describe θ without reference to a particular set of data is, in fact, what is implied by the idea of a prior distribution. Indeed, as Jackman notes, "the existence of a prior distribution over a parameter is a *result* of de Finetti's Representation Theorem (de Finetti, 1974), rather than an assumption" (p. 40, emphasis in original).

It is important to note that the assumption of exchangeability is weaker than the assumption of independence. In the case of two events—say A and B—independence implies that $p(A|B) = p(A)$. If these two events are independent, then they are exchangeable; however, exchangeability does not imply independence. A simple example in which an exchangeable process is not independent is the case of drawing balls from an urn without replacing them (Suppes, 1986, p. 348).

Our discussion of exchangeability has so far rested on the assumption of independent responses. In the social sciences it is well understood that this is a very heroic assumption. Perhaps the best example of a violation of this assumption concerns the problem of modeling data from clustered samples—such as assessing the responses of students nested in classrooms. To address this issue, we need to consider the problem of *conditional exchangeability*. This topic is covered in Chapter 8 where we discuss Bayesian multilevel modeling.

2.2 THE PRIOR DISTRIBUTION

As we move right to left in Equation 2.6, we begin with a discussion of the *prior distribution*. It is first useful to remind ourselves of why we specify a prior distribution on the parameters. The key philosophical reason concerns our view that progress in science generally comes about by learning from previous research findings and incorporating information from these findings into our present studies. Upon reflection, it seems obvious that no study is conducted in the complete absence of previous research. Whether we are designing randomized experiments or sketching out path diagrams, the information gleaned from previous research is almost always incorporated into our choice of designs, variables we choose to include in our models, or conceptual diagrams that we draw. Researchers who postulate a directional hypothesis for an effect are almost certainly using prior information about the direction that an estimate must take. Bayesian statistical inference, therefore, simply requires that our prior knowledge be made explicit, but then moderates our prior knowledge by the actual data in hand. Moderation of our prior knowledge by the data in hand is the key meaning behind Equations 2.5 and 2.6.

But how do we choose a prior? The general approach to considering the choice of a prior is based on how much information we believe we have *prior* to data collection and how accurate we believe that information to be (Lynch, 2007). This issue has also been discussed by Leamer (1983), who orders priors on the basis of degree of confidence. Leamer's hierarchy of confidence is as follows: truths (e.g., axioms) > facts (data) > opinions (e.g., expert judgment) > conventions (e.g., preset alpha levels). An interesting feature of this hierarchy, as noted by Leamer, concerns the inherent lack of "objectivity" in such choices as preset alpha levels, or any of a number of conventions used in frequentist statistics. Leamer (1983) goes on to argue that the problem should be to articulate exactly where a given investigation is located on this hierarchy. The strength of Bayesian inference lies precisely in its ability to incorporate existing knowledge into statistical specifications.

2.2.1 Noninformative Priors

In some cases we may not possess enough prior information to aid in drawing posterior inferences. From a Bayesian perspective, this lack of information is still important to consider and incorporate into our statistical specifications. In other words, it is as important to quantify our ignorance as it is to quantify our cumulative understanding of a problem at hand.

The standard approach to quantifying our ignorance is to incorporate a noninformative prior into our specification.[2] Noninformative priors are also referred to as *vague* or *diffuse* priors. In the situation in which there is no prior knowledge to draw from, perhaps the most sensible noninformative prior distribution to use is the uniform distribution $U(\alpha, \beta)$ over some sensible range of values from α to β.[3] In this case, the uniform distribution essential indicates that we believe that the value of our parameter of interest lies in the range $\beta - \alpha$ and that all values have equal probability. Care must be taken in the choice of the range of values over the uniform distribution. For example, a $U[-\infty, \infty]$ is an *improper* prior distribution insofar as it does not integrate to 1.0 as required of probability distributions. We discuss the uniform distribution in more detail in Chapter 3.

Jeffreys' Prior

A problem with the uniform prior distribution is that it is not invariant to simple transformations. In fact, a transformation of a uniform prior can result in a prior that is not uniform and will end up favoring some values more than others. As pointed out by Gill (2002), the invariance problem associated with uniform priors, and the use of uniform priors specifically, had been greeted with extreme skepticsm by many early statisticians and used as the foundation of major critiques of Bayesian statistics generally.

Despite the many criticisms against the uniform prior, its use dominates applied Bayesian work. The uniform prior is often used as the default setting for many Bayesian statistical software programs in R. Justification for the use of the uniform prior has been given in Bauwens, Lubrano, and Richard (2003), who point out that (1) the effect of the uniform prior tends to diminish with increasing sample size; (2) the uniform prior is useful when models contain nuisance parameters, such as the variance of the normal distribution when the mean is of interest, as they will be integrated out anyway; and (3) the uniform distribution

---

[2] It has been argued (see Kass & Wasserman, 1996) that there are many ways to quantify ignorance and there is no logical means of choosing among noninformative priors for this purpose. We will discuss this issue in Chapter 10.

[3] Application of the uniform distribution is based on the *principle of insufficient reason* first articulated by Laplace (1774/1951).

is the limit of certain conjugate distributions. In Bayesian statistics, conjugate distributions are those that, when multiplied by the likelihood via Bayes' theorem, yield posterior distributions in the same distributional family as the prior distribution.

In specifically addressing the invariance problem associated with the uniform distribution, Jeffreys (1961) proposed a general approach that yields a prior that is invariant under transformations. The central idea is that knowledge and information contained in the specification of the prior distribution of a parameter θ should not be lost when there is a one-to-one transformation from θ to another parameter, say φ. More specifically, using transformation-of-variables calculus, the prior distribution $p(\varphi)$ will be equivalent to $p(\theta)$ when obtained as

$$p(\varphi) = p(\theta) \left| \frac{d\theta}{d\varphi} \right| \qquad (2.9)$$

On the basis of the relationship in Equation 2.9, Jeffreys (1961) developed a noninformative prior distribution that is invariant under transformations, written as

$$p(\theta) \propto [I(\theta)]^{\frac{1}{2}} \qquad (2.10)$$

where $I(\theta)$ is the *Fisher information matrix* for θ. The derivation of this result can be found in Appendix 2.1.

Jeffreys' prior is part of a class of so-called *reference priors* that are designed to place the choice of priors on "objective" grounds based on a set of agreed-upon rules (Bernardo, 1979; Kass & Wasserman, 1996). Not all Bayesian statisticians agree with the overall goals of objective priors. We will take up this issue in Chapter 10.

2.2.2 Informative Priors

In the previous section, we considered the situation in which there may not be much prior information that can be brought to bear on a problem. In that situation we focused on objective priors. Alternatively, it may be the case that some information can be brought to bear on a problem and be systematically incorporated into the prior distribution. Such priors are referred to as *informative*.

To motivate the use of informative priors, consider the problem in education research of academic achievement and its relationship to class size. In this case, we have a considerable amount of prior information based on previous studies regarding the increase in academic achievement when reducing class size. It may be that previous investigations used different tests of academic achievement, but when examined together, it has been found that reducing class size to approximately 17 children per classroom results in one-quarter of a standard deviation increase (say about 8 points) in academic achievement. In addition to a prior estimate of the average achievement gain due to reduction in class size, we may also wish to quantify our uncertainty about the exact value of θ by specifying a probability distribution around the prior estimate of the average. Perhaps a sensible prior distribution would be a normal distribution centered at $\theta = 8$. However, let us imagine that previous research has shown that achievement gains due to class-size reduction are almost never less than 5 points and almost never more than 14 points (almost a full standard deviation). Taking this range of uncertainty into account, we might propose a prior distribution on θ that is $N(8, 1)$. The parameters of this prior distribution $\theta \sim N(8, 1)$ are referred to as *hyperparameters*.

The careful reader may have wondered if setting hyperparameters to fixed values violates the essence of Bayesian philosophy. To address that concern, note first that the Bayesian approach treats the hyperparameters as elicited quantities that are *known* and fixed. In contrast, the frequentist approach treats parameters as *unknown* and fixed. Second, it is not necessary to set hyperparameters to known and fixed quantities. In a fully hierarchical Bayesian model, it is possible to specify a probability distribution on the hyperparameters—referred to as a *hyperprior* distribution. Regardless, differences of opinion on the values specified for hyperparameters can be directly compared via Bayesian model testing and selection, which we will discuss in Chapter 5.

Informative–Conjugate Priors

One type of informative prior is based on the notion of a conjugate distribution. As noted earlier, a conjugate prior distribution is one that, when combined with the likelihood function, yields a posterior distribution that is in the same distributional family as the prior distribution.

Conjugacy is a very important and convenient feature because if a prior is not conjugate, the resulting posterior distribution may have a form that is not analytically simple to solve. Arguably, the existence of numerical simulation methods for Bayesian inference, such as Markov chain Monte Carlo (MCMC) estimation, may render conjugacy less of a problem. Chapter 3 outlines conjugate priors for probability distributions commonly encountered in the social sciences. Throughout this book, conjugate priors are used in examples when studying informative priors.

2.3 LIKELIHOOD

Whereas the prior distribution encodes our accumulated knowledge of the parameters of interest, this prior information must, of course, be moderated by the data in hand before yielding the posterior distribution—the source of our current inferences. In Equation 2.6 we saw that the probability distribution of the data given the model parameters, $p(y|\theta)$ could be written equivalently as the $L(\theta|y)$, the likelihood of the parameters given the data.

The concept of *likelihood* is extremely important for both frequentist and Bayesian schools of statistics. Excellent discussions of likelihood can be found in Edwards (1992) and Royall (1997). In this section, we briefly review the law of likelihood and then present simple expressions of the likelihood for the binomial probability and normal sampling models.

2.3.1 The Law of Likelihood

The likelihood can be defined as proportional to the probability of the data y given the parameter(s) θ. That is,

$$L(\theta|y) \propto p(y|\theta) \tag{2.11}$$

where the constant of proportionality does not depend on θ. As a standalone quantity, the likelihood is of little value. Rather, what matters is the ratio of the likelihoods, and this leads to the *law of likelihood*. We define the *law of likelihood* as follows (see also Royall, 1997):

Definition. If hypothesis θ_1 implies that Y takes on the value y with probability $p(y|\theta_1)$ while hypothesis θ_2 implies that Y takes on the value y with probability $p(y|\theta_2)$, then the law of likelihood states that the realization $Y = y$ is evidence in support of θ_1 over θ_2 if and only if $L(\theta_1|y) > L(\theta_2|y)$. The likelihood ratio, $L(\theta_1|y)/L(\theta_2|y)$, measures the strength of that evidence.

Notice that the law of likelihood implies that only the information in the data as summarized by the likelihood serves as evidence in corroboration (or refutation) of a hypothesis. This latter idea is referred to as the *likelihood principle*. Notice also that frequentist notions of repeated sampling do not enter into the law of likelihood or the likelihood principle.

EXAMPLE 2.1. THE BINOMIAL PROBABILITY MODEL

First, consider the number of correct answers on a test of length n. Each item on the test represents a "Bernoulli trial," with outcomes $0 =$ wrong and $1 =$ right. The natural probability model for data arising from n Bernoulli sequences is the binomial sampling model. Under the assumption of exchangeability—meaning the indices $1, \ldots, n$ provide no relevant information—we can summarize the total number of successes by y. Letting θ be the proportion of correct responses in the population, we can write the binomial sampling model as

$$p(y|\theta) = \text{Bin}(y|n, \theta) = \binom{n}{y}\theta^y(1 - \theta)^{(n-y)}$$

$$= L(\theta|n, y) \tag{2.12}$$

where $\binom{n}{y}$ is read as "n choose y" and refers to the number of successes y in a sequence of n "right/wrong" Bernoulli trials that can be obtained from an n item test. The abbreviation *Bin* is shorthand for the binomial density function.

EXAMPLE 2.2. THE NORMAL SAMPLING MODEL

Next consider the likelihood function for the parameters of the simple normal distribution, which we write as

$$p(y|\mu, \sigma^2) = \frac{1}{\sqrt{2\pi}\sigma} \exp\left(-\frac{(y - \mu)^2}{2\sigma^2}\right) \tag{2.13}$$

where μ is the population mean and σ^2 is the population variance. Under the assumption of independent observations, we can write Equation 2.13 as

$$p(y_1, y_2, \ldots, y_n | \mu, \sigma^2) = \prod_i^n p(y_i | \mu, \sigma^2)$$

$$= \left(\frac{1}{\sqrt{2\pi\sigma^2}}\right)^{n/2} \exp\left(-\frac{\sum_i (y_i - \mu)^2}{2\sigma^2}\right)$$

$$= L(\theta | y) \tag{2.14}$$

where $\theta = (\mu, \sigma)$. Thus, under the assumption of independence, the likelihood of model parameters given the data is simply the product of the individual probabilities of the data given the parameters.

2.4 THE POSTERIOR DISTRIBUTION

Continuing with our analysis of Equation 2.6, notice that the posterior distribution of the model parameters is determined by multiplying the likelihood by the prior. In modern Bayesian statistics, we typically use computational methods such as MCMC for drawing inferences about model parameters from the posterior distributions. We discuss MCMC methods in Chapter 4. Here we provide two small examples utilizing conjugate prior distributions. In Chapter 3, we consider the prior and posterior for other important distributions utilized in the social sciences.

EXAMPLE 2.3. THE BINOMIAL DISTRIBUTION WITH BETA PRIOR

Consider again the binomial distribution used to estimate probabilities for successes and failures, such as those obtained from responses to multiple-choice questions scored right/wrong. As an example of a conjugate prior, consider estimating the number of correct responses y on a test of length n. Let θ be the proportion of correct responses. We first assume that the responses are independent of one another. The binomial sampling model was given in Equation 2.12 and is reproduced here:

$$p(y | \theta) = \text{Bin}(y | n, \theta) = \binom{n}{y} \theta^y (1 - \theta)^{(n-y)} \tag{2.15}$$

One choice of a conjugate prior distribution for θ is the beta(a,b) distribution. The beta distribution is a continuous distribution appropriate for variables that range from zero to one. The terms a and b are the *shape* and *scale* parameters of the beta distribution, respectively.[4] For this example, a and b will serve as hyperparameters because the beta distribution is being used as a prior distribution for the binomial distribution. The form of the beta(a,b) distribution is

$$p(\theta; a, b) = \frac{\Gamma(a+b)}{\Gamma(a)\Gamma(b)} \theta^{a-1}(1-\theta)^{b-1} \tag{2.16}$$

where Γ is the gamma(a, b) function. Multiplying Equation 2.4 and Equation 2.16 and ignoring terms that don't involve model parameters, we obtain the posterior distribution by

$$p(\theta|y) = \frac{\Gamma(n+a+b)}{\Gamma(y+a)\Gamma(n-y+b)} \theta^{y+a-1}(1-\theta)^{n-y+b-1} \tag{2.17}$$

which is a beta distribution with parameters $a' = a + y$ and $b' = b + n - y$. Thus, the beta prior for the binomial sampling model is a conjugate prior and yields a posterior distribution that is also in the family of the beta distribution.

EXAMPLE 2.4. THE NORMAL DISTRIBUTION WITH NORMAL PRIOR: σ^2 KNOWN

This next example explores the normal prior for the normal sampling model in which the variance σ^2 is assumed to be known. Thus, the problem is one of estimating the mean μ. Let y denote a data vector of size n. We assume that y follows a normal distribution shown in Equation 2.13 and reproduced here:

$$p(y|\mu, \sigma^2) = \frac{1}{\sqrt{2\pi}\sigma} \exp\left(-\frac{(y-\mu)^2}{2\sigma^2}\right) \tag{2.18}$$

---

[4] The scale parameter affects spread of the distribution, in the sense of shrinking or stretching the distribution. The shape parameter, as the term implies, affects the shape of the distribution.

Consider that our prior distribution on the mean is normal with mean and variance hyperparameters, κ and τ^2, respectively, which for this example are known. The prior distribution can be written as

$$p(\mu|\kappa, \tau^2) = \frac{1}{\sqrt{2\pi\tau^2}} \exp\left(-\frac{(\mu - \kappa)^2}{2\tau^2}\right) \tag{2.19}$$

After some algebra, the posterior distribution can be obtained as

$$p(\mu|y) \sim N\left[\frac{\frac{\kappa}{\tau^2} + \frac{n\bar{y}}{\sigma^2}}{\frac{1}{\tau^2} + \frac{n}{\sigma^2}}, \frac{\tau^2\sigma^2}{\sigma^2 + n\tau^2}\right] \tag{2.20}$$

Thus, the posterior distribution of μ is normal with mean

$$\hat{\mu} = \frac{\frac{\kappa}{\tau^2} + \frac{n\bar{y}}{\sigma^2}}{\frac{1}{\tau^2} + \frac{n}{\sigma^2}} \tag{2.21}$$

and variance

$$\hat{\sigma}_\mu^2 = \frac{\tau^2\sigma^2}{\sigma^2 + n\tau^2} \tag{2.22}$$

We see from Equations 2.20, 2.21, and 2.22 that the normal prior is conjugate for the likelihood, yielding a normal posterior.

2.5 THE BAYESIAN CENTRAL LIMIT THEOREM AND BAYESIAN SHRINKAGE

When examining Equations 2.21 and 2.22 carefully, some interesting features emerge. For example, notice that as the sample size approaches infinity, there is no information in the prior distribution that is relevant to estimating the mean and variance of the posterior distribution. To see this, first we compute the asymptotic posterior mean by letting n go to infinity:

$$\lim_{n\to\infty} \hat{\mu} = \lim_{n\to\infty} \frac{\frac{\kappa}{\tau^2} + \frac{n\bar{y}}{\sigma^2}}{\frac{1}{\tau^2} + \frac{n}{\sigma^2}}$$

$$= \lim_{n\to\infty} \frac{\frac{\kappa\sigma^2}{n\tau^2} + \bar{y}}{\frac{\sigma^2}{n\tau^2} + 1} = \bar{y} \tag{2.23}$$

Thus as the sample size increases to infinity, the expected a posteriori estimate $\hat{\mu}$ converges to the maximum likelihood estimate $\bar{y}$.

In terms of the variance, first let $1/\tau^2$ and n/σ^2 refer to the *prior precision* and *data precision*, respectively. The role of these two measures of precision can be seen by once again examining the variance term for the normal distribution in Equation 2.22. Specifically, letting n approach infinity, we obtain

$$\lim_{n\to\infty} \hat{\sigma}^2_\mu = \lim_{n\to\infty} \frac{1}{\frac{1}{\tau^2} + \frac{n}{\sigma^2}}$$

$$= \lim_{n\to\infty} \frac{\sigma^2}{\frac{\sigma^2}{\tau^2} + n} = \frac{\sigma^2}{n} \tag{2.24}$$

which we recognize as the maximum likelihood estimator of the variance of the mean, the square root of which yields the standard error of the mean. A similar result emerges if we consider the case where we have very little information regarding the prior precision. That is, choosing a very large value for τ^2 gives the same result.

The fact that as n increases to infinity leads to the same result as we would obtain from the frequentist perspective has been referred to as the *Bayesian central limit theorem*. This point is important from a philosophical perspective insofar as it suggests that Bayesian and frequentist results will agree in the limit.

The posterior distribution in Equation 2.20 reveals another interesting feature regarding the relationship between the maximum likelihood estimator of the mean $\bar{y}$ and the prior mean κ. Specifically, the posterior mean μ can be seen as a compromise between the prior mean κ and the observed data mean $\bar{y}$. To see this clearly, notice that we can rewrite Equation 2.20 as

$$\hat{\mu} = \frac{\sigma^2}{\sigma^2 + n\tau^2}\kappa + \frac{n\tau^2}{\sigma^2 + n\tau^2}\bar{y} \qquad (2.25)$$

Thus, the posterior mean is a weighted combination of the prior mean and observed data mean. These weights are bounded by 0 and 1 and together are referred to as the *shrinkage factor*. The shrinkage factor represents the proportional distance that the posterior mean has shrunk back to the prior mean κ and away from the maximum likelihood estimator $\bar{y}$. Notice that if the sample size is large, the weight associated with κ will approach zero and the weight associated with $\bar{y}$ will approach one. Thus $\hat{\mu}$ will approach $\bar{y}$. Similarly, if the data variance σ^2 is very large relative to the prior variance τ^2, this suggests little precision in the data relative to the prior; therefore the posterior mean will approach the prior mean, κ. Conversely, if the prior variance is very large relative to the data variance, this suggests greater precision in the data compared to the prior; therefore the posterior mean will approach $\bar{y}$.

EXAMPLE 2.5. THE NORMAL DISTRIBUTION WITH NORMAL PRIOR:
σ^2 UNKNOWN

Perhaps a more realistic situation that arises in practice is when the mean *and* variance of the normal distribution are unknown. In this case, we need to specify a full probability model for both the mean μ and variance σ^2. If we assume that μ and σ^2 are independent of one another, then we can factor the joint prior distribution of μ and σ^2 as

$$p(\mu, \sigma^2) = p(\mu)p(\sigma^2) \qquad (2.26)$$

We now need to specify the prior distribution of σ^2. There are two approaches that we can take to specify the prior for σ^2. First, we can specify a uniform prior on μ and $\log(\sigma^2)$, because when converting the uniform prior on $\log(\sigma^2)$ to a density for σ^2, we obtain $p(\sigma^2) = 1/\sigma^2$.[5] With uniform priors on both μ and σ^2, the joint prior distribution $p(\mu, \sigma^2) \propto 1/\sigma^2$. However, the problem with this first approach is that the uniform prior over the real line is an improper prior. Therefore, a second approach would be to provide proper informative priors, but with a choice of hyperparameters such that the resulting priors are quite diffused. First, again we assume as before that $y \sim N(\mu, \sigma^2)$ and that $\mu \sim N(\kappa, \tau^2)$. As is discussed in the next chapter, the variance parameter σ^2 follows an inverse-gamma distribution with shape and scale parameters a and b, respectively. Succinctly, $\sigma^2 \sim IG(a, b)$ and the probability density function for σ^2 can be written as

$$p(\sigma^2|a, b) \propto (\sigma^2)^{-(a+1)}e^{-b/\sigma^2} \qquad (2.27)$$

Even though Equation 2.27 is a proper distribution for σ^2, we can see that as a and b approach 0, the proper prior approaches the noninformative prior $1/\sigma^2$. Thus, very small values of a and b can suffice to provide a prior on σ^2 to be used to estimate the joint posterior distribution of μ and σ^2.

The final step in this example is to obtain the joint posterior distribution for μ and σ^2. Assuming that the joint prior distribution is $1/\sigma^2$, then the joint posterior distribution can be written as

$$p(\mu, \sigma^2|y) \propto \frac{1}{\sigma^2}\prod_{i=1}^{n}\frac{1}{\sqrt{2\pi\sigma^2}}\exp\left\{-\frac{(y_i - \mu)^2}{2\sigma^2}\right\} \qquad (2.28)$$

Notice, however, that Equation 2.28 involves two parameters μ and σ^2. The solution to this problem is discussed in Lynch (2007). First, the posterior distribution of μ obtained from Equation 2.28 can be written as

$$p(\mu|y, \sigma^2) \propto \exp\left\{-\frac{n\mu^2 - 2n\bar{y}\mu}{2\sigma^2}\right\} \qquad (2.29)$$

---

[5] Following Lynch (2007), this result is obtained via a change of variable calculus. Specifically, let $k = \log(\sigma^2)$, and $p(k) \propto$ constant. Change of variable calculus involves the Jacobian $J = dk/d\sigma^2 = 1/\sigma^2$. Therefore, $p(\sigma^2) \propto$ constant $\times J$.

Solving for μ involves dividing by n and completing the square, yielding

$$p(\mu|y, \sigma^2) \propto \exp\left\{-\frac{(\mu - \bar{y})^2}{2\sigma^2/n}\right\} \tag{2.30}$$

There are several ways to determine the posterior distribution of σ^2. Perhaps the simplest is to recognize that the joint posterior distribution for μ and σ^2 can be factored into their respective conditional distributions:

$$p(\mu, \sigma^2|y) = p(\mu|\sigma^2, y)p(\sigma^2|y) \tag{2.31}$$

The first term on the right-hand side of Equation 2.31 was solved above assuming σ^2 is known. The second term on the right-hand side of Equation 2.31 is the marginal posterior distribution of σ^2. An exact expression for $p(\sigma^2|y)$ can be obtained by integrating the joint distribution over μ—that is,

$$p(\sigma^2|y) = \int p(\mu, \sigma^2|y)d\mu \tag{2.32}$$

Although this discussion shows that analytic expressions are possible for the solution of this simple case, in practice the advent of MCMC algorithms renders the solution to the joint posterior distribution of model parameters quite straightforward.

2.6 SUMMARY

This chapter provided a breakdown of Bayes' theorem as it functions with respect to statistical practice. With reference to any parameter of interest, be it a mean, variance, regression coefficient, or a factor loading, Bayes' theorem is composed of three parts: the prior distribution representing our cumulative knowledge about the parameter of interest; the likelihood representing the data in hand; and the posterior distribution representing our updated knowledge based on the moderation of the prior distribution by the likelihood. By carefully decomposing Bayes' theorem into its constituent parts, we also can see its relationship to frequentist statistics, particularly through the Bayesian central limit theorem and the notion of shrinkage. In the next chapter we focus on the relationship between the likelihood and the prior. Specifically, we examine a variety of common data distributions used in social and behavioral science research and define their conjugate prior distributions.

2.7 SUGGESTED READINGS

Edwards, A. W. F. (1992). *Likelihood.* Baltimore: Johns Hopkins University Press.

Jackman, S. (2009). *Bayesian analysis for the social sciences.* Hoboken, NJ: Wiley.

Kass, R. E., & Wasserman, L. (1996). The selection of prior distributions by formal rules. *Journal of the American Statistical Association, 91,* 1343–1370.

Press, S. J. (2003). *Subjective and objective Bayesian statistics: Principles, models, and applications* (2nd ed.). Hoboken, NJ: Wiley.

Royall, R. (1997). *Statistical evidence: A likelihood paradigm.* New York: Chapman and Hall.

APPENDIX 2.1
DERIVATION OF JEFFREYS' PRIOR

Jeffreys' prior is obtained as follows. Following Gelman, Carlin, Stern, and Rubin (2003), let $f(x|\theta)$ be the likelihood for θ and write its associated Fisher information matrix as

$$I(\theta) = \left[-E_{x|\theta}\left(\frac{\partial^2(\log f(x|\theta))}{\partial\theta^2} \right) \right]^{1/2} \tag{2.33}$$

Next, we write the Fisher information matrix for ϕ as

$$I(\phi) = \left[-E_{x|\theta}\left(\frac{\partial^2(\log f(x|\phi))}{\partial\phi^2} \right) \right]^{1/2} \tag{2.34}$$

From the change of variables expression in Equation 2.9, we can rewrite Equation 2.34 as

$$I(\phi) = \left[-E_{x|\theta}\left(\frac{\partial^2(\log f(x|\theta))}{\partial\theta^2} \times \left| \frac{d\theta}{d\phi} \right| \right) \right]^{1/2} \tag{2.35}$$

$$= I(\theta)\left| \frac{d\theta}{d\phi} \right|^2$$

Therefore,

$$I^{1/2}(\phi) = I^{1/2}(\theta) \times \left| \frac{d\theta}{d\phi} \right| \tag{2.36}$$

from which we obtain the relationship to Equation 2.10.

3

Common Probability Distributions

In Chapter 2, we introduced the core concepts of Bayesian statistical inference. The key idea of Bayesian statistics is that the distribution of the data is weighted by the prior distribution of the parameters in order to form a posterior distribution of all unknown quantities. Philosophically, we adopt the view that there is an external reality that generates data. We refer to this as the *data-generating process,* or DGP. We view the data that arises from the DGP as capable of being described by a probability distribution governed by unknown parameters. The difference between Bayesians and frequentists, as noted earlier, is that Bayesians hold that all unknowns, including parameters, are random and can be described by probability distributions. In contrast, frequentists hold that parameters are also unknown, but that they are fixed quantities. Deciding on the correct probability model for the data and the parameters (including possibly hyperparameters) is at the heart of Bayesian statistical modeling. Because the orientation of Bayesian statistical inference is the probability distribution, it is essential that we explore the major distributions that are used in the social sciences. This chapter, therefore, presents an overview of important distributions found in common statistical practice in the social sciences.

The organization of this chapter is as follows. We first explore the following distributions and their use in common statistical practice:

1. The normal distribution
   - Mean unknown/variance known
   - Mean known/variance unknown

2. The uniform distribution

3. The Poisson distribution

4. The binomial distribution

5. The multinomial distribution

6. The Wishart distribution

For each of these distributions, we discuss how they are commonly used in the social sciences and then describe their shape under a different set of parameter values. We then describe how each of these distributions is typically incorporated in Bayesian statistical modeling by describing their use as conjugate prior distributions. We also describe the posterior distribution that is derived from applying Bayes' theorem to each of these distributions. We do not devote space to the more technical details of these distributions, such as the moment-generating functions or characteristic functions. A succinct summary of the technical details of these and many more distributions can be found in Evans, Hastings, and Peacock (2000).

   To create the plots, artificial data were generated using a variety of R functions available in "scatterplot3d" (Ligges & Mächler, 2003), "pscl" (Jackman, 2012), "MCMCpack" (A. D. Martin et al., 2010), and "MVA" (Everitt & Hothorn, 2012). The R code is available in Appendix 3.1.

3.1 THE NORMAL DISTRIBUTION

The normal (Gaussian) distribution figures prominently in the field of statistics, owing perhaps mostly to its role in the central limit theorem. The quintessential example of a variable that possesses a normal distribution is the intelligence quotient (IQ). For a random variable X, such as IQ, we denote the normal distribution as

$$X \sim N(\mu, \sigma^2) \tag{3.1}$$

where

$$E[x] = \mu \tag{3.2}$$

$$\mathrm{var}[x] = \sigma^2 \tag{3.3}$$

where $E[\cdot]$ and var$[\cdot]$ are the expectation and variance operators, respectively. The probability density function of the normal distribution was given in Equation 2.13 and is reproduced here:

$$p(y|\mu, \sigma^2) = \frac{1}{\sqrt{2\pi}\sigma} \exp\left(-\frac{(y-\mu)^2}{2\sigma^2}\right) \tag{3.4}$$

3.1.1 The Conjugate Prior for the Normal Distribution

We consider the conjugate prior for two cases of the normal distribution. The first case is where the mean is unknown but the variance is known, and the second case is where the mean is known but the variance is unknown. A third case is where both the mean and variance are unknown and was shown in Example 2.5.

The normal distribution itself is often used as a conjugate prior for parameters that are assumed to be normal in the population, such as regression coefficients.

EXAMPLE 3.1. MEAN UNKNOWN, VARIANCE KNOWN

In the case where the mean is unknown but the variance is known, the prior distribution of the mean is normal, as we know from standard statistical theory. Thus, we can write the prior distribution for the mean as

$$p(\mu|\mu_0, \sigma_0^2) \propto \frac{1}{\sigma_0} \exp\left(-\frac{1}{2\sigma_0^2}(\mu-\mu_0)^2\right) \tag{3.5}$$

where μ_0 and σ_0^2 are hyperparameters. Figure 3.1 provides an illustration of the normal distribution with unknown prior mean and known variance under varying conjugate priors. This case makes quite clear the relationship between the prior distribution and the posterior distribution. Specifically, the greater the degree of precision on the prior distribution of the mean (upper left figure), the closer the posterior matches the prior distribution. However, in the case of a very flat prior distribution (bottom right figure), the more the posterior distribution matches the data distribution.

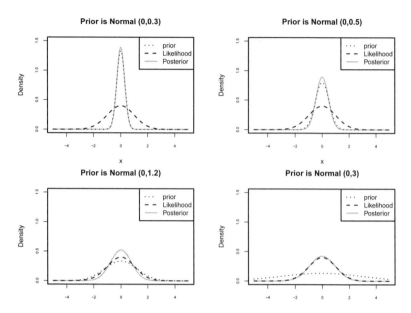

FIGURE 3.1. Normal distribution, mean unknown/variance known with varying conjugate priors.

EXAMPLE 3.2. MEAN KNOWN, VARIANCE UNKNOWN

When the mean of the normal distribution is known but the variance is unknown, the goal is to determine the prior distribution on the variance parameter. The *inverse-gamma distribution* is used as the conjugate prior for the variance parameter denoted as

$$\sigma^2 \sim \text{inverse-gamma}(a, b) \tag{3.6}$$

where α (> 0) is the shape parameter and β (> 0) is the scale parameter. The probability density function for the inverse-gamma distribution is written as

$$p(\sigma^2) = (\sigma^2)^{(a+1)} e^{-b/\sigma^2} \tag{3.7}$$

The expected value and variance of the inverse-gamma density are

$$E(\sigma^2) = \frac{b}{a-1}, \qquad \text{for } a > 0 \tag{3.8}$$

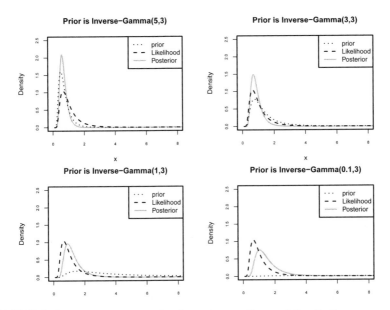

FIGURE 3.2. Inverse-gamma prior for variance of normal distribution.

and

$$\mathrm{var}(\sigma^2) = \frac{b^2}{(a-1)^2(a-2)}, \qquad \text{for } a > 2 \tag{3.9}$$

respectively. Figure 3.2 shows the posterior distribution of the variance for different inverse-gamma priors that differ only with respect to their shape. We see that the "peakedness" of the posterior distribution of the variance is dependent on the shape of the inverse-gamma prior.

3.2 THE UNIFORM DISTRIBUTION

The uniform distribution (also referred to as the *rectangular distribution*) is used to describe equally likely outcomes. For a continuous random variable X, we write the uniform distribution as

$$X \sim U(\alpha, \beta) \tag{3.10}$$

where α and β are the lower and upper limits of the uniform distribution, respectively. The uniform distribution has $\alpha = 0 \leq x \leq \beta = 1$. Under the uniform distribution

$$E[x] = \frac{\alpha + \beta}{2} \tag{3.11}$$

$$\text{var}[x] = \frac{(\beta - \alpha)^2}{12} \tag{3.12}$$

3.2.1 The Uniform Distribution as a Noninformative Prior

The uniform distribution is the typical choice for a noninformative prior. Specifically, if one lacks any prior information favoring one parameter value over another, then the uniform distribution is a good choice. Historically, Pierre-Simon Laplace (1774/1951) articulated the idea of assigning uniform probabilities in cases where prior information was lacking and referred to this as the *principle of insufficient reason.*

Generally speaking, it is useful to incorporate the uniform distribution as a noninformative prior for a distribution that has bounded support, such as $(-1, 1)$. As an example of the use of the uniform distribution as a prior, consider its role in forming the posterior distribution for a normal likelihood. Again, this would be the case where a researcher lacks prior information regarding the distribution of the parameter of interest.

EXAMPLE 3.3. UNIFORM PRIOR WITH DIFFERENT BOUNDS

Figure 3.3 shows how the influence of different bounds on the uniform prior results in different posterior distributions. We see from Figure 3.3 that the effect of the uniform prior on the posterior distribution is dependent on the bounds of the prior. For a prior with relatively narrow bounds (upper left-hand corner of figure), this is akin to having a fair amount of information, and therefore, the prior and posterior roughly match up. However, as in the case of Figure 3.1, if the uniform prior has very wide bounds indicating virtually no prior information (lower right-hand corner of figure), the posterior distribution will match the data distribution.

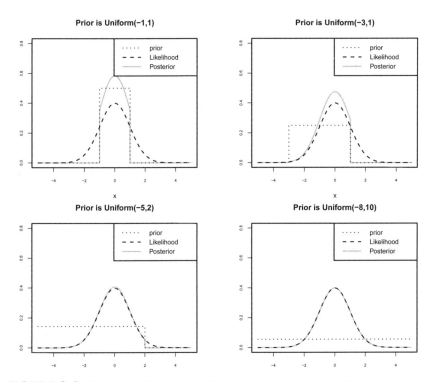

FIGURE 3.3. Influence of varying uniform priors on normal distribution.

3.3 THE POISSON DISTRIBUTION

Often, in the social sciences, the outcome of interest might be the count of the number of events that occur within a specified period of time. For example, one may be interested in the number of colds a child catches within a year—modeled as a function of access to good nutrition or health care. In another instance, the interest might be in the number of new teachers who drop out of the teaching profession after 5 years, modeled as a function of teacher training and demographic features of the school. In cases of this sort, the random variable k, representing the number of occurrences of the event, is assumed to follow a *Poisson* distribution with parameter θ. The probability density function for the Poisson distribution is written as

$$p(\theta) = \frac{e^{-\theta}\theta^k}{k!}, \ k = 0, 1, 2, \ldots, \qquad \theta > 0 \qquad (3.13)$$

3.3.1 The Gamma Density: Conjugate Prior for the Poisson Distribution

The conjugate prior for the parameter θ of the Poisson distribution is the gamma density with scale parameter a and shape parameter b. In this context, the gamma density is written as

$$g(\theta) = \theta^{a-1}e^{-b\theta} \tag{3.14}$$

The posterior density is formed by multiplying Equations 3.13 and 3.14, yielding

$$p(\theta|k, a, b) \propto \theta^{k+a-1}e^{-(b+1)\theta} \tag{3.15}$$

EXAMPLE 3.4. POISSON DISTRIBUTION WITH VARYING GAMMA-DENSITY
PRIORS

Figure 3.4 shows the posterior distribution under the Poisson likelihood with varying gamma-density priors. Here again we see the manner in which the data distribution moderates the influence on the prior distribution to obtain a posterior distribution that balances the data in hand with the prior information we can bring regarding the parameters of interest. The upper left of Figure 3.4 shows this perhaps most clearly with the posterior distribution balanced between the prior distribution and the data distribution. And again, in the case of a relatively noninformative gamma distribution, the posterior distribution matches up to the likelihood (lower right of Figure 3.4).

3.4 THE BINOMIAL DISTRIBUTION

We encountered the binomial distribution in Chapter 2. To reiterate, the binomial distribution is used to estimate probabilities for successes and failures, where any given event follows a Bernoulli distribution, such as right/wrong responses to a test, or agree/disagree responses to a survey item. The probability density function for the binomial distribution can be written as

$$\binom{n}{y}\theta^y(1-\theta)^{n-y} \tag{3.16}$$

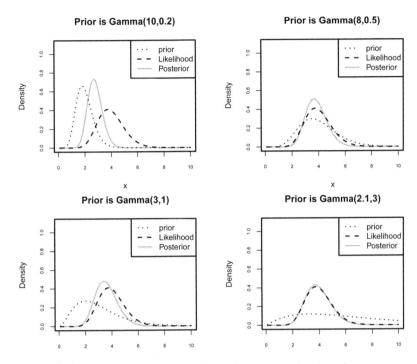

FIGURE 3.4. Poisson distribution with varying gamma-density priors.

where here $\theta \in [0, 1]$ is the success proportion, $y \in \{1, 2, \ldots, n\}$ is the number of successes, and n is the number of trials. Furthermore, $E(y) = n\theta$ and $\text{var}(y) = n\theta(1 - \theta)$.

3.4.1 The Beta Distribution: Conjugate Prior for the Binomial Distribution

Perhaps one of the most important distributions in statistics and one that is commonly encountered as a prior distribution in Bayesian statistics is the beta distribution. The probability density function of the beta distribution with respect to the success proportion parameter θ can be written as

$$f(\theta | a, b) = \frac{\Gamma(a + b)}{\Gamma(a)\Gamma(b)} \theta^{a-1}(1 - \theta)^{b-1} \qquad (3.17)$$

where a (> 0) and b (> 0) are scale and shape parameters, respectively, and Γ is the gamma distribution, discussed in the previous section. The mean and variance of the beta distribution can be written as

$$E(\theta|a, b) = \frac{a}{a + b} \tag{3.18}$$

$$\text{var}(\theta|a, b) = \frac{ab}{(a + b)^2(a + b + 1)} \tag{3.19}$$

Note also that the $U(0, 1)$ distribution is equivalent to the beta$(1, 1)$ distribution.

The beta distribution is typically used as the prior distribution when data are assumed to be generated from the binomial distribution, such as in Example 2.3, because the binomial parameter θ is continuous and ranges between 0 and 1.

EXAMPLE 3.5. BINOMIAL LIKELIHOOD WITH VARYING BETA PRIORS

Figure 3.5 shows the posterior distribution under the binomial likelihood with varying beta priors. We see that the role of the beta prior on the posterior distribution is quite similar to the role of the normal prior on the posterior distribution in Figure 3.1. Notice that the beta$(1.2, 1.5)$ distribution in the lower right-hand corner of Figure 3.1 is noninformative and would be equivalent to the $U(0, 1)$ distribution if $a = 1$ and $b = 1$.

3.5 THE MULTINOMIAL DISTRIBUTION

Another very important distribution used in the social sciences is the multinomial distribution. As an example, the multinomial distribution can be used to characterize responses to items on questionnaires where there are more than two alternatives. The multinomial distribution can also be used in models for categorical latent variables, such as latent class analysis (Clogg, 1995), where individuals are assigned to one and only one of, say, C latent classes. A special case of the multinomial distribution is the binomial distribution discussed earlier.

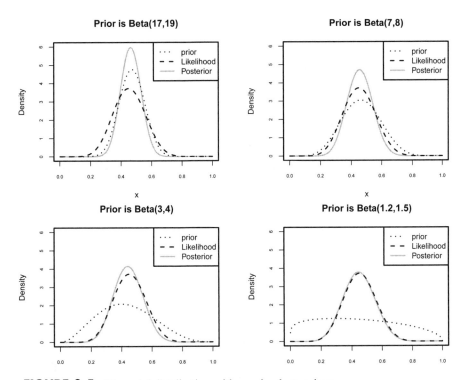

FIGURE 3.5. Binomial distribution with varying beta priors.

The probability density function for the multinomial distribution is written as

$$p(X_1 = x_1, \ldots, X_C = x_C) = \qquad (3.20)$$

$$\begin{cases} \dfrac{n!}{x_1! \cdots x_C!} \, \pi_1^{x_1} \cdots, \pi_C^{x_C}, & \text{when } \sum_{c=1}^{C} x_c = n \\ 0, \text{ otherwise} \end{cases}$$

where n is the sample size and $\pi_1, \ldots, \pi_C$ are parameters representing category proportions. The mean and variance of the multinomial distribution are written as

$$E(x_c) = n\pi_c \qquad (3.21)$$

$$\mathrm{var}(x_c) = n\pi_c(1 - \pi_c) \qquad (3.22)$$

and the covariances among any two categories c and d can be written as

$$\text{cov}(x_c, x_d) = -n\pi_c\pi_d \tag{3.23}$$

3.5.1 The Dirichlet Distribution: Conjugate Prior for the Multinomial Distribution

The conjugate prior distribution for the parameters of the multinomial distribution, π_c, follows a Dirichlet distribution. The Dirichlet distribution is the multivariate generalization of the beta distribution. The probability density function can be written as

$$f(\pi_1, \ldots, \pi_{C-1}; a_1, \ldots, a_C) = \frac{1}{\mathbf{B}(a)}\prod_{c=1}^{C}\pi_c^{a_c-1} \tag{3.24}$$

where

$$\mathbf{B}(a) = \frac{\prod_{c=1}^{C}\Gamma(a_c)}{\Gamma(\sum_{c=1}^{C}a_c)} \tag{3.25}$$

is the *multinomial beta function* expressed in terms of a gamma function.

EXAMPLE 3.6. MULTINOMIAL LIKELIHOOD WITH VARYING PRECISION ON DIRICHLET PRIORS

Figure 3.6 shows the multinomial likelihood and posterior distributions with varying degrees of precision on the Dirichlet prior. As in the other cases, we find that a highly informative Dirichlet prior (top row) yields a posterior distribution that is relatively precise, with a shape that is similar to that of the prior. For a relatively diffused Dirichlet prior (bottom row) the posterior more closely resembles the likelihood.

3.6 THE WISHART DISTRIBUTION

Until now, we have considered univariate distributions and their conjugate priors. However, many applied problems in the social sciences

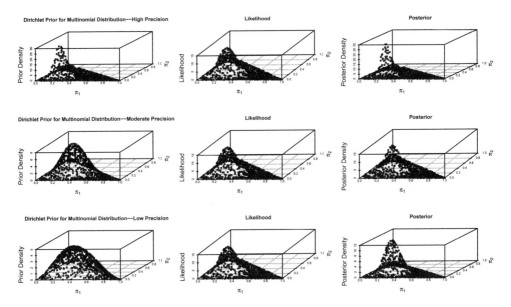

FIGURE 3.6. Multinomial distribution with varying Dirichlet priors.

focus on multivariate outcomes, and a large array of multivariate statistical models are available to address these problems. In the context of this book, we consider a number of models that focus on the covariance matrices of the observed data—in particular, factor analysis and structural equation modeling.[1]

Denote by $\mathbf{x}$ a p-dimensional vector of observed responses for n individuals. For example, these outcomes could be answers to items asking n students to answer a p item survey on their school environment. For simplicity, assume that $\mathbf{x}$ is generated from a multivariate normal distribution with a p-dimensional mean vector $\boldsymbol{\mu}$ and a $p \times p$ covariance matrix $\boldsymbol{\Sigma}$. Furthermore, let $\mathbf{W} = \mathbf{x}'\mathbf{x}$. Then $\mathbf{W}$ follows a *Wishart distribution* denoted as

$$\mathbf{W} \sim Wishart(\mathbf{S}, v) \tag{3.26}$$

---

[1] It is well known that observed means can be incorporated into factor models and structural equation models (see, e.g., Sörbom, 1974), but here we simply focus on the covariance matrix.

where $v = p - 1$ are the degrees of freedom and $\mathbf{S}$ is a scale matrix. The Wishart distribution is the multivariate generalization of the gamma distribution described in Section 3.3.1. As such, if $p = 1$ and $\mathbf{S} = 1$, the Wishart distribution reduces to the chi-square distribution with v degrees of freedom.

3.6.1 The Inverse-Wishart Distribution: Conjugate Prior for the Wishart Distribution

The conjugate prior for the Wishart distribution arising from a multivariate normal distribution is the *inverse-Wishart* distribution, denoted as

$$\mathbf{W}^{-1} \sim \textit{inverse-Wishart}(\mathbf{S}^{-1}, v) \tag{3.27}$$

Here too, if $p = 1$ and $\mathbf{S} = 1$, then the inverse-Wishart distribution reduces to the inverse-gamma distribution. Note that just as the inverse-Wishart distribution can be used as the conjugate prior for the covariance matrix, the Wishart distribution can be used as the conjugate prior for the precision matrix.

3.7 SUMMARY

This chapter presented the most common distributions encountered in the social sciences along with their conjugate priors. The manner in which the prior and the data distributions balance each other to result in the posterior distribution is the key point of this chapter. When priors are very precise, the posterior distribution will have shape closer to that of the prior. When the prior distribution is noninformative, the posterior distribution will adopt the shape of the data distribution. This finding can be deduced from an inspection of the shrinkage factor given in Equation 2.25. In the next chapter we focus our attention on the computational machinery for summarizing the posterior distribution.

3.8 SUGGESTED READINGS

Evans, M., Hastings, N. A. J., & Peacock, J. B. (2000). *Statistical distributions* (3rd ed.). New York: Wiley.

Kotz, S., Johnson, N. L., & Balakrishnan, N. (1994). *Continuous univariate distributions* (Vol. 1, 2nd ed.). New York: Wiley.

Kotz, S., Johnson, N. L., & Balakrishnan, N. (1995). *Continuous univariate distributions* (Vol. 2, 2nd ed.). New York: Wiley.

Kotz, S., Johnson, N. L., & Balakrishnan, N. (1997). *Discrete multivariate distributions*. New York: Wiley.

Kotz, S., Johnson, N. L., & Balakrishnan, N. (2000). *Continuous multivariate distributions* (Vol. 1, 2nd ed.). New York: Wiley.

APPENDIX 3.1
R CODE FOR CHAPTER 3

```
#-------------------------------------------------------------------#
# The following R code generates artificial data and plots the data distribution,
# the prior distribution under varying degrees of precision of the prior,
# and the resulting posterior distribution.
#
#             Program steps common for each plot
# 1. Create a sequence of values for the x-axis and artifical data for the y-axis.
# 2. Call a variety of available density functions in R.
# 3. Define the posterior as the product of the prior and the likelihood.
# 4. Generate plots.
#-------------------------------------------------------------------#

install.packages("scatterplot3d")
install.packages("pscl")
require(scatterplot3d)
require(pscl)

#-------------------------------------------------#
# Example 3.1. NORMAL DISTRIBUTION: MEAN KNOWN,  VARIANCE UNKNOWN
# PRIOR FOR SIGMA^2 IS INVERSE-GAMMA
#-------------------------------------------------#

x<- seq(0.1,10,by=.001)  y<- c(-1,-0.7,-0.5,-0.2,0.1,0.3,0.6,1.2)   n=8
par(mfrow=c(2,2),lwd=2,mar=c(3,3,4,4),cex.axis=.6)
```

```
# INVERSE-GAMMA(5,3)  -- HIGH PRECISION

prior = densigamma(x,5,3)
like = densigamma(x,sum(y^2),n/2-1)
and known mean parameter
post_propor = prior*like
#Approx. posterior density; sum(post)*0.001 = 1
post = post_propor / (0.001*sum(post_propor))
plot(x,post,type="l",ylab="Density",lty=1,xlim=c(0,8),ylim=c(0,2.5),
     lwd=2,col="gray",
     main=paste("Prior is Inverse-Gamma(5,3)"))
lines(x,like,lty=2,lwd=2)
lines(x,prior,lty=3,lwd=2)
legend("topright",c("prior","Likelihood","Posterior"),
lty=c(3,2,1),col=c("black","black","gray"))
# INVERSE GAMMA (3,3)
prior = densigamma(x,3,3) #scale parameter 3, shape parameter 3
like = densigamma(x,sum(y^2),n/2-1)
post_propor = prior*like
post = post_propor / (0.001*sum(post_propor))

plot(x,post,type="l",ylab="Density",lty=1,xlim=c(0,8),
     ylim=c(0,2.5),lwd=2,col="gray",
     main=paste("Prior is Inverse-Gamma(3,3)"))
lines(x,like,lty=2,lwd=2)
```

49

```r
lines(x,prior,lty=3,lwd=2)
legend("topright",c("prior","Likelihood","Posterior"),
    lty=c(3,2,1),col=c("black","black","gray"))

# INVERSE GAMMA (1,3)
prior = densigamma(x,1,3)
like = densigamma(x,sum(y^2),n/2-1)
post_propor = prior*like
post = post_propor / (0.001*sum(post_propor))

plot(x,post,type="l",ylab="Density",lty=1,xlim=c(0,8),
    ylim=c(0,2.5),lwd=2,col="gray",
    main=paste("Prior is Inverse-Gamma(1,3)"))
lines(x,like,lty=2,lwd=2)
lines(x,prior,lty=3,lwd=2)
legend("topright",c("prior","Likelihood","Posterior"),
    lty=c(3,2,1),col=c("black","black","gray"))

#-------- INVERSE GAMMA (0,3) -- VERY LOW PRECISION---------#
prior = densigamma(x,0.1,3)
like = densigamma(x,sum(y^2),n/2-1)
post_propor = prior*like
post = post_propor / (0.001*sum(post_propor))

plot(x,post,type="l",ylab="Density",lty=1,xlim=c(0,8),
    ylim=c(0,2.5),lwd=2,col="gray",
    main=paste("Prior is Inverse-Gamma(0.1,3)"))
```

```r
lines(x,like,lty=2,lwd=2)
lines(x,prior,lty=3,lwd=2)
legend("topright",c("prior","Likelihood","Posterior"),
    lty=c(3,2,1),col=c("black","black","gray"))

#--------NORMAL DISTRIBUTION: MEAN UNKNOWN, VARIANCE KNOWN---------#
x<- seq(-5,5,by=.001) #length(x)=10001
par(mfrow=c(2,2),lwd=2,mar=c(3,3,4,4),cex.axis=.6)

# Normal--High precision
prior = dnorm(x,0,0.3)

like = dnorm(x,0,1)
post_propor = prior*like
post = post_propor / (0.001*sum(post_propor)) #Approx. posterior density:
sum(post)*0.001
= 1

plot(x,post,type="l",ylab="Density",lty=1,lwd=2,col="gray",ylim=c(0,1.5),
    main=paste("Prior is Normal (0,0.3)"))
lines(x,like,lty=2,lwd=2)
lines(x,prior,lty=3,lwd=2)
legend(1.6,1.58,c("prior","Likelihood","Posterior"), lty=c(3,2,1),col=c("black","black",
"gray"))

# Normal--Intermediate precision
prior = dnorm(x,0,0.5)
```

51

```r
like = dnorm(x,0,1)
post_propor = prior*like
post = post_propor / (0.001*sum(post_propor))

plot(x,post,type="l",ylab="Density",lty=1,lwd=2,col="gray",ylim=c(0,1.5),
     main=paste("Prior is Normal (0,0.5)"))
lines(x,like,lty=2,lwd=2)
lines(x,prior,lty=3,lwd=2)
legend(1.6,1.58,c("prior","Likelihood","Posterior"), lty=c(3,2,1),col=c("black","black",
"gray"))

# Normal--low precision
prior = dnorm(x,0,1.2)
like = dnorm(x,0,1)
post_propor = prior*like
post = post_propor / (0.001*sum(post_propor))

plot(x,post,type="l",ylab="Density",lty=1,lwd=2,col="gray",ylim=c(0,1.5),
     main=paste("Prior is Normal (0,1.2)"))
lines(x,like,lty=2,lwd=2)
lines(x,prior,lty=3,lwd=2)
legend(1.6,1.58,c("prior","Likelihood","Posterior"), lty=c(3,2,1),col=c("black","black",
"gray"))

# Normal--very low precision
prior = dnorm(x,0,3)
like = dnorm(x,0,1)
```

```
post_propor = prior*like
post = post_propor / (0.001*sum(post_propor))

plot(x,post,type="l",ylab="Density",lty=1,lwd=2,col="gray",ylim=c(0,1.5),
     main=paste("Prior is Normal (0,3)"))
lines(x,like,lty=2,lwd=2)
lines(x,prior,lty=3,lwd=2)
legend(1.6,1.58,c("prior","Likelihood","Posterior"), lty=c(3,2,1),col=c("black","black",
"gray"))

# End

#------------UNIFORM PRIOR------------#
x<- seq(-5,5,by=.001)

par(mfrow=c(2,2),lwd=2,mar=c(3,3,4,4),cex.axis=.6)

# Prior: Uniform --High precision
prior = dunif(x,min=-1,max=1)
like = dnorm(x,0,1) #given parameter, the distribution of data
post_propor = prior*like
post = post_propor / (0.001*sum(post_propor)) #Approx. posterior density:
sum(post)*0.001
= 1

plot(x,post,type="l",ylab="",lty=1,lwd=2,col="gray",ylim=c(0,0.8),main=paste("Prior
is Uniform(-1,1)"))
```

```
lines(x,like,lty=2,lwd=2)
lines(x,prior,lty=3,lwd=2)
legend("topright",c("prior","Likelihood","Posterior"),lty=c(3,2,1),col=c("black",
"black","gray"))

# Prior: Uniform --Intermediate precision
prior = dunif(x,min=-3,max=1)
like = dnorm(x,0,1) #given parameter, the distribution of data
post_propor = prior*like
post = post_propor / (0.001*sum(post_propor)) #Approx. posterior density:
sum(post)*0.001
= 1

plot(x,post,type="l",ylab="",lty=1,lwd=2,col="gray",ylim=c(0,0.8),main=paste("Prior
is Uniform(-3,1)"))
lines(x,like,lty=2,lwd=2)
lines(x,prior,lty=3,lwd=2)
legend("topright",c("prior","Likelihood","Posterior"),lty=c(3,2,1),col=c("black",
"black","gray"))

# Prior: Uniform --Low precision
prior = dunif(x,min=-5,max=2)
like = dnorm(x,0,1) #given parameter, the distribution of data
post_propor = prior*like
post = post_propor / (0.001*sum(post_propor)) #Approx. posterior density:
sum(post)*0.001
= 1
```

```r
plot(x,post,type="l",ylab="",lty=1,lwd=2,col="gray",ylim=c(0,0.8),main=paste("Prior
is Uniform(-5,2)"))
  lines(x,like,lty=2,lwd=2)
  lines(x,prior,lty=3,lwd=2)
  legend("topright",c("prior","Likelihood","Posterior"),lty=c(3,2,1),col=c("black",
"black","gray"))

# Prior: Uniform --Very low precision
prior = dunif(x,min=-8,max=10)
like = dnorm(x,0,1) #given parameter, the distribution of data
post_propor = prior*like
post = post_propor / (0.001*sum(post_propor)) #Approx. posterior density:
sum(post)*0.001
= 1

plot(x,post,type="l",ylab="",lty=1,lwd=2,col="gray",ylim=c(0,0.8),main=paste("Prior
is Uniform(-8,10)"))
  lines(x,like,lty=2,lwd=2)
  lines(x,prior,lty=3,lwd=2)
  legend("topright",c("prior","Likelihood","Posterior"),lty=c(3,2,1),col=c("black",
"black","gray"))
# End

#------------POISSON DISTRIBUTION----------#

x<- seq(0.1,10,by=.001) #length(x)=9901;
y=c(1,3,4,7)
n=4
```

```r
par(mfrow=c(2,2),lwd=2,mar=c(3,3,4,4),cex.axis=.6)

# Prior: Gamma(10,0.2)--High precision
prior = dgamma(x,shape=10,scale=0.2)
like=dgamma(x,shape=sum(y)+1,scale=1/n)
post_propor = prior*like
post = post_propor / (0.001*sum(post_propor))  #Approx. posterior density:
#sum(post)*0.001
= 1

plot(x,post,type="l",ylab="Density",lty=1,lwd=2,col="gray",ylim=c(0,1.1),
        main=paste("Prior is Gamma(10,0.2)"))
lines(x,like,lty=2,lwd=2)
lines(x,prior,lty=3,lwd=2)
legend(5.5,1.15,c("prior","Likelihood","Posterior"), lty=c(3,2,1),col=c("black","black",
"gray"))

# Prior: Gamma(8,0.5)--Intermediate precision
prior = dgamma(x,shape=8,scale=0.5)
like=dgamma(x,shape=sum(y)+1,scale=1/n)
post_propor = prior*like
post = post_propor / (0.001*sum(post_propor))  #Approx. posterior density:
#sum(post)*0.001
= 1

plot(x,post,type="l",ylab="Density",lty=1,lwd=2,col="gray",ylim=c(0,1.1),
        main=paste("Prior is Gamma(8,0.5)"))
```

```r
lines(x,like,lty=2,lwd=2)
lines(x,prior,lty=3,lwd=2)

legend(5.5,1.15,c("prior","Likelihood","Posterior"), lty=c(3,2,1),col=c("black","black",
"gray"))

# Prior: Gamma(3,1)--Low precision
prior = dgamma(x,shape=3,scale=1)
like=dgamma(x,shape=sum(y)+1,scale=1/n)
post_propor = prior*like
post = post_propor / (0.001*sum(post_propor)) #Approx. posterior density:
#sum(post)*0.001
= 1

plot(x,post,type="l",ylab="Density",lty=1,lwd=2,col="gray",ylim=c(0,1.1),
     main=paste("Prior is Gamma(3,1)"))
lines(x,like,lty=2,lwd=2)
lines(x,prior,lty=3,lwd=2)
legend(5.5,1.15,c("prior","Likelihood","Posterior"), lty=c(3,2,1),col=c("black","black",
"gray"))

# Prior: Gamma(2.1,3)--Very low precision
prior = dgamma(x,shape=2.1,scale=3)
like=dgamma(x,shape=sum(y)+1,scale=1/n)
post_propor = prior*like
post = post_propor / (0.001*sum(post_propor)) #Approx. posterior density:
#sum(post)*0.001
= 1
```

```
plot(x,post,type="l",ylab="Density",lty=1,lwd=2,col="gray",ylim=c(0,1.1),
     main=paste("Prior is Gamma(2.1,3)"))
lines(x,like,lty=2,lwd=2)
lines(x,prior,lty=3,lwd=2)
legend(5.5,1.15,c("prior","Likelihood","Posterior"), lty=c(3,2,1),col=c("black","black",
"gray"))
# End


#-------BINOMIAL DISTRIBUTION-----------#
x<- seq(0.001,1,by=.001) #length(x)=1000; parameter
y=9
n=20

par(mfrow=c(2,2),lwd=2,mar=c(3,3,4,4),cex.axis=.6)

# Prior: Beta--High Precision
prior = dbeta(x,17,19)
like=dbeta(x,y+1,n-y+1)
post_propor = prior*like
post = post_propor / (0.001*sum(post_propor)) #Approx. posterior density:
#sum(post)*0.001
= 1

plot(x,post,type="l",ylab="Density",lty=1,lwd=2,col="gray",ylim=c(0,6),
     main=paste("Prior is Beta(17,19)"))
lines(x,like,lty=2,lwd=2)
lines(x,prior,lty=3,lwd=2)
```

```r
legend("topright",c("prior","Likelihood","Posterior"), lty=c(3,2,1),col=c("black",
"black","gray"))

# Prior: Beta--Intermediate Precision
prior = dbeta(x,7,8)
like=dbeta(x,y+1,n-y+1)
post_propor = prior*like
post = post_propor / (0.001*sum(post_propor)) #Approx. posterior density:
#sum(post)*0.001
= 1

plot(x,post,type="l",ylab="Density",lty=1,lwd=2,col="gray",ylim=c(0,6),
        main=paste("Prior is Beta(7,8)"))
lines(x,like,lty=2,lwd=2)
lines(x,prior,lty=3,lwd=2)
legend("topright",c("prior","Likelihood","Posterior"), lty=c(3,2,1),col=c("black",
"black","gray"))

# Prior: Beta--Low Precision
prior = dbeta(x,3,4)
like=dbeta(x,y+1,n-y+1)
post_propor = prior*like
post = post_propor / (0.001*sum(post_propor)) #Approx. posterior density:
#sum(post)*0.001
= 1
```

59

```
plot(x,post,type="l",ylab="Density",lty=1,lwd=2,col="gray",ylim=c(0,6),
    main=paste("Prior is Beta(3,4)"))
lines(x,like,lty=2,lwd=2)
lines(x,prior,lty=3,lwd=2)
legend("topright",c("prior","Likelihood","Posterior"), lty=c(3,2,1),col=c("black",
"black","gray"))

# Prior: Beta--Very low Precision
prior = dbeta(x,1.2,1.5)
like=dbeta(x,y+1,n-y+1)
post_propor = prior*like
post = post_propor / (0.001*sum(post_propor)) #Approx. posterior density:
#sum(post)*0.001
= 1

plot(x,post,type="l",ylab="Density",lty=1,lwd=2,col="gray",ylim=c(0,6),
    main=paste("Prior is Beta(1.2,1.5)"))
lines(x,like,lty=2,lwd=2)
lines(x,prior,lty=3,lwd=2)
legend("topright",c("prior","Likelihood","Posterior"), lty=c(3,2,1),col=c("black",
"black","gray"))
# End

#-------MULTINOMIAL DISTRIBUTION-----------# library(MCMCpack)          # For dirichlet
distribution library(MVA)        # For 3D plot

x<-matrix(rep(0,1000*3),nrow=1000)
```

```r
x[,1] <- sample(seq(0.001,1,by=.001))  #length(x[,1])=1000; parameter theta1
x[,2] <- runif(1000,0,1-x[,1])          #length(x[,2])=1000; parameter theta2
x[,3] <-1-x[,1]-x[,2]                    #length(x[,3])=1000; parameter theta3
y1=3
y2=5
y3=6
n=14

# Prior: Dirichlet (High Precision)
par(mfrow=c(3,3),lwd=2,mar=c(3,4,4),cex.axis=.6)

prior1 = ddirichlet(x, alpha=c(5,10,14))
likel=ddirichlet(x,alpha=c(y1+1,y2+1,y3+1))
post_propor = prior1*likel
post1 = post_propor / (0.001*sum(post_propor))  #Approx. posterior density:
#sum(post)*0.001
= 1

scatterplot3d(x[,1],x[,2],prior1,type="p",angle=55,color="black",
xlab=expression(pi[1]),
          ylab=expression(pi[2]),zlab="Prior Density",main="Dirichlet Prior for
Multinomial Distribution--High Precision")
scatterplot3d(x[,1],x[,2],likel,type="p",angle=55,color="black",
xlab=expression(pi[1]),
          ylab=expression(pi[2]), zlab="Likelihood",main="Likelihood")
scatterplot3d(x[,1],x[,2],post1,type="p",angle=55,color="black",
xlab=expression(pi[1]),
```

61

```r
         ylab=expression(pi[2]), zlab="Posterior Density",main="Posterior")

# Prior: Dirichlet (Intermediate Precision)

prior2 = ddirichlet(x, alpha=c(3,4,3))
like2=ddirichlet(x,alpha=c(y1+1,y2+1,y3+1))
post_propor = prior2*like2
post2 = post_propor / (0.001*sum(post_propor))  #Approx. posterior density:
#sum(post)*0.001
= 1

scatterplot3d(x[,1],x[,2],prior2,type="p",angle=55,color="black",
xlab=expression(pi[1]),
         ylab=expression(pi[2]),zlab="Prior Density",main="Dirichlet Prior for
Multinomial Distribution--Moderate Precision")
scatterplot3d(x[,1],x[,2],like2,type="p",angle=55,color="black",
xlab=expression(pi[1]),
         ylab=expression(pi[2]),
         zlab="Likelihood",main="Likelihood")
scatterplot3d(x[,1],x[,2],post2,type="p",angle=55,color="black",xlab=expression(pi[1]),
         ylab=expression(pi[2]), zlab="Posterior Density",main="Posterior")

# Prior: Dirichlet (Low Precision)

prior3 = ddirichlet(x, alpha=c(2,2,2))
like3=ddirichlet(x,alpha=c(y1+1,y2+1,y3+1))
post_propor = prior3*like3
```

```r
post3 = post_propor / (0.001*sum(post_propor)) #Approx. posterior density:
#sum(post)*0.001
= 1

scatterplot3d(x[,1],x[,2],prior3,type="p",angle=55,color="black",
xlab=expression(pi[1]),
            ylab=expression(pi[2]),zlab="Prior Density",main="Dirichlet Prior for
Multinomial Distribution--Low Precision")
scatterplot3d(x[,1],x[,2],like3,type="p",angle=55,color="black",
xlab=expression(pi[1]),
ylab=expression(pi[2]),
            zlab="Likelihood",main="Likelihood")
scatterplot3d(x[,1],x[,2],post3,type="p",angle=55,color="black",
xlab=expression(pi[1]),
ylab=expression(pi[2]),
            zlab="Posterior Density",main="Posterior")

# End
```

4

Markov Chain Monte Carlo Sampling

As stated in the Preface, the key reason for the increased popularity of Bayesian methods in the social sciences has been the (re)discovery of numerical algorithms for estimating posterior distributions of the model parameters given the data. Prior to these developments, it was virtually impossible to analytically derive summary measures of the posterior distribution, particularly for complex models with many parameters. The numerical algorithms that we describe in this chapter involve Monte Carlo integration using Markov chains—also referred to as Markov chain Monte Carlo (MCMC) sampling. These algorithms have a rather long history, arising out of statistical physics and image analysis (Geman & Geman, 1984; Metropolis, Rosenbluth, Rosenbluth, Teller, & Teller, 1953).

MCMC sampling encompasses a number of different algorithms. For the purposes of this chapter, we consider two of the most common algorithms that are available in both open source and commercially available software—the Metropolis–Hastings algorithm and the Gibbs sampler. First, however, we introduce some of the general features of Markov chains. This is followed by a discussion of the Metropolis–Hastings algorithm and the Gibbs sampler. Then, we turn to a discussion of the criteria used to evaluate the quality of an MCMC algorithm.

A number of very important papers and books have been written about MCMC sampling. This chapter draws on introductions given in

Gilks, Richardson, and Spiegelhalter (1996b), Kim and Bolt (2007), and Kaplan and Depaoli (2012a).

4.1 BASIC IDEAS OF MCMC SAMPLING

Within the frequentist school of statistics, a large number of popular estimation approaches are available to obtain point estimates and standard errors of model parameters. Perhaps the most common approach to parameter estimation is *maximum likelihood*. The focus of frequentist parameter estimation is the derivation of point estimates of model parameters that have desirable asymptotic properties. Under the assumptions required for maximum likelihood estimation (e.g., normality), point estimates are consistent, asymptotically normal, and efficient (see, e.g., Silvey, 1975).

In contrast to maximum likelihood estimation and other estimation methods within the frequentist paradigm, Bayesian inference focuses on estimating features of the posterior distribution, such as point estimates (e.g., the expected a posteriori or maximum a posteriori) and posterior probability intervals. The difficulty arises when attempting to summarize the posterior distribution.

Summarizing the posterior distribution requires calculating expectations. For simple problems, such as obtaining the mean or variance of a distribution, this can be handled analytically. However, for complex, high-dimensional problems involving multiple integrals, the task of calculating expectations can be virtually impossible. Rather than attempting the impossible task of analytically solving high-dimensional problems, we can instead draw samples from the posterior distribution and summarize the distribution formed by those samples. This approach is referred to as *Monte Carlo integration*. It is based on first drawing T samples of the parameters of interest $\{\theta_t,\ t = 1, \dots, T\}$ from the posterior distribution $p(\theta|y)$ and approximating the expectation by

$$E[p(\theta|y)] \approx \frac{1}{T}\sum_{t=1}^{T} p(\theta_t|y) \qquad (4.1)$$

Assuming the samples are independent of one another, we find that the law of large numbers ensures that the approximation in Equation 4.1

will be increasingly accurate as T increases. However, an important feature of Monte Carlo integration, and of particular relevance to Bayesian inference, is that the samples do not have to be drawn independently. All that is required is that the sequence $\{\theta_t, t = 1, \ldots, T\}$ will result in samples throughout the support of the distribution (Gilks, Richardson, & Spiegelhalter, 1996a).[1] One approach to sampling throughout the support of a distribution while also relaxing the assumption of independent sampling is through the use of a Markov chain.

Formally, a *Markov chain* is a sequence of dependent random variables $\{\theta^s\}$

$$\theta^0, \theta^1, \ldots, \theta^s, \ldots \tag{4.2}$$

such that the conditional probability of θ^s given all of the past variables depends only on θ^{s-1}—that is, only on the immediate past variable. This conditional probability is referred to as the *transition kernel K* of the Markov chain.[2]

The Markov chain has a number of very important properties, not the least of which is that over a long sequence, the chain will "forget" its initial state θ^0 and converge to its stationary distribution $p(\theta|y)$, which depends neither on the number of samples T nor on the initial state θ^0. The number of iterations prior to the stability of the distribution is referred to as the *burn-in* samples. Letting m represent the initial number of burn-in samples, we can obtain an *ergodic average* of the posterior distribution $p(\theta|y)$ as

$$\bar{p}(\theta|y) = \frac{1}{T - m} \sum_{t=m+1}^{T} p(\theta_t|y) \tag{4.3}$$

4.2 THE METROPOLIS–HASTINGS ALGORITHM

One of the earliest, yet still common, methods for constructing a Markov chain is referred to as the *Metropolis–Hastings* algorithm (Metropolis et

[1] The *support* of a distribution is the smallest closed interval (or set in the multivariate case) where the elements of the interval/set are members of the distribution. Outside the support of the distribution, the probability of the element is zero.

[2] For discrete random variables, K is referred to as the *transition matrix*.

al., 1953). Following Gilks et al. (1996a), the basic idea of the Metropolis–Hastings algorithm is as follows. First, a *candidate* value x is sampled from a so-called *proposal* distribution (also referred to as a *jumping distribution*, which we will denote as $q(.|y_t)$. This proposal distribution could be, for example, a standard normal distribution. Next, the algorithm *accepts* the candidate value with a probability

$$p(y, x) = \min \left\{ 1, \frac{p(x)q(y|x)}{p(y)q(x|y)} \right\} \tag{4.4}$$

Notice that the numerator of Equation 4.4 is the probability of the candidate value and the denominator is the probability of the current value. In essence, Equation 4.4 states that if the ratio $p(x)q(y|x) > p(y)q(x|y)$, then the probability of acceptance is 1.0—that is, we accept the candidate value with certainty. However, if the ratio is less than 1.0, then we can either move to the next value or stay at the current value. To render this decision, the algorithm then draws a value from a $U(0, 1)$ distribution. If the sample value is between 0 and $p(y, x)$, then the algorithm moves to the next state. That is, if x is accepted, then the algorithm moves to $y_{t+1} = x$. Otherwise, if it is rejected, then the algorithm does not move, and $y_{t+1} = y_t$. A remarkable feature of the Metropolis–Hastings algorithm is that, regardless of the proposal distribution, the stationary distribution of the algorithm will be $p(\cdot)$. The technical details of this fact can be found in Gilks et al. (1996a).

EXAMPLE 4.1. A SIMPLE DEMONSTRATION OF THE METROPOLIS–HASTINGS ALGORITHM

Two simple examples of the Metropolis–Hastings algorithm are presented in this section, and the R programs are presented in Appendix 4.1. The former uses the normal distribution as the proposal distribution from which a candidate point is sampled, while the latter program uses the uniform distribution as the proposal distribution. Trace plots and density plots for both analyses are given in Figure 4.1. Both plots are virtually indistinguishable, demonstrating that, regardless of the proposal distribution, we end up with the same stationary distribution. Moreover, there is good evidence from the trace plot that convergence was achieved. We discuss methods for determining convergence of the MCMC algorithm in Section 4.4.

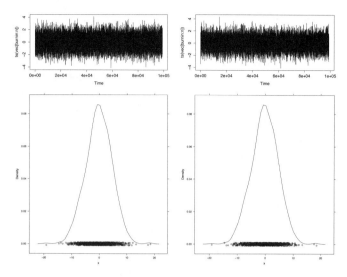

FIGURE 4.1. Metropolis–Hastings trace and density plots for normal (left column) and uniform (right column) proposal distributions.

4.3 THE GIBBS SAMPLER

In this section, we outline the general form of the Gibbs sampler. First, we discuss the Gibbs sampler in conceptual terms, and then we examine the formal algorithm.

Informally, the Gibbs sampler proceeds as follows. Consider that the goal is to obtain the joint posterior distribution of two model parameters—say, θ_1 and θ_2, given some data y, written as $p(\theta_1, \theta_2|y)$. These two model parameters can, for example, be regression coefficients from a simple multiple regression model. Dropping the conditioning on y for notational simplicity, what is required is to sample from $p(\theta_1|\theta_2)$ and $p(\theta_2|\theta_1)$. In the first step, an arbitrary value for θ_2 is chosen, say θ_2^0. We next obtain a sample from $p(\theta_1|\theta_2^0)$. Denote this value as θ_1^1. With this new value, we then obtain a sample θ_2^1 from $p(\theta_2|\theta_1^1)$. The Gibbs algorithm continues to draw samples using previously obtained values until two long chains of values for both θ_1 and θ_2 are formed. After discarding the burn-in samples, the remaining samples are then considered to be drawn from the marginal distributions of $p(\theta_1)$ and $p(\theta_2)$.

The formal algorithm can be specified as follows. Now, for notational clarity, let $\boldsymbol{\theta}$ be a vector of model parameters with elements $\boldsymbol{\theta} = \{\theta_1, \ldots, \theta_q\}$. The elements of $\boldsymbol{\theta}$ could be the parameters of a regression model, structural equation model, and so on. Note that information regarding $\boldsymbol{\theta}$ is contained in the prior distribution $p(\boldsymbol{\theta})$. Following the description given in Gilks et al. (1996b), the Gibbs sampler begins with an initial set of starting values for the parameters, denoted as $\boldsymbol{\theta}^{(0)} = (\theta_1^{(0)}, \ldots, \theta_q^{(0)})$. Given this starting point, the Gibbs sampler generates $\theta^{(s)}$ from $\theta^{(s-1)}$ as follows:

1. Sample $\theta_1^{(s)} \sim p(\theta_1 | \theta_2^{(s-1)}, \theta_3^{(s-1)}, \ldots, \theta_q^{(s-1)}, y)$

2. Sample $\theta_2^{(s)} \sim p(\theta_2 | \theta_1^{(s)}, \theta_3^{(s-1)}, \ldots, \theta_q^{(s-1)}, y)$

$\vdots$

q. Sample $\theta_q^{(s)} \sim p(\theta_q | \theta_1^{(s)}, \theta_2^{(s)}, \ldots, \theta_{q-1}^{(s)}, y)$

So, for example, in Step 1, a value for θ_1 at, say, iteration one is drawn from the conditional distribution of θ_1, given other parameters with start values at iteration zero and the data y. At Step 2, the algorithm draws a value for θ_2 at iteration one from the conditional distribution of θ_2, given the value of θ_1 drawn in Step 1, the remaining parameters at iteration zero, and the data. This process continues, and ultimately a sequence of dependent vectors are formed

$$\theta^{(1)} = \{\theta_1^{(1)}, \ldots, \theta_q^{(1)}\}$$
$$\theta^{(2)} = \{\theta_1^{(2)}, \ldots, \theta_q^{(2)}\}$$
$$\vdots$$
$$\theta^{(S)} = \{\theta_1^{(S)}, \ldots, \theta_q^{(S)}\}$$

This sequence exhibits the so-called *Markov property* insofar as $\theta^{(s)}$ is conditionally independent of $\{\theta_1^{(0)}, \ldots, \theta_q^{(s-2)}\}$ given $\theta^{(s-1)}$. Under some general conditions, the sampling distribution resulting from this sequence will converge to the target distribution as $s \to \infty$. See Gilks et al. (1996b) for additional details on the properties of MCMC.

In setting up the Gibbs sampler, a decision must be made regarding the number of Markov chains to be generated, as well as the number of iterations of the sampler. With regard to the number of chains to be generated, it is not uncommon to specify multiple chains. Each chain samples from another location of the posterior distribution based on starting values. With multiple chains it may be the case that fewer iterations are required, particularly if there is evidence for the chains converging to the same posterior mean for each parameter. In some cases, the same result can be obtained from one chain, although often requiring a considerably larger number of iterations. Once the chain has stabilized, the burn-in samples are discarded. Summary statistics, including the posterior mean, mode, standard deviation, and posterior probability intervals, are calculated on the post-burn-in iterations. Also, convergence diagnostics (discussed in Section 4.4) are calculated on the post-burn-in iterations.

EXAMPLE 4.2. A SIMPLE DEMONSTRATION OF THE GIBBS SAMPLER

The goal of this simple example is to obtain the posterior distribution of the mean and the precision of data generated from normal distribution with mean 0 and variance 5. The prior distribution was also normal with mean 0 and precision 0.001. The precision parameter was generated with a noninformative gamma distribution with shape and scale of 0.001. This demonstration makes use of the R packages "rjags" (Plummer, 2011) and "coda" (Plummer et al., 2006). The "rjags" program requires the user to download the program "JAGS," which stands for "Just Another Gibbs Sampler" (Plummer, 2003). The "JAGS" program is based on the "WinBUGS" language (Lunn, Thomas, Best, & Spiegelhalter, 2000) and provides considerable flexibility in specifiying and estimating Bayesian models. The R package "rjags" provides an R "wrapper" to "JAGS" and allows one to process and manipulate data using the flexible features of R and to send "JAGS" output also to R programs such as "coda" for postanalysis processing of diagnostics and summaries.

For this example, the algorithm was set to produce 1,000 burn-in iterations, with 99,000 post-burn-in draws and a thinning interval of 10, from two chains starting at different locations of the posterior distribution. Figure 4.2 shows the posterior distribution for the two chains.

4.4 CONVERGENCE DIAGNOSTICS

Assessing the convergence of the MCMC algorithm is a difficult task that has received attention in the literature for many years (see, e.g.,

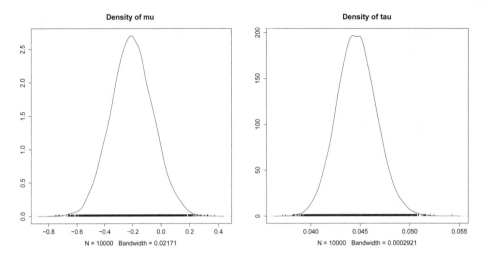

FIGURE 4.2. Posterior density of the mean and precision.

Mengersen, Robery, & Guihenneuc-Jouyax, 1999; Sinharay, 2004). The difficulty of assessing convergence stems from the very nature of MCMC in that the MCMC algorithm is designed to converge in distribution rather than to a point estimate. Because there is not a single adequate assessment of convergence, it is common to inspect several different diagnostics that examine varying aspects of convergence.

Perhaps the most common form of assessing MCMC convergence is to examine the convergence (also called *trace* or *history*) plots produced for a chain. Typically, a parameter will appear to converge if the sample estimates form a tight horizontal band across this history plot. However, using this method as an assessment for convergence is rather crude since merely viewing a tight plot does not indicate that convergence was actually obtained. As a result, this method is more likely to be an indicator of nonconvergence (Mengersen et al., 1999). For example, if two chains for the same parameter are sampling from different areas of the target distribution, there is evidence of nonconvergence. Likewise, if a plot shows substantial fluctuation or jumps in the chain, it is likely that the parameter has not reached convergence.

In addition to the trace plots, it is important to examine the speed in which the draws from the posterior distribution achieve independence.

As noted earlier, draws from the posterior distribution using a Markov chain are not, in the beginning, independent of one another. However, we expect that the chain will eventually "forget" its initial state and converge to a set of independent and stationary draws from the posterior distribution. We can determine how quickly the chain has forgotten its initial state by inspecting the autocorrelation function (ACF) plot. We prefer that the ACF drop off quickly over the number of iterations.

EXAMPLE 4.3. GIBBS SAMPLING TRACE AND ACF PLOTS FOR THE MEAN: TWO CHAINS

For this example, we use "coda" (Plummer et al., 2006) in R to present a complete set of diagnostics from the MCMC analysis in Example 4.2. We see from Figure 4.3 that there is evidence for convergence of the two chains. The trace plots show a nice horizontal band. Moreover, inspection of the ACF plots indicate that independent draws from the posterior distribution occur very quickly.

Although it is useful to examine trace and ACF plots, merely viewing these plots may not be sufficient to determine convergence (or nonconvergence). Thus it is common to reference additional diagnostics. Although the following list of diagnostics is not exhaustive, we focus on several of the most commonly used diagnostics for single-chain situations.

EXAMPLE 4.4. GEWEKE PLOTS FOR BOTH CHAINS SEPARATELY

The Geweke convergence diagnostic (Geweke, 1992) is used with a single chain to determine whether or not the first part of a chain differs significantly from the last part of a chain. The motivation for this diagnostic is rooted in the dependent nature of an MCMC chain. Specifically, since samples in a chain are not independently and identically distributed, it can be problematic to assess convergence due to the inherent dependence between adjacent samples. As a result of this dilemma, Geweke constructed a diagnostic that aims at assessing two independent sections of the chain. The program "coda" allows the user to set the proportion of iterations to be assessed at the beginning and the end of the chain. The default for the program mimics the standard suggested by

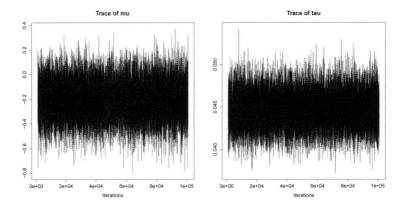

Chains 1 and 2

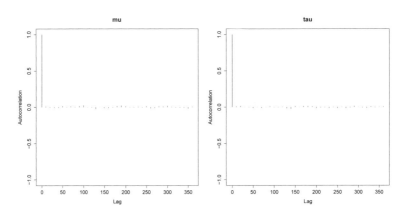

Chain 1

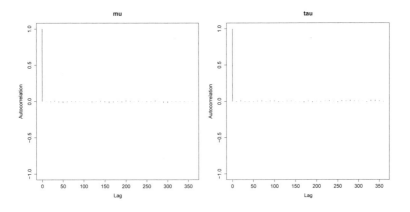

Chain 2

FIGURE 4.3. Trace and ACF plots for two chains.

74

Geweke (1992), which is to compare the first 10% of the chain and the last 50% of the chain. Although the user can modify this default, it is important to note that there should be a sufficient number of iterations between the two samples to ensure that the means for the two samples are independent. This method computes a z-statistic whereby the difference in the two sample means is divided by the asymptotic standard error of their difference. A z-statistic falling in the extreme tail of a standard normal distribution suggests that the sample from the beginning of the chain has not yet converged (Smith, 2005). The program "coda" produces an observed z-statistic and two-sided p-value. It is common to conclude that there is evidence against convergence with a p-value less than .05. We see from Figure 4.4 that the sample points within the first 10% of the chain all fall within -2 and $+2$ z-score units, and the same holds true for the last 50%. The Geweke diagnostic also produces a z-score for the difference between the means (adjusted for autocorrelation). In this example, the z-score is 0.530 ($p > .05$).

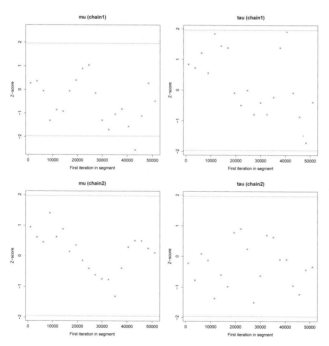

FIGURE 4.4. Geweke plots.

EXAMPLE 4.5. THE GELMAN–RUBIN–BROOKS PLOT

When implementing an MCMC algorithm such as the Gibbs sampler with multiple chains, one of the most common diagnostics is the Brooks, Gelman, and Rubin diagnostic (see, e.g., Gelman & Rubin, 1992a; Gelman, 1996; Gelman & Rubin, 1992b). This diagnostic is based on analysis of variance and is intended to assess convergence among several parallel chains with varying starting values. Specifically, Gelman and Rubin (1992a) proposed a method in which an overestimate and an underestimate of the variance of the target distribution is formed. The overestimate of the variance of the target distribution is measured by the between-chain variance, and the underestimate is measured by the within-chain variance (Gelman, 1996). The theory is that these two estimates should be approximately equal at the point of convergence. The comparison of between and within variances is referred to as the *potential scale reduction factor* (PSRF), and larger values typically indicate that the chains have not fully explored the target distribution. Specifically, a variance ratio that is computed with values approximately equal to 1.0 indicates convergence. Brooks and Gelman (1998) added an adjustment for sampling variability in the variance estimates and also proposed a multivariate extension (MPSRF) that does not include the sampling variability correction. We see from Figure 4.5 that the potential scale reduction factor indicates convergence of the chains insofar as the variance ratio is nearly 1.0.

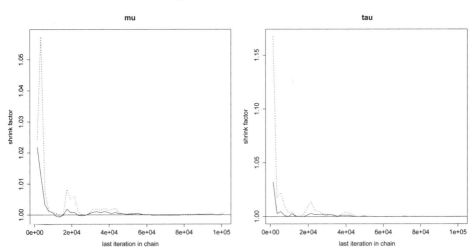

FIGURE 4.5. Gelman–Rubin–Brooks plot.

EXAMPLE 4.6. THE HEIDELBERGER—WELCH DIAGNOSTIC

The Heidelberger and Welch convergence diagnostic (Heidelberger & Welch, 1983) is a stationary test that determines whether or not the last part of a Markov chain has stabilized. This test uses the Cramér–von Mises statistic to assess evidence of nonstationarity. If there is evidence of nonstationarity, the first 10% of the iterations will be discarded and the test will be repeated until either the chain has passed the test or more than 50% of the iterations are discarded. If the latter situation occurs, it suffices to conclude there was not a sufficiently long stationary portion of the chain to properly assess convergence (Heidelberger & Welch, 1983). The results presented in "coda" report the number of iterations that were retained as well as the Cramér–von Mises statistic. Each parameter is given a status of having either passed the test or not passed the test based on the Cramér–von Mises statistic. If a parameter does not pass this test, this is an indication that the chain needs to run longer before achieving convergence. A second stage of this diagnostic examines the portion of the iterations that pass the stationary test for accuracy. Specifically, if the half-width of the estimate's confidence interval is less than a preset fraction of the mean, then the test implies that the mean was estimated with sufficient accuracy. If a parameter fails under this diagnostic stage (indicating low estimate accuracy), it may be necessary for a longer run of the MCMC sampler.

For this current example, the Heidelberger–Welch diagnostic suggests that Markov chains have stabilized and there is no need to run the chains out any longer.

EXAMPLE 4.7. THE RAFTERY—LEWIS DIAGNOSTIC

The Raftery and Lewis convergence diagnostic (Raftery & Lewis, 1992) was originally developed for Gibbs sampling and is used to help determine three of the main features of MCMC: the burn-in length, the total number of iterations, and the thinning interval (if any). A process is carried out that identifies this information for all of the model parameters being estimated. This diagnostic is specified for a particular quantile of interest with a set degree of accuracy within the "coda" program. Once the quantiles of interest and accuracy are set, "coda" will produce the number of iterations needed for a burn-in and a range of necessary post-burn-in iterations for a particular parameter to converge. For each of these iterations, a lower-bound value is produced which represents the minimum number of iterations (burn-in or post-burn-in) needed to estimate the specified quantile using independent samples. Note, however, that the minimum value recommended for the burn-in phase can be optimistic and larger values are often required for this phase (Mengersen et al., 1999).

Finally, information is also provided about the thinning interval that should be used for each parameter. This process involves comparing first-order and second-order Markov chains together for several different thinning intervals. This comparison is accomplished through computing G^2, a likelihood-ratio test statistic between the Markov models (Raftery & Lewis, 1996). After computing G^2, the Bayesian information criterion (BIC) can then be computed in order to compare the models directly.[3] The BIC is discussed in Chapter 5. The most appropriate thinning interval is chosen by adopting the smallest thinning value produced where the first-order Markov chain fits better than the second-order chain.

Although the default in the "coda" program is to estimate the 0.025 quantile, the 0.5 quantile is often of more interest in determining the number of iterations needed for convergence because interest typically focuses on the central tendency of the distribution. Using this diagnostic is often an iterative process in that the results from an initial chain may indicate that a longer chain is needed to obtain parameter convergence. A word of caution is that "bad" starting values can contribute to the Raftery and Lewis diagnostic requesting a larger number of burn-in and post-burn-in iterations. On a related note, Raftery and Lewis (1996) recommend that the maximum number of burn-in and post-burn-in iterations produced from the diagnostic be used in the final analysis. However, this may not always be practical when models are complex (e.g., longitudinal mixture models) or starting values are purposefully overdispersed.

For this example, we ran the Raftery–Lewis diagnostic for the 0.025 quantile and the 0.50 quantile using the default tolerance and

---

[3]Note that the BIC can be assessed by using the likelihood-ratio test statistic G^2; specifically, $BIC = G^2 - 2 \log n$. Raftery and Lewis (1996) discuss how this can be used to compare first-order and second-order Markov chains in relation to determining the most appropriate thinning interval for a chain.

probability levels (0.005 and 0.95, respectively). For the 0.025 quantile, we find that the Raftery–Lewis diagnostic suggests two burn-in iterations followed by a total of 3,680 iterations to obtain convergence of the chain. As noted by Mengersen et al. (1999), the number of burn-in iterations for this example appears optimistic. For the 0.50 quantile analysis, we find that 38,415 iterations are required for convergence using these tolerance and p-value levels, which we believe reflects poor automatic start values for the diagnostic. Given the information from the other diagnostics, we believe that the 10,000 iterations used in this example are sufficient for convergence of the chains.

4.5 SUMMARY

Markov chain Monte Carlo sampling revolutionized Bayesian statistical practice by making it possible to accurately estimate the posterior distribution of model parameters. Two algorithms were reviewed in this chapter—the Metropolis–Hastings algorithm and the Gibbs sampler. Convergence diagnostics were presented along with some simple examples. Monitoring convergence cannot be overstated insofar as MCMC can be computationally intensive, especially for complex models.

This chapter ends Part I of the book. We now turn from the theoretical and technical details of Bayesian inference to Bayesian statistical practice.

4.6 SUGGESTED READINGS

Albert, J. (2009). *Bayesian computation with R* (2nd ed.). New York: Springer.

Brooks, S., Gelman, A., Jones, G. L., & Meng, X.-L. (2011). *Handbook of Markov chain Monte Carlo*. Boca Raton, FL: Chapman and Hall/CRC Press.

Casella, G., & Robert, C. (2003). *Monte Carlo statistical methods*. New York: Springer.

Cowles, M. K., & Carlin, B. P. (1996). Markov chain Monte Carlo convergence diagnostics: A comparative review. *Journal of the American Statistical Association, 91*, 883–904.

Gilks, W. R., Richardson, S., & Spiegelhalter, D. J. (Eds.). (1996). *Markov chain Monte Carlo in practice*. London: Chapman and Hall.

Kim, J.-S., & Bolt, D. M. (2007). Estimating item response theory models using Markov chain Monte Carlo methods. *Educational Measurement: Issues and Practice, 26,* 38–51.

Sinharay, S. (2004). Experiences with Markov chain Monte Carlo convergence assessment in two psychometric examples. *Journal of Educational and Behavioral Statistics, 29,* 461–488.

APPENDIX 4.1
R CODE FOR CHAPTER 4

```
install.packages("pastecs")
install.packages("coda")
require(pastecs)
require(coda)

#-----------------------------------------------------------------------#
# EXAMPLE 4.1: Metropolis-Hastings Algorithm with a normal proposal distribution
#                      Program Steps:
# 1. Define a numeric vector of length n and set the first value to zero
# 2. Draw one value from a proposal normal distribution with mean 0 and variance 1
# 3. Define a candidate value as the value of the target plus the first value
# 4. Define the acceptance probability "aprob" as the minimum value of 1 or the
#    ratio of the density values of candidate value and x.
# 5. Decide to accept or reject the candidate value by comparing ``aprob" to a random
#    draw from a uniform(0, 1) distribution
# 6. Summarize and plot the results
#-----------------------------------------------------------------------#

MHNorm <- function (n,burnin,print=FALSE)
{
        vec <- vector("numeric", n)
        x <- 0 vec[1] <- x
        for (i in 2:n) {
```

```r
        target <- rnorm(1,0,1)
        can <- x + target
        aprob <- min(1, dnorm(can)/dnorm(x))
        u <- runif(1)
        if (u < aprob)
            x <- can
        vec[i] <- x
    }
    summary <- stat.desc(vec[burnin:n], basic=F)
    print(summary)

    if (print==TRUE) print(vec[burnin:n])

par(mfrow=c(2,1))
plot(ts(vec[burnin:n]))
hist(vec[burnin:n],30,main=NULL,xlab=NULL)
par(mfrow=c(1,1))
}
# End

#--Metropolis-Hastings Algorithm with a Uniform Proposal Distribution--#
require(pastecs)
require(coda)

MHunif <- function (n,burnin,tau,print=FALSE)
```

82

```
{
vec <- vector("numeric",n)
x <- 0 vec[1] <- x
for (i in 2:n) {
    target <- runif(1, -tau, tau)
    can <- x + target
    aprob <- min(1, dnorm(can)/dnorm(x))
    u <- runif(1)
    if (u < aprob)
        x <- can

        vec[i] <- x
}

summary <- stat.desc(vec[burnin:n], basic=F)
print(summary)

if (print==TRUE) print(vec[burnin:n])
}

par(mfrow=c(2,1))
plot(ts(vec[burnin:n]))
hist(vec[burnin:n],30)
par(mfrow=c(1,1))
boa.geweke(vec[burnin:n],.10,.90)
}
# End
```

83

```
#------------------------------------------------------------------
# EXAMPLE 4.2: Gibbs Sampler
#              Program Steps
# 1. Define a sample of size N and generate data from a normal distribution with
#              chosen mean and variance (here, 0 and 5, respectively)
# 2. Create a table to be filled in later
# 3. Write JAGS code beginning with "modelstring="
# 4. Define a probability distribution for x and for hyperparameters mu and tau
# 5. End JAGS code and return to rjags
# 6. Create a .bug file that contains the model string
# 7. Define rjags parameters
# 8. Run jags.model which reads in model.bug and model parameters
# 9. Summarize with coda and diagnostics
#------------------------------------------------------------------

install.packages("rjags") # requires that "jags" be installed"
install.packages("coda")
require(rjags)
require(coda)

N <- 1000
x <- rnorm(N, 0, 5)

write.table(x,
            file = 'example1.data',
            row.names = FALSE,
            col.names = FALSE)
```

84

```
#-----------------------------------------#
# JAGS code starts here
#-----------------------------------------#

modelstring="
model {
for (i in 1:N) {
x[i] ~ dnorm(mu, tau)
}
mu ~ dnorm(0, .0001)
tau ~ dgamma(0.001,0.001)
} "
#-----------------------------------------#
# JAGS code ends here
#-----------------------------------------#
writeLines(modelstring,con="model.bug")
parameters = c("mu","tau") #Specify the Parameters to Be Estimated
adaptSteps = 500
burnInSteps = 1000
nChains = 2
thinSteps = 10
nPerChain = 100000

foo <- jags.model("model.bug",
                  data = list('x' = x,
                              'N' = N),
```

```
                      n.chains = nChains,
                      n.adapt = adaptSteps)

cat("Burning in the MCMC chain ...\n")

update(foo, n.iter=burnInSteps)
cat("Sampling from the final MCMC chain ...  \n")

codaSamples1 = coda.samples(foo, variable.names=parameters,
                      n.iter=nPerChain, thin=thinSteps, seed=2847)

summary(codaSamples1[[1]])      #Posterior Mean, posterior SD and posterior probablity
interval (PPI) for the first chain

plot(codaSamples1, trace=F)
plot(codaSamples1, density=F, col="black")

par(mfrow=c(2,2))
autocorr.plot(codaSamples1[[1]])
autocorr.plot(codaSamples1[[2]])

geweke.plot(codaSamples1)
geweke.diag(codaSamples1)

#Gelman Plot
gelman.diag(codaSamples1)
gelman.plot(codaSamples1)
```

```
#Heidelberger-Welch diagnostics
heidel.diag(codaSamples1[[1]])

#Raftery.diag
raftery.diag(codaSamples1[[1]])

# End
```

Part II

Topics in Bayesian Modeling

5

Bayesian Hypothesis Testing

5.1 SETTING THE STAGE: THE CLASSICAL APPROACH TO HYPOTHESIS TESTING AND ITS LIMITATIONS

A critically important component of applied statistics is inference and model building. Indeed, a considerable amount of time is spent in introductory statistics courses laying the foundation for the frequentist perspective on hypothesis testing, culminating in the Neyman–Pearson approach which can be considered the conventional approach to hypothesis testing in the social sciences. An interesting aspect of the Neyman–Pearson approach to hypothesis testing is that students (as well as many seasoned researchers) appear to have a very difficult time grasping its principles. In a review of the problem of hypothesis testing in the social sciences, Gigerenzer et al. (2004) argued that much of the difficulty in grasping frequentist hypothesis testing lies in the conflation of Fisherian hypothesis testing and the Neyman–Pearson approach to hypothesis testing. For interesting discussions on this problem, see, for example, Cohen (1994), Gigerenzer et al. (2004), and Harlow, Mulaik, and Steiger (1997).

Briefly, Fisher's early approach to hypothesis testing required specifying only the null hypothesis. A conventional significance level is chosen (usually the 5% level). Once the test is conducted, the result is either significant ($p < .05$) or it is not ($p > .05$). If the resulting test is significant, then the null hypothesis is rejected. However, if the resulting test is not significant, then no conclusion can be drawn. As Gigerenzer et al. (2004) have pointed out, Fisher developed a later version of his ideas wherein one only reports the exact significance level arising from the test and does not place a "significant" or "nonsignificant" value label to the result. In other words, one reports, say, $p = .045$ but does not label the result as "significant" (Gigerenzer et al., 2004, p. 399).

In contrast to Fisher's ideas, the approach advocated by Neyman and Pearson requires that two hypotheses be specified—the null and alternative hypothesis. By specifying two hypotheses, one can compute a desired trade-off between two types of errors: Type I errors (the probability of rejecting the null when it is true, denoted as α) and Type II errors (the probability of not rejecting the null when it is false, denoted as β, where $1 - \beta$ denotes the *power* of the test). As Raftery (1995) has pointed out, the dimensions of this hypothesis are not relevant—that is, the problem can be as simple as the difference between a treatment group and a control group, or as complex as a structural equation model. The point remains that only two hypotheses are of interest in the conventional practice. Moreover, as Raftery (1995) notes, it is often far from the case that only two hypotheses are of interest. This is particularly true in the early stages of a research program, when a large number of models might be of interest to explore, with equally large numbers of variables that can be plausibly entertained as relevant to the problem. The goal is not, typically, the comparison of any one model taken as "true" against an alternative model. Rather, it is whether the data provide evidence in support for one of the competing models.

The conflation of Fisherian and Neyman–Pearson hypothesis testing lies in the use and interpretation of the p-value. In Fisher's paradigm, the p-value is a matter of convention with the resulting outcome being based on the data. In contrast, in the Neyman–Pearson paradigm, α and β are determined prior to the experiment being conducted and refer to a consideration of the cost of making one or the other error. Indeed, in the Neyman–Pearson approach, the problem is one of finding a balance between α, power, and sample size. However, even a casual perusal of the top journals in the social sciences will reveal that this balance is virtually always ignored and $\alpha = 0.05$ is used. The conventional 0.05 level itself is the result of Fisher's experience with small agricultural experiments. The point is that the p-value and α are not the same thing. The confusion between these two concepts is made worse

by the fact that statistical software packages often report a number of
p-values that a researcher can choose from after having conducted the
analysis (e.g., .001, .01, .05). This can lead a researcher to set α ahead
of time, as per the Neyman–Pearson school, but then communicate a
different level of "significance" after running the test.[1]

Of course, misunderstanding the Fisher or Neyman–Pearson framework for hypothesis testing and/or poor methodological practice is not
a criticism of the approach per se. However, from the frequentist point
of view, a criticism often leveled at the Bayesian approach to statistical inference is that it is "subjective," while the frequentist approach is
"objective." This criticism also appears in discussions of the differences
in these approaches to hypothesis testing. The objection to "subjectivism" is somewhat perplexing insofar as frequentist hypothesis testing
also rests on assumptions that do not involve data. A clear example of
this problem is the definition of a statistically significant effect—that is,
the *p*-value is properly interpreted as the probability of observing data
at least as extreme as the data that were actually observed under the
assumption that the null hypothesis is true. In fact, classical significance
testing violates the likelihood principle discussed in Section 2.3 (see
also Kadane, 2011). These issues are taken up in Chapter 10. Suffice to
say here that a key difference between Bayesian and frequentist approaches to hypothesis testing is that Bayesian inference is based on the
data at hand and makes prior information explicit. Moreover, Bayesians do not find the idea that parameters possess probability distributions in conflict with a coherent framework for hypothesis testing.

5.2 POINT ESTIMATES OF THE POSTERIOR DISTRIBUTION

For frequentists and Bayesians alike, model building and hypothesis
testing proceeds after obtaining summaries of relevant distributions.
For example, in testing for the differences between two groups (e.g., a
treatment group and a control group), we first summarize the data, obtaining the means and standard deviations for both groups and then

---

[1] The conventional practice is even worse than described, as evidenced by nonsensi-
cal phrases such as results "trending toward significance."

perform the relevant statistical tests. These summary statistics are considered "sufficient" summaries of the data; in a sense, they stand in for the data. The difference between Bayesian and frequentist statistics is that with Bayesian statistics we wish to obtain summaries of the posterior distribution. The expressions for the mean and variance of the posterior distribution come from expressions for the mean and variance of conditional distributions generally. Specifically, for the continuous case, the mean of the posterior distribution of θ given the data y is referred to as the *expected a posteriori* or EAP estimate and can be written as

$$E(\theta|y) = \int_{-\infty}^{+\infty} \theta p(\theta|y)d\theta \qquad (5.1)$$

Similarly, the variance of posterior distribution of θ given y can be obtained as

$$\text{var}(\theta|y) = E[(\theta - E[(\theta|y)])^2|y]$$
$$= \int_{-\infty}^{+\infty} (\theta - E[\theta|y])^2 p(\theta|y)d\theta$$
$$= \int_{-\infty}^{+\infty} (\theta^2 - 2\theta E[\theta|y]) + E[\theta|y]^2)p(\theta|y)d\theta$$
$$= E[\theta^2|y] - E[\theta|y]^2 \qquad (5.2)$$

The mean and variance provide two simple summary values of the posterior distribution. Another common summary measure is the mode of the posterior distribution—referred to as the *maximum a posteriori* (MAP) estimate. The MAP begins with the idea of maximum likelihood estimation. Maximum likelihood estimation obtains the value of θ, say $\hat{\theta}_{ML}$, which maximizes the likelihood function $L(\theta|y)$, written succinctly as

$$\hat{\theta}_{ML} = \arg\max_{\theta} L(\theta|y) \qquad (5.3)$$

where $\arg\max_{\theta}$ stands for the value of the argument for which the function attains its maximum. In Bayesian inference, however, we treat θ as random and specify a prior distribution on θ to reflect our uncertainty about θ. By adding the prior distribution to Equation 5.3, we obtain

$$\hat{\theta}_{MAP} = \arg \max_{\theta} L(\theta|y)p(\theta) \tag{5.4}$$

Recalling that $p(\theta|y) = L(\theta|y)p(\theta)$ is the posterior distribution, we see that Equation 5.4 provides the maximum value of the posterior distribution of θ given y, corresponding to the mode of the posterior distribution.

5.2.1 Interval Summaries of the Posterior Distribution

Along with point summary measures and posterior probabilities, it is usually desirable to provide interval summaries of the posterior distribution. There are two general approaches to obtaining interval summaries of the posterior distribution. The first is the so-called *posterior probability interval* (also referred to as the *credible interval*), and the second is the *highest posterior density interval*.

Posterior Probability Intervals

One important consequence of viewing parameters probabilistically concerns the interpretation of *confidence intervals*. Recall that the frequentist confidence interval requires that we imagine a fixed parameter, say the population mean μ. Then, we imagine an infinite number of repeated samples from the population characterized by μ. For any given sample, we can obtain the sample mean $\bar{x}$ and then form a $100(1 - \alpha)\%$ confidence interval. The correct frequentist interpretation is that $100(1 - \alpha)\%$ of the confidence intervals formed this way capture the true parameter μ under the null hypothesis. Notice that from this perspective, the probability that the parameter is in the interval is either 0 or 1.

In contrast, the Bayesian framework assumes that a parameter has a probability distribution. Sampling from the posterior distribution of the model parameters, we can obtain its quantiles. From the quantiles, we can directly obtain the probability that a parameter lies within a particular interval. So here, a 95% posterior probability interval would mean that the probability that the parameter lies in the interval is 0.95. Notice that this is entirely different from the frequentist interpretation and arguably aligns with common sense.[2]

---

[2] Interestingly, the Bayesian interpretation is often the one incorrectly ascribed to the frequentist interpretation of the confidence interval.

In formal terms, a $100(1 - \alpha)\%$ posterior probability interval for a particular subset of the parameter space Θ is defined as

$$1 - \alpha = \int_C p(\theta|x)d\theta \qquad (5.5)$$

The posterior probability interval will be demonstrated by way of the examples presented throughout this book.

Highest Posterior Density

The simplicity of the posterior probability interval notwithstanding, it is not the only way to provide an interval estimate of a parameter. Following arguments set down by Box and Tiao (1973), when considering the posterior distribution of a parameter θ, there is a substantial part of the region of that distribution where the density is quite small. It may be reasonable, therefore, to construct an interval in which every point inside the interval has a higher probability than any point outside the interval. Such a construction is referred to as the *highest posterior density (HPD)* interval. More formally,

> **Definition.** Let $p(\theta|y)$ be the posterior probability density function. A region R of the parameter space θ is called the HPD region of the interval $1 - \alpha$ if
>
> 1. $p(\theta \in R|y) = 1 - \alpha$
> 2. For $\theta_1 \in R$ and $\theta_2 \notin R$, $p(\theta_1|y) \geq p(\theta_2|y)$

In words, the first part says that given the data y, the probability that θ is in a particular region is equal to $1 - \alpha$, where α is determined ahead of time. The second part says that for two different values of θ, denoted as θ_1 and θ_2, if θ_1 is in the region defined by $1 - \alpha$ but θ_2 is not, then θ_1 has a higher probability than θ_2 given the data. Note that for unimodal and symmetric distributions, such as the uniform distribution or the normal distribution, the HPD is formed by choosing tails of equal density. The advantage of the HPD arises when densities are not symmetric and/or are not unimodal. This is an important property of the HPD and sets it apart from posterior probability intervals. Following Box and Tiao (1973), if $p(\theta|y)$ is not uniform over every region in θ, then the HPD region $1 - \alpha$ is unique. Also, if $p(\theta_1|y) = p(\theta_2|y)$, then these points are included (or excluded) by a $1 - \alpha$ HPD region. The opposite is true as well: namely, if $p(\theta_1|y) \neq p(\theta_2|y)$, then a $1 - \alpha$ HPD region includes one point but not the other (Box & Tiao, 1973, p. 123).

EXAMPLE 5.1. HPD PLOTS

Figure 5.1 shows the HPDs for a symmetric distribution centered at zero on the left and an asymmetric distribution on the right. We see that for the symmetric distribution, the 95% HPD aligns with the 95% confidence interval as well as the posterior probability interval, as expected. Perhaps more importantly, we see the role of the HPD in the case of the asymmetric distribution on the right. Such distributions could arise from the mixture of two normal distributions. Here, the value of the posterior probability interval would be misleading. The HPD, by contrast, indicates that, due to the asymmetric nature of this particular distribution, there is very little difference in the probability that the parameter of interest lies within the 95% or 99% intervals of the highest posterior density.

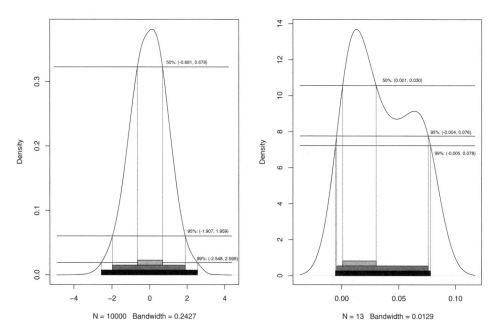

FIGURE 5.1. HPD plot for symmetric and nonsymmetric distributions.

5.3 BAYESIAN MODEL EVALUATION AND COMPARISON

In many respects, the frequentist and Bayesian goals of model building are the same. First, a researcher will specify an initial model relying on a lesser or greater degree of prior theoretical knowledge. At this first stage, a number of different models may be specified according to different theories, with the goal being to choose the "best" model, in some sense of the word. Second, these models will be fit to data obtained from a sample from some relevant population. Third, an evaluation of the quality of the models will be undertaken, examining where each model might deviate from the data, as well as assessing any possible model violations. At this point, model respecification may come into play. Finally, depending on the goals of the research, the "best model" will be chosen for some purpose.

Despite the similarities between the two approaches with regard to the broad goals of model building, there are important differences. A major difference between the Bayesian and frequentist goals of model building lies in the model specification stage. In particular, because the Bayesian perspective explicitly incorporates uncertainty regarding model parameters in terms of probability distributions, the first phase of model building will require the specification of a full probability model for the data and the parameters of the model, where the latter require the specification of prior distributions. The notion of model fit, therefore, implies that the full probability model fits the data. Lack of model fit may well be due to incorrect specification of likelihood, the prior distribution, or both.

Arguably, another difference between the Bayesian and frequentist goals of model building relates to the justification for choosing a particular model among a set of competing models. Specifically, model building and model choice in the frequentist domain are based primarily on choosing the model that best fits the data. This has certainly been the key motivation for model building, respecification, and model choice in the context of popular methods in the social sciences such as structural equation modeling (see, e.g., Kaplan, 2009). In the Bayesian domain, the choice among a set of competing models is based on which model provides the best posterior predictions. That is, the choice among a set of competing models should be based on which model will best predict what actually happened.

In this section, we examine the notion of model building and model fit and discuss a number of commonly used Bayesian approaches. We first introduce a familiar approach to model checking—namely, whether predictive values generated by the model actually fit the observed data. Next, we introduce Bayes factors as a very general means of choosing from a set of competing models. This is followed by a special case of the Bayes factor, referred to as the Bayesian information criterion. Then, we consider the deviance information criterion. Finally, we will consider the idea of borrowing strength from a number of competing models in the form of Bayesian model averaging.

5.3.1 Posterior Predictive Checks

A very natural way of evaluating the quality of a model is to examine how well the model fits the actual data. Examples of such approaches abound in frequentist statistics, often based on "badness-of-fit" measures. In the context of Bayesian statistics, the approach to examining how well a model fits the data is based on the notion of *posterior predictive checks* and the accompanying *posterior predictive p-value*. An important philosophical defense of the use of posterior predictive checks can be found in Gelman and Shalizi (2013).

The general idea behind posterior predictive checking is that there should be little, if any, discrepancy between data generated by the model and the actual data itself. In essence, posterior predictive checking is a method for assessing the specification quality of the model. Any deviation between the data generated from the model and the actual data implies model misspecification.

In the Bayesian context, the approach to examining model fit and specification utilizes the posterior predictive distribution of replicated data. Following Gelman, Carlin, Stern, and Rubin (2003), let y^{rep} be data replicated from our current model. That is,

$$p(y^{\text{rep}}|y) = \int p(y^{\text{rep}}|\theta)p(\theta|y)d\theta,$$
$$= \int p(y^{\text{rep}}|\theta)p(y|\theta)p(\theta)d\theta \qquad (5.6)$$

Notice that Equation 5.6 derives from the fact that the second term on the right-hand side of Equation 5.6 is simply the posterior distribution of the model parameters. In words, Equation 5.6 states that the distribution of future observations given the present data, $p(y^{rep}|y)$, is equal to the probability distribution of the future observations given the parameters, $p(y^{rep}|\theta)$, weighted by the posterior distribution of the model parameters. This is then integrated (or summed) over the model parameters, yielding the distribution of future observations given the present data. Thus, posterior predictive checking accounts for the uncertainty in the model parameters and the uncertainty in the data.

As a means of assessing the fit of the model, posterior predictive checking implies that the replicated data should match the observed data quite closely if we are to conclude that the model fits the data. One approach to quantifying model fit in the context of posterior predictive checking incorporates the notion of Bayesian p-values. Denote by $T(y)$ a test statistic based on the data, and let $T(y^{rep})$ be the same test statistic but defined for the replicated data. Then, the Bayesian p-value is defined to be

$$p\text{-value} = p(T(y^{rep}) \geq T(y)|y) \tag{5.7}$$

Equation 5.7 measures the proportion of test statistics based on replicated data that equal or exceed those of the test statistics based on the actual data.

One way to consider posterior predictive p-values is in terms of *calibration,* as in weather forecasting (Gelman, 2013; see also Dawid, 1982). That is, if the posterior predictive p-value is .30, then, assuming we believe the model to be true, this means that we believe there is a 30% chance that future observations predicted by the model will exceed the current observations. Thus, if we were to obtain many actual replications of the model, then we would expect that 30% would indeed exceed the current observations when the p-value is .3, assuming the model is true. Therefore, as long as the posterior predictive p-values are treated as model-generated probabilities, then they are calibrated.

In the context of the examples presented in this book, the interpretation of the posterior predictive p-value is as follows. First, as noted by Gelman (2013), when the uncertainty in the model parameters is passed to the test statistic T through the posterior predictive distribution, then the resulting p-values will concentrate around .5, under the assumption that the model is true. Therefore, values closer to 0 or 1 are indicative of a model with poor posterior predictive qualities. Because the focus is on assessing the predictive quality of a model, the degree of deviation from .5 that would constitute "poor predictive quality" is a matter of substantive judgment and will depend, in part, on expected uses of the model.

For the purposes of this book, we demonstrate two different choices for $T(y)$. For Chapters 6 and 8, on Bayesian regression and Bayesian multilevel modeling, respectively, we use the discrepancy function based on the Pearson χ^2 test as discussed in Gelman et al. (2003, p. 175). Specifically, Gelman et al. write their discrepancy function $T(y)$ as

$$T(y|\theta) = \sum_i \frac{(y_i - E(y_i|\theta))^2}{\text{var}(y_i|\theta)} \tag{5.8}$$

where the summation is over the sample of predicted observations. For Chapter 9, covering confirmatory factor analysis and structural equation modeling, we use the expression for the likelihood ratio chi-square as provided by Asparouhov and Muthén (2010) and implemented in "Mplus" (L. K. Muthén & Muthén, 1998–2012)—namely,

$$F_{ML} = \frac{1}{2} \log |\mathbf{\Sigma}| + Tr(\mathbf{\Sigma}^{-1}(\mathbf{S} + (\boldsymbol{\mu} - \mathbf{\bar{x}})(\boldsymbol{\mu} - \mathbf{\bar{x}}))) - \log |\mathbf{S}| - p - q \tag{5.9}$$

where $\mathbf{\Sigma}$ is the model implied covariance matrix, $\mathbf{S}$ is the sample covariance matrix, $\boldsymbol{\mu}$ is the model implied mean vector, $\mathbf{\bar{x}}$ is the sample mean vector, and p and q are the number of outcomes and predictors, respectively. The product $N \times F_{ML}$ is asymptotically distributed as chi-square.

5.3.2 Bayes Factors

A very simple and intuitive approach to model building and model selection uses so-called *Bayes factors* (Kass & Raftery, 1995). An excellent discussion of Bayes factors and the problem of hypothesis testing from the Bayesian perspective can be found in Raftery (1995). In essence, the Bayes factor provides a way to quantify the odds that the data favor one hypothesis over another. A key benefit of Bayes factors is that models do not have to be nested.

To motivate Bayes factors, consider two competing models, denoted as M_1 and M_2, that could be nested within a larger space of alternative models. For example, these could be two regression models with a different number of variables, or two structural equation models specifying very different directions of mediating effects. Further, let θ_1 and θ_2 be the two parameter vectors associated with these two models. From Bayes' theorem, the posterior probability that, say, M_1, is the correct model can be written as

$$p(M_1|y) = \frac{p(y|M_1)p(M_1)}{p(y|M_1)p(M_1) + p(y|M_2)p(M_2)} \tag{5.10}$$

Notice that $p(y|M_1)$ does not contain model parameters θ_1. To obtain $p(y|M_1)$ requires integrating over θ_1. That is

$$p(y|M_1) = \int p(y|\theta_1, M_1)p(\theta_1|M_1)d\theta_1 \tag{5.11}$$

where the terms inside the integral are the likelihood and the prior, respectively. The quantity $p(y|M_1)$ is referred to as the *integrated likelihood* for model M_1 (Raftery, 1995). Perhaps a more useful term is the *predictive probability of the data* given M_1. A similar expression can be written for M_2.

With these expressions, we can move to the comparison of our two models, M_1 and M_2. The goal is to develop a quantity that expresses the extent to which the data support M_1 over M_2. One quantity could be the posterior odds of M_1 over M_2, expressed as

$$\frac{p(M_1|y)}{p(M_2|y)} = \frac{p(y|M_1)}{p(y|M_2)} \times \left[\frac{p(M_1)}{p(M_2)}\right] \tag{5.12}$$

Notice that the first term on the right-hand side of Equation 5.12 is the ratio of two integrated likelihoods. This ratio is referred to as the *Bayes factor* for M_1 over M_2, denoted here as B_{12}. In line with Kass and Raftery (1995, p. 776), our prior opinion regarding the odds of M_1 over M_2, given by $p(M_1)/p(M_2)$, is weighted by our consideration of the data, given by $p(y|M_1)/p(y|M_2)$. This weighting gives rise to our updated view of evidence provided by the data for either hypothesis, denoted as $p(M_1|y)/p(M_2|y)$. An inspection of Equation 5.12 also suggests that the Bayes factor is the ratio of the posterior odds to the prior odds.

In practice, there might not be a prior preference for one model over the other. In this case, the prior odds are neutral and $p(M_1) = p(M_2) = \frac{1}{2}$. When the prior odds ratio equals 1, then the posterior odds is equal to the Bayes factor. We demonstrate the use of Bayes factors in Chapter 6.

5.3.3 The Bayesian Information Criterion

A popular measure for model selection used in both frequentist and Bayesian applications is based on an approximation of the Bayes factor and is referred to as the *Bayesian information criterion* (BIC), also referred to as the Schwarz criterion (Schwarz, 1978). A detailed mathematical derivation for the BIC can be found in Raftery (1995), who also examines generalizations of the BIC to a broad class of statistical models.

Consider once again two models, M_j and M_k, with M_k nested in M_j. For example, M_j could represent a set of predictors in a regression model and M_k could be a subset of those predictors. Or M_j could be an initially specified structural equation model and M_k could be the same model with one path deleted. Under conditions where there is little prior information, Raftery (1995) has shown that an approximation of the Bayes factor can be written as

$$2 \log B_{jk} \approx \chi^2_{jk} - df_{jk} \log n \qquad (5.13)$$

where χ^2_{jk} is the conventional likelihood ratio chi-square obtained from testing M_j against M_k and df_{jk} is the difference in the degrees of freedom associated with each test.

Next, consider the comparison of some model of interest, M_k, to a saturated model, M_s. In path analysis, for example, M_s would be a model with all paths freely estimated. In this case, the BIC for M_s would be zero with $df_s = 0$. The BIC for M_k is then approximated by Equation 5.13 and is written as

$$BIC_k = \chi^2 - df_k \log n \qquad (5.14)$$

In practice, the saturated model, M_s, would be preferred if $BIC_k > 0$ and M_k would be preferred if $BIC_k < 0$.

Notice that when comparing two models, M_j and M_k, we have

$$B_{jk} = \frac{p(y|M_j)}{p(y|M_k)} \tag{5.15}$$

$$= \left\{ \frac{p(y|M_s)}{p(y|M_j)} \Big/ \frac{p(y|M_s)}{p(y|M_k)} \right\} \tag{5.16}$$

$$= B_{sk}/B_{sj} \tag{5.17}$$

Again, because $\mathrm{BIC}_s = 0$ we have

$$2 \log B_{jk} = 2 \log B_{sk} - 2 \log B_{sj} \tag{5.18}$$

$$\approx BIC_k - BIC_j \tag{5.19}$$

Two models can therefore be compared by taking the difference in their BIC values, with the smaller (more negative) of the two being preferred. Rules of thumb have been developed to assess the quality of the evidence favoring one hypothesis over another using Bayes factors and the comparison of BIC values from two competing models. Following Kass and Raftery (1995, p. 777; see also Jeffreys, 1961) and using M_k as the reference model,

BIC difference	Bayes factor	Evidence against M_k
0 to 2	1 to 3	Weak
2 to 6	3 to 20	Positive
6 to 10	20 to 150	Strong
> 10	> 150	Very strong

Now consider the case of comparing a model of interest M_k to a null model M_0. In regression analysis, for example, a null model would have no predictors. Following Raftery (1995), the approximation of the BIC when comparing M_0 against M_k is given as

$$BIC'_k = -\chi^2_{k0} + df_k \log n \tag{5.20}$$

where χ^2_{k0} is the likelihood ratio chi-square statistic comparing M_0 against M_k and df_k is the number of degrees of freedom for M_k. In the regression case, $BIC'_0 = 0$. Hence, if BIC'_k is positive, then the null model would be preferred. As noted by Raftery (1995), this could mean that the model is overparameterized and a submodel of M_k containing fewer variables might fit better than M_0 or M_k. Conversely, if BIC_k' is negative, then M_k is preferred to M_0.

5.3.4 The Deviance Information Criterion

Although the BIC is derived from a fundamentally Bayesian perspective, it is often productively used for model comparison in the frequentist domain. This is because within a non-Bayesian modeling framework, the BIC requires the calculation of the maximum likelihood estimate of θ. From a Bayesian framework, we consider the unknown θ as a random variable described by a probability distribution. It is preferable, therefore, to have a fully Bayesian approach to model comparison. An explicitly Bayesian approach to model comparison was developed by Spiegelhalter, Best, Carlin, and van der Linde (2002) based on the notion of *Bayesian deviance*.

Consider a particular model proposed for a set of data, denoted as $p(y|\theta)$. Then, we begin by defining *Bayesian deviance* as

$$D(\theta) = -2 \log[p(y|\theta)] + 2 \log[h(y)] \qquad (5.21)$$

where, according to Spiegelhalter et al. (2002), the term $h(y)$ is a standardizing factor that does not involve model parameters and thus is not involved in model selection. Note that although Equation 5.21 is similar to the BIC, it is not, as currently defined, an explicit Bayesian measure of model fit. To obtain a Bayesian measure of model fit, we first obtain a posterior expectation of the deviance in Equation 5.21 by

$$\overline{D(\theta)} = E_\theta[-2\log[p(y|\theta)|y] + 2\log[h(y)] \qquad (5.22)$$

Note that Equation 5.22 can be obtained from MCMC sampling by taking the average of the posterior distribution of the deviance. Next, define the deviance of the mean $D(\bar{\theta})$ as the value of D at the EAP estimates of θ. From here, we can define the *effective dimension* of the model as

$$q_D = \overline{D(\theta)} - D(\bar{\theta}) \qquad (5.23)$$

which is the mean deviance minus the deviance of the means. Notice that q_D is a Bayesian measure of model complexity. With q_D in hand, we simply add the model fit term $\overline{D(\theta)}$ to obtain the *deviance information criterion* (DIC), namely,

$$DIC = \overline{D(\theta)} + q_D = 2\overline{D(\theta)} - D(\bar{\theta}) \tag{5.24}$$

As with the BIC, the model with the smallest DIC value is preferred.

5.4 BAYESIAN MODEL AVERAGING

A key characteristic that separates Bayesian statistical inference from frequentist statistical inference is its focus on characterizing uncertainty. Up to this point, we have concentrated on uncertainty in model parameters, addressing that uncertainty through the specification of a prior distribution on the model parameters. In a related but perhaps more general fashion, the selection of a particular model from a universe of possible models can also be characterized as a problem of uncertainty. This problem was succinctly stated by Hoeting, Madigan, Raftery, and Volinsky (1999), who write:

> Standard statistical practice ignores model uncertainty. Data analysts typically select a model from some class of models and then proceed as if the selected model had generated the data. This approach ignores the uncertainty in model selection, leading to over-confident inferences and decisions that are more risky than one thinks they are. (p. 382)

An interesting approach to addressing the problem of uncertainty lies in the method of *Bayesian model averaging* (BMA).

To begin, consider a quantity of interest such as a future observation or a parameter. Following Madigan and Raftery (1994), we will denote this quantity as Δ. Next, consider a set of competing models M_k, $k = 1, 2, \ldots, K$, that are not necessarily nested. The posterior distribution of Δ given data y can be written as

$$p(\Delta|y) = \sum_{k=1}^{K} p(\Delta|M_k)p(M_k|y) \tag{5.25}$$

where $p(M_k|y)$ is the posterior probability of model M_k written as

$$p(M_k|y) = \frac{p(y|M_k)p(M_k)}{\sum_{l=1}^{K} p(y|M_l)p(M_l)}, \qquad l \neq k \qquad (5.26)$$

The interesting feature of Equation 5.26 is that $p(M_k)$ is a prior on the kth model and will likely be different for different models. The term $p(y|M_k)$ can be expressed as an integrated likelihood

$$p(y|M_k) = \int p(y|\theta_k, M_k)p(\theta_k|M_k)d\theta_k \qquad (5.27)$$

where $p(\theta_k|M_k)$ is the prior density of θ_k under model M_k (Raftery, Madigan, & Hoeting, 1997). Thus, Bayesian model averaging provides an approach for combining models specified by researchers, or perhaps elicited by key stakeholders. The advantage of BMA has been discussed in Madigan and Raftery (1994), who showed that Bayesian model averaging provides better predictive performance than that of a single model.

   As pointed out by Hoeting et al. (1999), BMA is difficult to implement. In particular, they note that the number of terms in Equation 5.25 can be quite large, the corresponding integrals are hard to compute (though possibly less so with the advent of MCMC), the specification of $p(M_k)$ may not be straightforward, and choosing the class of models to average over is also challenging. To address the problem of computing Equation 5.27, the Laplace method can be used, and this will lead to a simple BIC approximation under certain circumstances (Tierney & Kadane, 1986; cited in Hoeting et al., 1999). The problem of reducing the overall number of models that one could incorporate in the summation of Equation 5.25 has led to two interesting solutions. One solution is based on the so-called *Occam's window* (Madigan & Raftery, 1994), and the other is based on *Markov chain Monte Carlo model composition* (MC³).

5.4.1 Occam's Window

To motivate the idea behind Occam's window, consider the problem of finding the best subset of predictors in a linear regression model. Following closely the discussion given in Raftery et al. (1997), we consider an initially large number of predictors, but perhaps the goal is to find a subset that provides accurate predictions.[3] As noted in the earlier quote by Hoeting et al. (1999), the concern in drawing inferences from a single "best" model is that the choice of a single set of predictors ignores uncertainty in model selection. Occam's window (Madigan & Raftery, 1994) provides an approach to Bayesian model averaging that reduces the subset of models under consideration.

The algorithm proceeds in two steps (Raftery et al., 1997). In the first step, models are eliminated if they predict the data less well than the model that provides the best predictions. Formally, consider a set of models M_k, $k = 1, \ldots, K$, and a cutoff value C chosen in advance by the analyst. Then, the set A'

$$A' = \left\{ M_k : \frac{\max_l \{ p(M_l | y) \}}{p(M_k | y)} \leq C \right\} \qquad (5.28)$$

In words, Equation 5.28 compares the model with the largest posterior model probability, $\max_l \{ p(M_l | y) \}$, to a given model $p(M_k | y)$. If the ratio in Equation 5.28 is less than or equal to a chosen value C, then it is discarded from the set of models to be included in the model averaging.

In the second step, models are discarded from consideration if they receive less support from the data than simpler submodels. Formally, we consider a set B, where

$$B = \left\{ M_k : \exists M_l \in A', M_l \subset M_k, \frac{p(M_l | y)}{p(M_k | y)} > 1 \right\} \qquad (5.29)$$

Again, in words Equation 5.29 states that there exists a model M_l within the set A' and where M_l is simpler than M_k. If the simpler model receives more support from the data than the more complex model, then it is included in the set B. Notice that the second step corresponds to the principle of Occam's razor (Madigan & Raftery, 1994).

---

[3]The notion of "best subset regression" is controversial in the frequentist framework because of concern over capitalization on chance. However, in the Bayesian framework with its focus on predictive accuracy, finding the best subset of predictors is not a problem.

With Step 1 and Step 2, the problem of Bayesian model averaging is simplified by replacing Equation 5.25 with

$$p(\Delta|y, A) = \sum_{M_k \in A} p(\Delta|M_k, y)p(M_k|y, A) \tag{5.30}$$

where A is the relative complement of A' and B. That is, the models under consideration for Bayesian model averaging are those that are in A' but not in B.

Madigan and Raftery (1994) then outline an approach to the choice between two models to be considered for Bayesian model averaging. Specifically, now consider just two models M_1 and M_0, where M_0 is the smaller of the two models. This could be the case where M_0 contains fewer predictors than M_1 in a regression analysis. In terms of log-posterior odds, if the log-posterior odds are positive, indicating support for M_0, then we reject M_1. If the log-posterior odds are large and negative, then we reject M_0 in favor of M_1. Finally, if the log-posterior odds lie in between the preset criterion, then both models are retained.

5.4.2 Markov Chain Monte Carlo Model Composition

The goal of Markov chain Monte Carlo model composition (MC^3) is the same as that of Occam's window: namely, to reduce the space of possible models that can be explored in a Bayesian model averaging exercise. Following Hoeting, Raftery, and Madigan (1996), the MC^3 algorithm proceeds as follows. First, let M represent the space of models of interest; in the case of linear regression, this would be the space of all possible combinations of variables. Next, the theory behind MCMC allows us to construct a Markov chain $\{M(t), t = 1, 2, \ldots, T\}$ which converges to the posterior distribution of model k, that is, $p(M_k|y)$.

The manner in which models are retained under MC^3 is as follows. First, for any given model currently explored by the Markov chain, we can define a neighborhood for that model which includes one more variable and one less variable than the current model. So, for example, if our model has four predictors x_1, x_2, x_3, and x_4, and the Markov chain is currently examining the model with x_2 and x_3, then the neighborhood of this model would include $\{x_2\}$, $\{x_3\}$, $\{x_2, x_3, x_4\}$, and $\{x_1, x_2, x_3\}$. Now, a transition matrix is formed such that moving from the current model M to a new model M' has probability zero if M' is not in the neighborhood of M and has a constant probability if M' is in the neighborhood of M. The model M' is then accepted for model averaging with probability

$$\min \left\{ 1, \frac{pr(M'|y)}{pr(M|y)} \right\} \tag{5.31}$$

Otherwise, the chain stays in model M.

5.5 SUMMARY

This chapter considered the elements of Bayesian hypothesis testing beginning with describing the posterior distribution of the parameters of interest, followed by checking model fit via posterior predictive checks, and culminating with choosing among competing models using Bayes factors, the BIC, and/or the DIC. In addition, we introduced the method of Bayesian model averaging which accounts for uncertainty in model specification. In the next chapter, we provide a detailed example of these ideas by way of Bayesian linear and generalized linear regression.

5.6 SUGGESTED READINGS

Clyde, M. (1999). Bayesian model averaging and model search strategies (with discussion). In J. M. Bernardo, A. P. Dawid, J. O. Berger, & A. F. M. Smith (Eds.), *Bayesian statistics, 6* (pp. 157–185). Oxford, UK: Oxford University Press.

Clyde, M., & George, E. I. (2004). Model uncertainty. *Statistical Science, 19*, 81–84.

Gigerenzer, G., Krauss, S., & Vitouch, O. (2004). The null ritual: What you always wanted to know about significance testing but were afraid to ask. In D. Kaplan (Ed.), *The Sage handbook of quantitative methodology for the social sciences* (pp. 391–408). Thousand Oaks, CA: Sage.

Harlow, L. L., Mulaik, S. A., & Steiger, J. H. (1997). *What if there were no significance tests?* Mahwah, NJ: Erlbaum.

Hoeting, J. A., Madigan, D., Raftery, A. E., & Volinsky, C. T. (1999). Bayesian model averaging: A tutorial. *Statistical Science, 14*, 382–417.

Kass, R. E., & Raftery, A. E. (1995). Bayes factors. *Journal of the American Statistical Association, 90,* 773–795.

Raftery, A. E. (1995). Bayesian model selection in social research (with discussion). In P. V. Marsden (Ed.), *Sociological methodology* (Vol. 25, pp. 111–196). New York: Blackwell.

6

Bayesian Linear and Generalized Linear Models

This chapter focuses on Bayesian linear and generalized linear models and sets the groundwork for later chapters insofar as many, if not most, of the statistical methodologies used in the social sciences have, at their core, the general and generalized linear regression model. We begin by providing a motivating example that is used throughout this chapter and that concerns the predictors of reading literacy among 15-year-olds. Then we discuss maximum likelihood estimation of the conventional linear regression model. This is followed by the specification of the Bayesian linear regression model with noninformative priors. Next, we incorporate informative conjugate priors into the analysis. Finally, we provide an example of Bayesian model comparison and model averaging. After discussion of the general linear model, we turn our attention to the generalized linear model, with specific focus on Bayesian logistic regression. An example using noninformative and informative priors is provided.

6.1 A MOTIVATING EXAMPLE

The example used throughout this chapter utilizes data from the 2009 *Program on International Student Assessment* (PISA), conducted by the Organisation for Economic Co-operation and Development (OECD, 2010). As defined by the OECD, "PISA is a collaborative effort among the OECD member countries (and many partner countries) to measure how well 15-year-old students approaching the end of compulsory schooling are prepared to meet the challenges of today's knowledge societies" (OECD, 2012).

PISA takes place every three years, with each cycle of PISA concentrating on a major domain and two minor domains. The first cycle of PISA was in 2000 and concentrated on reading competency as the major domain. This was followed by a focus on mathematics in 2003, science in 2006, and a return to reading in 2009. For PISA 2009, approximately 400,000 students representative of 20 million 15-year-olds enrolled in the schools of 66 participating countries and economies.

The PISA assessments take a literacy perspective that focuses on the extent to which students can use the knowledge and skills they have learned and practiced at school when confronted with situations and challenges for which that knowledge may be relevant. For reading, the main question concerns whether students can use their reading skills to understand and interpret various kinds of written material that they are likely to meet as they negotiate their daily lives. For mathematics, the main question concerns whether students can use their mathematical knowledge and skills to solve various kinds of mathematics-related challenges and problems. Finally, for science, the main question concerns whether students can use their scientific knowledge and skills to understand, interpret, and resolve various kinds of scientific situations and challenges.

The PISA background questionnaire collects information from students on various aspects of their home, family, and school background; and information from schools about various aspects of organization and educational provision in schools. This information is collected to facilitate a detailed study of factors within and between countries that are associated with varying levels of reading, mathematical, and scientific literacy among the 15-year-old students of each country.

The outcomes of the PISA survey consist of, among other things, (1) a profile of the knowledge and skills of 15-year-olds, (2) contextual indicators relating results to student and school characteristics, (3) a knowledge base for policy analysis and research, and (4) trend indicators at the country level showing how results change over time.

6.2 THE NORMAL LINEAR REGRESSION MODEL

We start with a very simple model linking student background characteristics to scores on the PISA reading assessment. To begin, let $\mathbf{y}$ be an n-dimensional vector $(y_1, y_2, \ldots, y_n)'$ $(i = 1, 2, \ldots, n)$ of scores from n students on the PISA reading assessment, and let $\mathbf{X}$ be an $n \times P$ matrix containing P $(p = 1, 2, \ldots, P)$ background measures, such as gender, ethnicity, metacognitive reading strategies, and so on. Then, the normal linear regression model can be written as

$$\mathbf{y} = \mathbf{X}\boldsymbol{\beta} + \mathbf{u} \tag{6.1}$$

where $\boldsymbol{\beta}$ is an $P \times 1$ vector of regression coefficients and where the first column of $\boldsymbol{\beta}$ contains an n-dimensional unit vector to capture the intercept term. We assume that the PISA reading scores are generated from a normal distribution—specifically,

$$\mathbf{y} \sim N(\mathbf{X}\boldsymbol{\beta}, \sigma^2 \mathbf{I}) \tag{6.2}$$

where $\mathbf{I}$ is an identity matrix. Moreover, we assume that the n-dimensional vector $\mathbf{u}$ are disturbance terms assumed to be independently, identically, and normally distributed, specifically,

$$\mathbf{u} \sim N(\mathbf{0}, \sigma^2 \mathbf{I}) \tag{6.3}$$

The assumptions in Equations 6.2 and 6.3 give rise to the normal linear regression model with homoskedastic disturbances (see, e.g., Fox, 2008).

From standard linear regression theory, the likelihood of the model parameters $\boldsymbol{\beta}$ and σ^2 can be written as

$$L(\boldsymbol{\beta}, \sigma^2 | \mathbf{X}, \mathbf{y}) = (2\pi\sigma^2)^{-n/2} \exp\left\{ -\frac{1}{2\sigma^2} (\mathbf{y} - \mathbf{X}\boldsymbol{\beta})'(\mathbf{y} - \mathbf{X}\boldsymbol{\beta}) \right\} \tag{6.4}$$

Notice that estimation of $\boldsymbol{\beta}$ hinges on minimizing the residual sum of squares $(\mathbf{y} - \mathbf{X}\boldsymbol{\beta})'(\mathbf{y} - \mathbf{X}\boldsymbol{\beta})$ in the exponent of the likelihood. Expanding the residual sum of squares, we obtain

$$
\begin{aligned}
RSS &= (\mathbf{y} - \mathbf{X}\boldsymbol{\beta})'(\mathbf{y} - \mathbf{X}\boldsymbol{\beta}) \\
&= \mathbf{y}'\mathbf{y} - 2\boldsymbol{\beta}'\mathbf{X}'\mathbf{y} + \boldsymbol{\beta}'\mathbf{X}'\mathbf{X}\boldsymbol{\beta}
\end{aligned} \tag{6.5}
$$

To minimize involves taking the derivative of Equation 6.5 with respect to β, setting it to zero, and solving. Thus,

$$\frac{\partial}{\partial \beta}(\mathbf{y'y} - 2\boldsymbol{\beta'}\mathbf{X'y} + \boldsymbol{\beta'}\mathbf{X'X}\boldsymbol{\beta})$$

$$= -2\mathbf{X'y} + 2\mathbf{X'X}\boldsymbol{\beta} \qquad (6.6)$$

Setting to zero and solving for β, we obtain

$$\mathbf{X'X}\boldsymbol{\beta} = \mathbf{X'y},$$

$$\hat{\boldsymbol{\beta}} = (\mathbf{X'X})^{-1}\mathbf{X'y} \qquad (6.7)$$

where the solution depends on whether the inverse of $\mathbf{X'X}$ exists.

Continuing, maximizing the likelihood with respect to σ^2 yields the estimator

$$\hat{\sigma}^2 = \frac{(\mathbf{y} - \mathbf{X}\hat{\boldsymbol{\beta}})'(\mathbf{y} - \mathbf{X}\hat{\boldsymbol{\beta}})}{n} \qquad (6.8)$$

We recognize that Equation 6.7 is the same as that obtained under ordinary least squares. However, Equation 6.8 differs from the least squares estimator $[(\mathbf{y} - \mathbf{X}\hat{\boldsymbol{\beta}})'(\mathbf{y} - \mathbf{X}\hat{\boldsymbol{\beta}})]/(n - P)$.

6.3 THE BAYESIAN LINEAR REGRESSION MODEL

Recall from Chapter 2 that the first step in a Bayesian analysis is the specification of the prior distributions for all model parameters. Recall also that we can consider two broad classes of prior distributions: (1) noninformative priors that reflect no prior knowledge or information about the location or shape of the distribution of the model parameters, or (2) informative–conjugate priors that specify prior knowledge or information about model parameters. Multiplying the likelihood and the conjugate prior yields a posterior distribution that is in the same family of distributions as the likelihood.

6.3.1 Noninformative Priors in the Linear Regression Model

In the context of the normal linear regression model, the uniform distribution is typically used as a noninformative prior and is specified in a manner similar to the normal model case we discussed in Chapter 2. First, we assign an improper uniform prior to the regression coefficient vector β that allows β to take on values over the support $[-\infty, \infty]$. This can be written as $p(\beta) \propto c$, where c is a constant.

Next, we assign a uniform prior to $\log(\sigma^2)$ because, as noted in Example 2.5 in Chapter 2, this transformation also allows values over the support $[0, \infty]$. From here, the joint posterior distribution of the model parameters is obtained by multiplying the prior distributions of β and σ^2 by the likelihood given in Equation 6.4. Assuming that β and σ^2 are independent, we obtain

$$p(\beta, \sigma^2 | \mathbf{y}, \mathbf{X}) \propto L(\beta, \sigma^2 | \mathbf{y}, \mathbf{X}) p(\beta) p(\sigma^2),$$

$$\propto (\sigma^2)^{-n/2} \exp\left\{-\frac{1}{2\sigma^2}(\mathbf{y} - \mathbf{X}\beta)'(\mathbf{y} - \mathbf{X}\beta)\right\} \times c \times \sigma^{-2}$$

Noting that c does not contain model parameters, and so drops out with the proportionality, we obtain

$$p(\beta, \sigma^2 | \mathbf{y}, \mathbf{X}) \propto (\sigma^2)^{-n/(2+1)} \exp\left\{-\frac{1}{2\sigma2}(\mathbf{y} - \mathbf{X}\beta)'(\mathbf{y} - \mathbf{X}\beta)\right\} \quad (6.9)$$

As pointed out by Lynch (2007), the posterior distribution of the model parameters in Equation 6.9 differs from the likelihood only in the leading exponent, $-n/(2 + 1)$, which is of no consequence in large samples. Here again, we see how the Bayesian approach and the frequentist approach align when samples are large and priors are noninformative.

EXAMPLE 6.1. BAYESIAN LINEAR REGRESSION MODEL USING PISA 2009
DATA: NONINFORMATIVE PRIORS[1]

For this example we use data from PISA 2009 to estimate a model relating reading proficiency to a set of background, attitudinal, and reading strategy variables. The sample comes from approximately 5,000
PISA-eligible students in the United States. Background variables include GENDER (female = 1, male = 0), immigrant status (NATIVE),
language that they use (SLANG; coded 1 if test language is the same as
language at home, 0 otherwise), and a measure of the economic, social,
and cultural status of the student (ESCS). In addition, measures of student reading attitudes include enjoyment of reading (JOYREAD), di-
versity in reading (DIVREAD); variables measuring student reading
strategies including memorization strategies (MEMOR), elaboration
strategies (ELAB), and control strategies (CSTRAT). The first plausible
value of the reading assessment was used as the dependent variable[2]:

$$\text{Reading} = \beta_0 + \beta_1(\text{GENDER}) + \beta_2(\text{NATIVE}) + \beta_3(\text{SLANG}) \quad (6.10)$$
$$+ \beta_4(\text{ESCS}) + \beta_5(\text{JOYREAD}) + \beta_6(\text{DIVREAD})$$
$$+ \beta_7(\text{MEMOR}) + \beta_8(\text{ELAB}) + \beta_9(\text{CSTRAT}) + u$$

The regression model with noninformative priors was estimated using
the Gibbs sampler as implemented in the "MCMCregress" program
within the "MCMCpack" package (A. D. Martin et al., 2010). Within
this package noninformative priors were specified by setting the means
for all regression coefficients to zero and the precisions of all regression coefficients to 0.01 (variance = 100). This specification results in
a highly diffused prior for all regression coefficients. The variance of
the disturbance term was set to have a noninformative inverse-gamma

---

[1] This example is adapted from Kaplan and Park (2014). Copyright 2014. Reproduced
by permission of Taylor & Francis Group, LLC, a division of Informa plc.

[2] Plausible values were developed as a means of obtaining consistent estimates of population characteristics in large-scale assessment such as PISA where students are administered too few items to allow precise ability estimates. Plausible values represent random
draws from an empirical proficiency distribution conditioned on the observed responses to
the assessment items and background variables.

distribution with shape and scale of 0.001. This analysis used 100,000 iterations, with 5,000 burn-in iterations and a thinning interval of 10.

Convergence Diagnostics.   We begin with a detailed assessment of the convergence of the Gibbs sampler. Figure 6.1 shows the autocorrelation plots for selected parameters. The plots reveal that the MCMC algorithm converges immediately to independent sampling from the posterior distribution. Figure 6.2 shows the trace plots and density plots for selected parameters. It can be seen that the plots indicate convergence of the iterations. Final evidence of convergence is provided by the Gelman–Rubin plot, the Geweke plot, the Heidelberger–Welch diagnos-

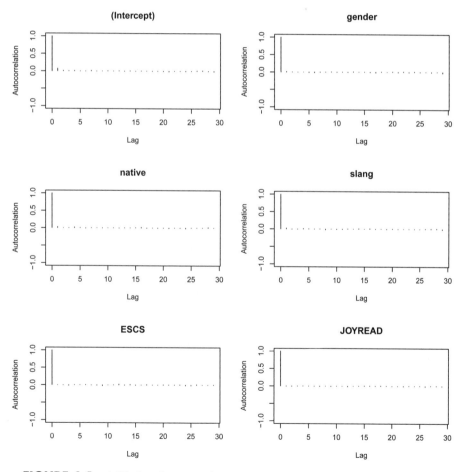

FIGURE 6.1. ACF plots for regression example: Selected parameters.

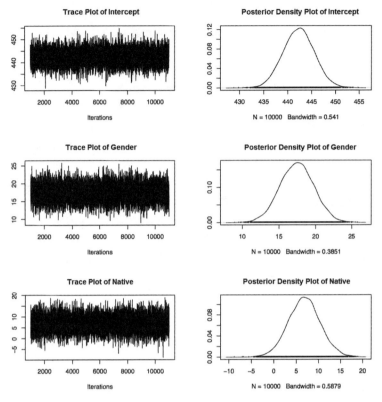

FIGURE 6.2. Trace and density plots for regression example: Selected parameters.

tic, and the Raftery diagnostic. These diagnostics were discussed in Chapter 4. The Gelman plot in Figure 6.3 shows that, for the selected parameters, the algorithm converges. Results for the remaining parameters also show good convergence of the algorithm. The Geweke plot in Figure 6.4 shows for selected parameters that the samples within the first 10% of the chain mostly fall within −2 and +2 z-score units, and the same holds true for the last 50%. The same results hold for the remaining parameters.

The Heidelberger–Welch diagnostic indicated that each parameter passed the stationarity test. Finally, the Raftery–Lewis diagnostic suggested much fewer burn-in runs and much less total number of iterations than were used. Taken together, the diagnostics indicate that the Gibbs sampler for this analysis converged.

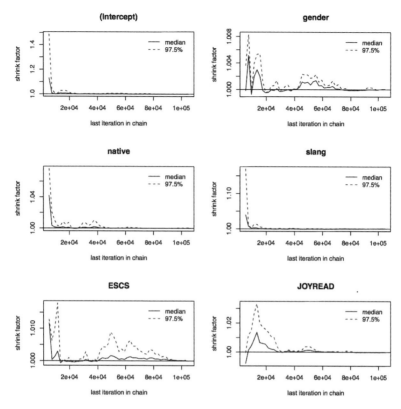

FIGURE 6.3. Gelman plot for regression example: Selected parameters.

Results.   Table 6.1 shows the results of the Bayesian regression analysis with noninformative priors. The EAP estimates correspond to the mean of the posterior distribution for each model parameter. The column labeled SD is the standard deviation of the posterior distribution of the relevant parameter and is the Bayesian counterpart to the frequentist standard error. To take a specific example, The EAP estimate for READING on JOYREAD is 27.47, with a posterior standard deviation of 1.28. The EAP is positive, indicating that higher reported joy in reading is associated with higher reading scores. The 95% PPI indicates that there is a 95% probability that the effect of JOYREAD on READING is between 24.97 and 29.93. Notice also that the 95% PPI for the effect of NATIVE on READING contains zero. This indicates that zero is a "credible" value. It is important to note again that our

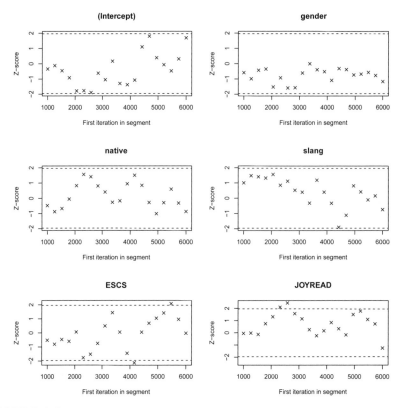

FIGURE 6.4. Geweke plot for regression example: Selected parameters.

**TABLE 6.1. Bayesian Linear Regression Estimates:
Non-informative Prior Case**

Parameter	EAP	*SD*	95% PPI
Full model			
INTERCEPT	490.40	3.34	483.94, 497.08
READING on GENDER	6.44	2.31	1.90, 10.91
READING on NATIVE	−5.68	3.85	−13.33, 1.92
READING on SLANG	6.75	4.50	−1.94, 15.47
READING on ESCS	30.28	1.30	27.67, 32.82
READING on JOYREAD	28.90	1.26	26.46, 31.40
READING on DIVREAD	−4.33	1.19	−6.65, −2.03
READING on MEMOR	−18.85	1.30	−21.38, −16.28
READING on ELAB	−14.88	1.25	−17.31, −12.41
READING on CSTRAT	27.39	1.46	24.52, 30.25

Note. EAP, expected a posteriori; *SD*, standard deviation; PPI, posterior probability interval.

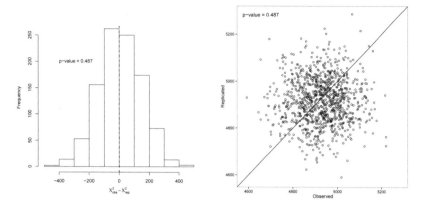

FIGURE 6.5. PPC scatterplot and histogram for regression model: Noninformative Priors.

decision regarding the importance of these effects is different from the frequentist reasoning we would use to conclude whether these effects are important.

Posterior Predictive Check for Regression Model: Noninformative Priors.   Figure 6.5 shows the posterior predictive check for the regression model. The left-hand figure displays the histogram of the difference between the observed and replicated chi-square values based on Equation 5.8 and the right-hand side displays the scatterplot of the observed and replicated chi-square values.

Recall from our earlier discussion that when the uncertainty in the model parameters is passed to the test statistic T through the posterior predictive distribution, then the resulting p-values will concentrate around .5, under the assumption that the model is true (Gelman, 2013). Therefore, values closer to 0 or 1 are indicative of a model with poor posterior predictive qualities. For this example, the posterior predictive p-value is .49, indicating very good posterior predictive quality of the regression model based on noninformative priors.

6.3.2 Informative Conjugate Priors

The previous section presented Bayesian linear regression with noninformative priors—the case in which no information can be brought to bear on the distributions of the model parameters. In that case, we are, in essence, quantifying our lack of prior information by choosing a prior that allows all possible values of the parameters to be equally likely. There may be some cases, however, in which statistical theory as well as prior information can be brought to bear on the analysis. In this case, we would want to employ informative priors.

In this section we demonstrate the application of informative conjugate priors for the Bayesian linear regression model. As discussed in Chapter 2, conjugate priors are those that, when multiplied by the likelihood, yield a posterior distribution in the same family as the prior distribution. The degree to which the prior distribution is informative depends on the values of the hyperparameters of the prior distribution, and in particular the value of the precision of the hyperparameters.

The most sensible conjugate prior distribution for the vector of regression coefficients β of the linear regression model is the multivariate normal prior. The argument for using the multivariate normal distribution as the prior for β lies in the fact that the asymptotic distribution of the regression coefficients is normal (Fox, 2008). Moreover, the normal prior is a conjugate distribution for the regression coefficients and will result in a normal posterior distribution for these model parameters.

The conditional prior distribution of the vector β given σ^2 can be written as

$$p(\beta|\sigma^2) = (2\pi)^{P/2}|\Sigma|^{1/2}\exp\left[-\frac{1}{2}(\beta - \mathbf{B})'\Sigma^{-1}(\beta - \mathbf{B})\right] \quad (6.11)$$

where P is the number of variables, $\mathbf{B}$ is the vector of mean hyperparameters assigned to β, and $\Sigma = \sigma^2\mathbf{I}$ is the diagonal matrix of constant disturbance variances.

The conjugate prior for the variance of the disturbance term σ^2 is (from Chapter 3) the inverse-gamma distribution, with hyperparameters a and b. We write the conjugate prior density for σ^2 as

$$p(\sigma^2) \propto (\sigma^2)^{-(a+1)}e^{-b/\sigma^2} \quad (6.12)$$

With the likelihood $L(\beta, \sigma^2|\mathbf{X}, \mathbf{y})$ defined in Equation 6.4, as well as the prior distributions $p(\beta|\sigma^2)$ and $p(\sigma^2)$, we have the necessary components to obtain the joint posterior distribution of the model parameters given the data. Specifically, the joint posterior distribution of the parameters $\boldsymbol{\beta}$ and σ^2 is given as

$$p(\boldsymbol{\beta}, \sigma^2 | \mathbf{y}, \mathbf{X}) \propto L(\boldsymbol{\beta}, \sigma^2 | \mathbf{X}, \mathbf{y}) \times p(\boldsymbol{\beta} | \sigma^2) \times p(\sigma^2) \qquad (6.13)$$

which, after some algebra, yields

$$p(\boldsymbol{\beta}, \sigma^2 | \mathbf{y}, \mathbf{X}) \propto \sigma^{-n-a} \exp\left[-\frac{1}{2\sigma^2} (\hat{\sigma}^2(n-P) + (\boldsymbol{\beta} - \hat{\boldsymbol{\beta}})' \mathbf{X}' \mathbf{X} (\boldsymbol{\beta} - \hat{\boldsymbol{\beta}}) \right.$$
$$\left. + 2b + (\boldsymbol{\beta} - \mathbf{B})'(\boldsymbol{\beta} - \mathbf{B}) \right] (6.14)$$

which has the form of a multivariate normal distribution.

EXAMPLE 6.2: BAYESIAN ESTIMATION OF THE LINEAR REGRESSION MODEL
            USING PISA 2009 DATA: INFORMATIVE PRIORS BASED ON
            PISA 2000

This example utilizes the same model as that used in Example 6.1. However, for this example, priors are specified using estimated regression coefficients based on a conventional regression analysis of the United States sample who were administered PISA 2000. Recall that the OECD/PISA program is administered every three years and cycles through the major domains of reading, mathematics, and science literacy. The major domain for the first cycle of PISA (PISA 2000) was reading. It should be pointed out that use of a prior cycle of data collection obtained on comparable samples is, perhaps, a fortuitous situation. Here, because the cycles of PISA are implemented and administered under comparable conditions, we can use results from prior cycles as strongly warranted subjective priors. In cases where such prior information is not available, we are often left to rely on less comparable prior data or to elicit expert opinion. We discuss these issues in more detail in Chapter 10.

Priors for this analysis were set for the means and precisions of the regression coefficients. For each model parameter, we set the precisions to be equal to $1/(SE_p)^2$, where SE is the standard error of the pth regression coefficient obtained from the frequentist regression analysis. As with Example 6.1, this analysis used 100,000 iterations, with 5,000 burn-in iterations and a thinning interval of 10.

TABLE 6.2. Bayesian Regression Estimates: Informative Priors Based on PISA 2000

Parameter	EAP	SD	95% PPI
Full model			
INTERCEPT	487.94	2.82	482.52, 493.59
READING on FEMALE	9.46	1.86	5.81, 13.07
READING on NATIVE	−6.87	3.28	−13.30, −0.26
READING on SLANG	9.53	3.56	2.44, 16.48
READING on ESCS	31.19	1.04	29.20, 33.23
READING on JOYREAD	26.50	1.00	24.53, 28.43
READING on DIVREAD	−2.52	0.97	−4.40, −0.59
READING on MEMOR	−18.77	1.09	−20.91, −16.64
READING on ELAB	−13.62	1.06	−15.76, −11.60
READING on CSTRAT	26.06	1.17	23.77, 28.36

Note. EAP, expected a posteriori; *SD*, standard deviation; PPI, posterior probability interval.

Results.   First, as with the noninformative priors case, the convergence plots and diagnostics for the informative priors case indicated good convergence of the Gibbs sampler. They are not presented here. Table 6.2 provides roughly similar results to those shown in Table 6.1.

Important differences lie in the posterior standard deviation and the 95% PPI. Again, taking the example of the regression of READING on JOYREAD, we find that the effect is roughly the same, but the standard deviation of the posterior distribution is smaller and the 95% PPI is narrower than comparable findings in the noninformative case. This reflects the use of a highly informative and empirically based prior, even in the case of a large sample. Although the results of READING on JOYREAD are roughly comparable, an inspection of the EAP associated with female on READING shows a dramatic effect of incorporating an informative prior, when compared to the results of the noninformative case in Table 6.1.

Posterior Predictive Check for Regression Model: Informative Priors.   The posterior predictive histogram and scatterplot are shown in Figure 6.6. The use of informative priors based on the results of PISA 2000 does not appreciably improve the predictive quality of the model insofar as the posterior predictive *p*-value is slightly above .50.

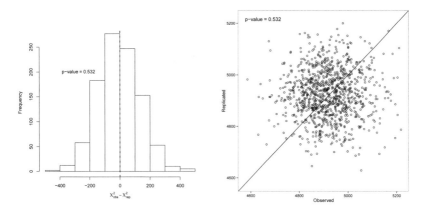

FIGURE 6.6. PPC histogram and scatterplot for regression model: Informative Priors.

EXAMPLE 6.3. MODEL COMPARISON WITH PISA 2009 EXAMPLE

Consider that researchers wish to compare different models for the prediction of reading proficiency. For this example, Model 1 is the full model containing all of the variables listed earlier. Model 2 focuses on only the background variables as predictors of reading proficiency. Model 3 focuses on only the attitudinal variables as predictors of reading proficiency. Model 4 focuses only on the reading strategy variables as predictors of reading literacy. Focusing for now on only the informative priors case, we note that there are a total of four models to be compared. Table 6.3 shows the results for the four separate submodels. Choosing among these competing models will utilize Bayes factors as implemented in "MCMCpack" (A. D. Martin et al., 2010). The natural log Bayes factors are shown in Table 6.4. Table 6.4 represents a matrix comparing models in row i against models in column j. The values can be interpreted as the strength of evidence in favor of model i relative to model j. So, for example, among the submodels, the model based on using only background variables as predictors of reading competency (first row) is decisively more favored by the data than either the learning strategies model or the attitude model. However, the full model enjoys clear support from the data compared to the other three submodels.

TABLE 6.3. Separate Submodels: Informative Priors Case

Parameter	EAP	SD	95% PPI
Background model			
INTERCEPT	478.33	3.04	472.31, 484.24
READING on GENDER	28.01	1.95	24.18, 31.85
READING on NATIVE	−9.17	3.51	−15.97, −2.31
READING on SLANG	11.24	3.78	3.90, 18.66
READING on ESCS	40.00	1.07	37.88, 42.11
Attitude model			
INTERCEPT	503.92	1.00	501.97, 505.90
READING on JOYREAD	33.63	1.01	31.66, 35.61
READING on DIVREAD	1.64	1.03	−0.35, 3.67
Learning strategy model			
INTERCEPT	503.80	1.01	501.83, 505.83
READING on MEMOR	−25.07	1.22	−27.45, −22.69
READING on ELAB	−13.01	1.16	−15.36, −10.82
READING on CSTRAT	42.89	1.27	40.40, 45.40

Note. EAP, expected a posteriori; *SD*, standard deviation; PPI, posterior probability interval.

TABLE 6.4. Natural Log Bayes Factors: Informative Priors Case

Submodel	BG model	ATT model	LS model	Full model
BG model	0.0	27.8	85.6	−539
ATT model	−27.8	0.0	57.8	−567
LS model	−85.6	−57.8	0.0	−625
Full model	539.2	567.0	624.8	0

Note. BG model, background variables model; ATT model, attitude variables model; LS model, learning strategies model; Full model, model with all variables.

EXAMPLE 6.4. BAYESIAN MODEL AVERAGING USING PISA 2009

Recall from our discussion in Section 5.3 that although Bayesian statistical methods take into account uncertainty in model parameters through the specification of the prior distribution, these methods do not directly account for model uncertainty. Specifically, in the standard practice of regression modeling, the choice of variables to include in a model is typically fixed as a result of the research question under investigation. However, for any given outcome, such as scores on a reading literacy assessment, a universe of possible models is available. Nevertheless, the researcher typically selects one model from that universe and treats it as though it was the one that generated the observed data. In a very real sense, model selection is a form of uncertainty, and consistent with Bayesian philosophy, it may be reasonable to try to model this form of uncertainty as well. The method of Bayesian model averaging (Madigan & Raftery, 1994; Hoeting et al., 1999) discussed in Section 5.3 represents an approach to accounting for model uncertainty.

The technical details of Bayesian model averaging were provided in Section 5.3. To reiterate, we start with some quantity of interest such as a future observation or a parameter denoted as Δ. It is assumed that there are a set of competing models M_k, $k = 1, 2, \ldots, K$ that are not necessarily nested. Bayesian model averaging derives the posterior distribution Δ given the data y, which is written as (cf. Equation 5.25)

$$p(\Delta|y) = \sum_{k=1}^{K} p(\Delta|M_k)p(M_k|y) \qquad (6.15)$$

where $p(M_k|y)$ is the posterior probability of model M_k which will vary across different models. Essentially, Equation 6.15 is combining models for a quantity of interest. Again, as shown by Madigan and Raftery (1994), Bayesian model averaging can often outperform single models in terms of predictive performance.

The problem with Bayesian model averaging is that it is difficult to implement, particularly when there is a large number of competing models. Fortunately, the problem of reducing the set of competing models has been addressed using the notion of Occam's window (Madigan & Raftery, 1994) or the MC^3 algorithm (Madigan & York, 1995), as discussed in Sections 5.4.1 and 5.4.2, respectively. For this analysis, the program "bicreg" within the R package "BMA" (Raftery et al., 2009) was used, which incorporates Occam's window to reduce the model space. The results of Bayesian model averaging for the PISA example are given in Table 6.5.

Table 6.5 can be interpreted as follows (see Madigan & Raftery, 1994; Hoeting et al., 1999). First, Models 1 through 4 refer to the top four models retained after narrowing down the number of models via Occam's window, discussed in Chapter 5. For each of these models, the regression coefficients are provided as well as the R^2's, BICs, and posterior model probabilities associated with each model. These are arranged in descending order in terms of the posterior model probabilities.

TABLE 6.5. Bayesian Model Averaging Results for Full Multiple Regression Model

Predictor	Avg coef	SD	Model 1	Model 2	Model 3	Model 4
Full model						
INTERCEPT	493.63	2.11	494.86	491.67	492.77	496.19
GENDER	2.72	3.54	.	6.46	6.84	.
NATIVE	0.00	0.00	.	.	.	.
SLANG	0.00	0.00	.	.	.	.
ESCS	30.19	1.24	30.10	30.36	30.18	29.90
JOYREAD	29.40	1.40	29.97	28.93	27.31	28.35
DIVREAD	−4.01	1.68	−4.44	−4.28	.	.
MEMOR	−18.61	1.31	−18.47	−18.76	−18.99	−18.70
ELAB	−15.24	1.26	−15.37	−14.95	−15.43	−15.90
CSTRAT	27.53	1.46	27.62	27.43	27.27	27.45
R^2			0.34	0.34	0.34	0.34
BIC			−1993.72	−1992.98	−1988.72	−1988.51
PMP			0.54	0.37	0.05	0.04

Note. Avg coef, average unstandardized coefficient for all variables in the model; *SD*, standard deviation for the averaged coefficients; R^2, percent of variance accounted for by each model; BIC, Bayesian information criteria; PMP, posterior model probability for each of the four models.

So, for example, Model 1 has the highest posterior model probability, followed by Model 2, and so on. Note that the posterior model probabiltiy for Model 1 accounts for a little over half (54%) of the total posterior probability. Continuing, the column labeled "Avg coef" includes the Bayesian model averaged coefficients obtained from a weighted average of the coefficients for each model weighted by the posterior model probability. The standard deviation for each coefficient is also provided.

6.4 BAYESIAN GENERALIZED LINEAR MODELS

The previous section examined Bayesian linear regression. The conventional form of the linear regression model assumes that the outcome variable is continuous and normally distributed, as specified in Equation 6.2. Note that when this assumption holds, the conditional distribution of **y** given the predictors **X** will be normally distributed as well. This then leads to asymptotically unbiased, consistent, and efficient estimates of the model parameters.

For many applications of linear regression in the social sciences, the assumption of a continuous and normally distributed outcome is largely untenable or not even appropriate for the research question at hand. In the former case, the data might have been generated from a population in which the assumption of normality might arguably hold, but where the data in the finite sample is non-normal. In those cases, transformations of the original variables to achieve a more normal shape might be justified. In the latter case, the population distribution might not be normal at all. For example, an outcome of interest might be dichotomous, such as a response to the question "Did you vote in the last national election? (Yes/No)." Or, an outcome might be in the form of a count—for example, a response to a question such as "How many times this week did you read to your child?"

In both of these examples, the use of normal theory-based linear regression would lead to biased and inefficient estimates. Moreover, there would be loss in the richness of interpretation if the normal theory model were used for these data. Rather, it is best to apply models that explicitly account for the probability model generating the data. In the example of the dichotomous outcome, the appropriate probability model would be based on the binomial distribution, and in the example of the count outcome, the appropriate probability model would be based on the Poisson distribution. Both distributions (along with their conjugate priors) were discussed in Chapter 3. Incorporating alternative probability models in the context of regression has led to the *generalized linear model*.

For this section, we describe the so-called link function which provides a convenient framework for moving among nonlinear and linear models (McCullagh & Nelder, 1989). We then provide an empirical example utilizing Bayesian logistic regression.

6.4.1 The Link Function

In considering generalized linear models, the notion of the *link function* has unified a large number of models and has shown that the linear model discussed in the previous chapter is also a special case of the generalized linear model. Specifically, the link function is designed to relate (or "link") a noncontinuous and/or nonlinear outcome variable y_i ($i = 1, 2, \ldots, n$) to its linear predictor $\mathbf{x}'_i \boldsymbol{\beta}$. Take, as an example, the linear model discussed in the previous chapter. Letting $E(y_i) = \mu_i$, we have

$\mu_i = \mathbf{x}'_i\boldsymbol{\beta}$. Thus, the link function for the linear model is $F(\mu) = \mu$. From McCullagh and Nelder (1989), this is referred to as the *identity link*.

The idea is to determine link functions for noncontinuous and/or nonlinear outcome variables such as those we model in the context of logistic regression and Poisson regression. As we describe in more detail later, the link functions for the logistic model, multinomial model, and Poisson model are as follows:

Link function, $F(\mu)$	Model
μ	Linear
$\ln\left(\frac{\mu}{1-\mu}\right)$	Logistic regression
$\ln\left(\frac{\mu}{1-\mu}\right)$	Multinomial regression
$\ln(\mu)$	Poisson regression

6.4.2 The Logit–Link Function for Logistic and Multinomial Models

Notice from the above table that the logit-link function $\ln[\mu/(1-\mu)]$ is appropriate for cases where the outcome is binary (e.g., yes/no) or multinomial (e.g., agree/neutral/disagree). We address both cases in this section.

To begin our discussion of the logistic regression model, consider an outcome variable y_i, which can take on values 1 or 0. As before, this outcome variable could be a right/wrong answer on a math test or agree/disagree on an attitude survey item. For individual i, the outcome is generated from a binomial distribution, namely,

$$y_i | \theta \sim \text{Bin}(n, \theta) \tag{6.16}$$

Recall that the link function is the logarithm of the odds ratio, that is,

$$\ln\left(\frac{\mu}{1-\mu}\right) \tag{6.17}$$

where $\mu_i = \beta_0 + \beta_1 x_1 + \ldots + \beta_p x_p$. The first step in a Bayesian analysis is to define the likelihood. In the case of logistic regression, the likelihood of a single observation y_i is assumed to generate from a binomial probability model. That is, the likelihood function for this model can be written as

$$l(\beta_0, \ldots, \beta_p | y_i) = \theta_i^{y_i}(1 - \theta_i)^{1-y_i} \qquad (6.18)$$

For n independent observations, the likelihood can be written as

$$l(\beta_0, \ldots, \beta_p | y_1, \ldots, y_n) = \prod_{i=1}^{n} l(\beta_0, \ldots, \beta_p | y_i) \qquad (6.19)$$

As usual, the goal is to find the joint posterior distribution of the model parameters via Bayes' theorem, that is,

$$p(\beta_0, \ldots, \beta_p | y_1, \ldots, y_n) \propto l(\beta_0, \ldots, \beta_p | y_1, \ldots, y_n) \times p(\beta_0, \ldots, \beta_p) \qquad (6.20)$$

From here, uniform priors could be chosen for the intercept β_0 and the slopes $\beta_1, \ldots, \beta_p$ reflecting no prior information on the model parameters. The resulting joint posterior distribution $p(\beta_0, \ldots, \beta_p | y_1, \ldots, y_n)$ will be multivariate normal. In the case where one has prior information on the intercept and slopes, a multivariate normal prior can be chosen, resulting in a multivariate normal joint posterior distribution.

EXAMPLE 6.5. BAYESIAN LOGISTIC REGRESSION USING PISA 2009

In this example, we use data from PISA 2009, exploring whether private school attendance in the United States can be predicted by the student's gender (GENDER), immigrant status (NATIVE), language that he/she uses (SLANG; coded 1 if test language is the same as language at home, 0 otherwise), and a measure of the economic, social, and cultural status of the student (ESCS). The R program *MCMClogit* within MCMCpack (A. D. Martin et al., 2010) was used. A total of 100,000 iterations after 1,000 burn-in iterations were performed.

Convergence Diagnostics. The trace and density plots for the logistic model parameters in Figure 6.7 do not indicate problems of convergence. The Geweke plot shown in Figure 6.8 suggests convergence

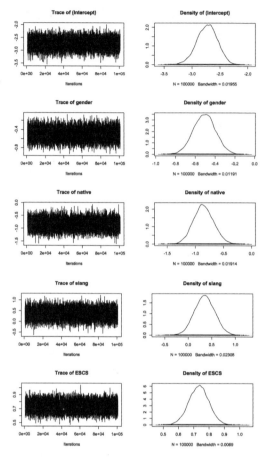

FIGURE 6.7. Trace and density plots for logistic regression model parameters.

of the single chain. In addition, the Heidelberger–Welch diagnostic also shows that the stationarity test for all model parameters was passed.

Results. Results comparing noninformative priors to priors based on PISA 2000 can be found in Table 6.6. We find that, with the exception of the effect of SLANG on PRIVATE, all coefficients are associated with 95% PPIs that do not contain zero.

The results of Bayesian model averaging for the logistic regression model using BMA are shown in Table 6.7.

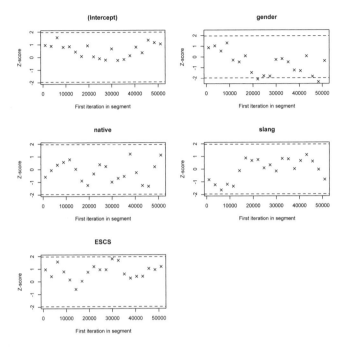

FIGURE 6.8. Geweke plot for logistic regression model parameters.

TABLE 6.6. Bayesian Logistic Regression of Private School Attendance: Comparison of Noninformative and Informative Priors

Parameter	EAP	SD	95% PPI
With noninformative prior			
INTERCEPT	−2.66	0.23	−3.12, −2.24
PRIVATE on GENDER	−1.01	0.16	−1.32, −0.71
PRIVATE on NATIVE	−1.32	0.20	−1.69, −0.92
PRIVATE on SLANG	0.57	0.28	0.04, 1.12
PRIVATE on ESCS	1.11	0.09	0.93, 1.29
With informative priors based on PISA 2000			
INTERCEPT	−2.73	0.18	−3.11, −2.38
PRIVATE on GENDER	−0.51	0.11	−0.73, −0.29
PRIVATE on NATIVE	−0.85	0.18	−1.20, −0.49
PRIVATE on SLANG	0.35	0.22	−0.07, 0.78
PRIVATE on ESCS	0.73	0.07	0.61, 0.86

Note. EAP, expected a posteriori; *SD*, standard deviation; *p*-value, Bayesian *p*-value; PPI, posterior probability interval.

TABLE 6.7. Bayesian Model Averaging Results for Logistic Regression Model

Predictor	Avg coef	SD	Model 1	Model 2
Full model				
INTERCEPT	−2.37	0.19	−2.34	−2.64
GENDER	−0.99	0.15	−0.99	−1.00
NATIVE	−1.11	0.18	−1.08	−1.32
SLANG	0.06	0.20	.	0.56
ESCS	1.12	0.09	1.12	1.10
BIC			−4.02e + 04	−4.02e + .04
PMP			0.89	0.11

Note. Avg coef, average unstandardized coefficient for all variables in the model; *SD*, standard deviation for the averaged coefficients; BIC, Bayesian information criteria; PMP, posterior model probability for each of the four models. Note that the R^2 is not included because this is a nonlinear model.

6.5 SUMMARY

This chapter provided the first complete analysis of a substantive problem using Bayesian regression. The general approach follows closely the steps of model building, evaluation, and selection within the frequentist domain. The key differences between the Bayesian and frequentist approaches to model building are (1) incorporation of prior knowledge as encoded into the prior distribution; (2) interpretation, particularly of posterior probability intervals; (3) model comparison using Bayes factors, where the focus of attention is on the evidence in the data in support of a model; and (4) incorporating model uncertainty via Bayesian model averaging. This chapter also demonstrated a Bayesian analysis for logistic regression—arguably the most popular of the generalized linear models. The link functions for other generalized linear models were provided. From a Bayesian perspective, as long as the probability model for the outcome variable is correctly specified, the issue then centers on the specification of the priors.

6.6 SUGGESTED READINGS

Gelman, A., Carlin, J. B., Stern, H. S., & Rubin, D. B. (2003). *Bayesian data analysis* (2nd ed.). London: Chapman and Hall.

Gelman, A., & Hill, J. (2003). *Data analysis using regression and multilevel/hierarchical models.* Cambridge, UK: Cambridge University Press.

Gill, J. (2002). *Bayesian methods: A social and behavioral sciences approach.* London: Chapman and Hall/CRC Press.

Lynch, S. M. (2007). *Introduction to applied Bayesian statistics and estimation for social scientists.* New York: Springer.

APPENDIX 6.1
R CODE FOR CHAPTER 6

```
#---------------------------------------------------------------
# EXAMPLE 6:1: BAYESIAN MULTIPLE REGRESSION WITH NON-INFORMATIVE PRIORS
#                       Program Steps
# 1. Read in data and apply tranformations or handle missing data as needed
# 2. Call MCMCregress
# 3. Default prior mean b0=0 precision B0=0 tells MCMCregress to use to use an improper
#      uniform prior
# 4. Summarize and obtain diagnostic plots
#---------------------------------------------------------------

install.packages("MCMCpack")
install.packages("BMA")
install.packages("coda")
require(MCMCpack) require(coda)
require (BMA)

# Read in data

datafile <- read.csv(file.choose(),header=T)
datafile9 <- subset(datafile, select=c(RCOMB1, GENDER, NATIVE, SLANG, ESCS,
    JOYREAD, DIVREAD, MEMOR, ELAB, CSTRAT))
head(datafile9)
nrow(datafile9)
```

```
datafile9<-na.omit(datafile9)
nrow(datafile9)

# Run model

FullModel <- MCMCregress(RCOMB1~GENDER+NATIVE+ SLANG+ESCS+
        JOYREAD+ DIVREAD+ MEMOR+ ELAB+ CSTRAT,
        data=datafile9,burnin=5000,mcmc=100000,thin=10,b0=0,B0=0)
plot(FullModel)
autocorr.plot(FullModel)
dev.off()
summary(FullModel)

# Diagnostics
geweke.diag(FullModel, frac1=0.1, frac2=0.5)
heidel.diag(FullModel,eps=0.1,pvalue=0.05)
raftery.diag(FullModel,q=0.5,r=0.05,s=0.95,converge.eps=0.001)

#-------------------------------------------------------------------
# EXAMPLE 6.2: BAYESIAN MULTIPLE REGRESSION WITH INFORMATIVE PRIORS
#        Program Steps
# Same as Example 6.1 except now priors are specified for the regression coefficients
# b0 and precisions B0.
#-------------------------------------------------------------------
```

```
FullModel_inf <- MCMCregress(RCOMB1~GENDER+NATIVE+ SLANG+ ESCS+
    JOYREAD+ DIVREAD+ MEMOR+ ELAB+ CSTRAT,data=datafile9,
    marginal.likelihood="Chib95",mcmc=10000,
b0=c(491.2, 12.9, 3.4, 21.4, 32.6, 22.9, 0.01, -18.6, -11.1, 22.8),
B0=c(0.0173, 0.0932, 0.0141, 0.0216, 0.3354, 0.3210, 0.3245, 0.2101, 0.2111, 0.1707))

pdf('FullModel_inf.trace.pdf')
plot(FullModel_inf) # Produces the convergence plots and the posterior densities
pdf('FullModel_inf.acf.pdf')
autocorr.plot(FullModel_inf)
dev.off()
summary(FullModel_inf)


geweke.diag(FullModel_inf, frac1=0.1, frac2=0.5)
heidel.diag(FullModel_inf,eps=0.1,pvalue=0.05)
raftery.diag(FullModel_inf,q=0.5,r=0.05,s=0.95,converge.eps=0.001)

#----------EXAMPLE 6.3: MODEL COMPARISON-----------------#

# Model Comparison: Background variables only

BGModel_inf <- MCMCregress(RCOMB1~GENDER+NATIVE+ SLANG+ ESCS
    ,data=datafile9,marginal.likelihood="Chib95",mcmc=10000,
b0=c(470.9, 26.3, 4.7, 23.3, 39.9 ),
B0=c( 0.0185, 0.0952, 0.0151, 0.0222, 0.3541 ))
plot(BGModel_inf)
```

```
dev.off()
summary(BGModel_inf)

# Model Comparison: Attitudinal variables only

ATTModel_inf <- MCMCregress(rcomb1~JOYREAD+ DIVREAD,
data=datafile9,marginal.likelihood="Chib95",mcmc=10000,
b0=c( 505.4, 27.2, 8.4 ),B0=c(0.3643, 0.3147, 0.3497))
plot(ATTModel_inf)
dev.off()
summary(ATTModel_inf)

# Model Comparison: Learning strategies variables only

LSModel_inf <- MCMCregress(rcomb1~ MEMOR+ ELAB+ CSTRAT,
data=datafile9,marginal.likelihood="Chib95",mcmc=10000,
b0=c( 509.7, -24.2, -9.8, 38.9),B0=c( 0.3327, 0.1829, 0.1848, 0.1563))
plot(LSModel_inf)
dev.off()
summary(LSModel_inf)

# Calculation of Bayes Factors

bf <- BayesFactor(BGModel_inf, ATTModel_inf, LSModel_inf, FullModel_inf)
print(bf)
```

```r
#--------EXAMPLE 6.4: BAYESIAN MODEL AVERAGING-----------#

attach(datafile9)
bma=bicreg(cbind(GENDER, NATIVE, SLANG, ESCS,
JOYREAD, DIVREAD, MEMOR, ELAB, CSTRAT),rcomb1,strict=FALSE,OR=20)
summary(bma)
plot(bma,include.intercept=FALSE)

#-------- EXAMPLE 6.5 BAYESIAN LOGISTIC REGRESSION--------#

install.packages("MCMCpack")
install.packages("BMA")

#Multiple Regression Analysis :
library(MCMCpack)
datafile <- read.csv(file.choose(),header=T)
datafile5 <- subset (datafile, select=c(private, gender, native, slang, ESCS))

head(datafile5)
nrow(datafile5)
datafile5<-na.omit(datafile5)
nrow(datafile5)

#FullModel
FullModel <- MCMClogit(private~gender+ native+ slang+ ESCS
,data=datafile5,marginal.likelihood="Laplace",mcmc=100000,b0=0,
```

142

```r
B0=(.01))
plot(FullModel) # Produces the convergence plots and the posterior densities
dev.off()
summary(FullModel)

FullModel_inf <- MCMClogit(private~gender+ native+ slang+ ESCS
,data=datafile5,marginal.likelihood="Laplace",mcmc=100000,
b0=c(-3.4118, 0.2513, 0.6171, -0.3057, 0.2446 ),

B0=c( 3.454347, 27.272662, 3.018396, 6.184967, 93.873638))
plot(FullModel_inf) # Produces the convergence plots and the posterior densities
dev.off()
summary(FullModel_inf)

#Convergence Diagnostics
library(coda)
geweke.diag(FullModel_inf, frac1=0.1, frac2=0.5)
heidel.diag(FullModel_inf, eps=0.1,pvalue=0.05)
raftery.diag(FullModel_inf,q=0.5,r=0.05,s=0.95,converge.eps=0.001)

geweke.diag(FullModel_inf, frac1=0.1, frac2=0.5)
heidel.diag(FullModel_inf, eps=0.1,pvalue=0.05)
raftery.diag(FullModel_inf,q=0.5,r=0.05,s=0.95,converge.eps=0.001)

#Bayesian Model Averaging
library(BMA)
```

143

```
attach(datafile5)
bma=bic.glm(cbind(gender, native, slang, ESCS),private,
glm.family=binomial("logit"), strict=FALSE,OR=20)
summary(bma)
plot(bma) # Plots of BMA posterior distributions
imageplot.bma(bma) # The image plot shows which predictors are included in each model

#------------------------POSTERIOR PREDICTIVE CHECK ------------------------------#

library(gridExtra)
library(coda)
require(MCMCpack)

#set.seed(515)
###These grab the data from the MCMC object
beta.df <- data.frame(as.matrix(FullModel_inf))
beta.mat <- as.matrix(beta.df[sample(8000:10000,1000),])?beta.non.df <- data.frame(as.
matrix(FullMod beta.non.mat <- as.matrix(beta.non.df[sample(8000:10000,1000),])

ppc <- function(x, df1) {

obs <- as.matrix(cbind(Intercept = 1,datafile9[,2:10])) ## Independent variables in
regression model
betas <- as.matrix(df1[x,1:10]) ## betas drawn from the posterior distribution
y.rep.ev <- obs %*% betas    ## expected value y
y.rep.var <- df1[x,11] ## variance of y
```

```r
#print(c(y.rep.ev,y.rep.var))
y.rep <- obs %*% betas + rnorm(nrow(datafile9),0,sqrt(df1[x,11])) ## replicated data
val1 <- ((y.rep - y.rep.ev)^2)/y.rep.var ##y.rep chi.square ## Replicated Chi Square Statistic
val2 <- ((datafile9$rcomb1 - y.rep.ev)^2)/y.rep.var ## Observed Chi Square Statistic
return(list(y.rep,c(chi.rep = sum(val1),chi.obs = sum(val2))))

}##END function ppc

## SIMULATED THE REPLICATED DATA AND OBTAIN THE DISCREPANCY STATISTIC
ppc.data <- lapply(1:1000,ppc, df1 = beta.mat)
ppc.non.data <- lapply(1:1000,ppc, df1 = beta.non.mat)
posterior.check <- t(sapply(ppc.data, function(x) return(x[[2]])))
posterior.non.check <- t(sapply(ppc.non.data, function(x) return(x[[2]])))
chi.obs <- posterior.non.check[,2]
chi.rep <- posterior.non.check[,1]
chi.discrepancy <- posterior.non.check[,2] - posterior.non.check[,1] #get the
difference between y.obs and y.rep
p.value <- round(length(which(chi.discrepancy < 0))/length(chi.discrepancy),3)
range <- max(chi.discrepancy) - min(chi.discrepancy) ##range

##SAVE PDF POSTERIOR CHECKING PLOTS
liks.dif <- chi.obs - chi.rep
range <- max(liks.dif) - min(liks.dif)
p.value <- round(length(which(liks.dif < 0))/length(liks.dif),3)
pdf(file=' ') ####ADD FILE PATH#####
```

145

```r
par(ask = FALSE)
hist(liks.dif, xlab = expression(Chi["obs"]^2 - Chi["rep"]^2), main = "")
abline(v = 0, lty = 2, lwd = 2)
text(x = min(liks.dif) + range/5, y = 200, label = paste("p-value = ",p.value,sep =
""))
dev.off()
pdf(file=' ') ####ADD FILE PATH#####
qplot(chi.obs,chi.rep, shape = I(1)) +
geom_abline(slope = 1, intercept = 0) +
theme_bw() +
geom_text(aes(x = 65 + min(chi.obs,chi.rep), y = - 2 + max(chi.obs,chi.rep), label
= paste("p-value =",p.value)), size = 4.5) +
theme(panel.grid.major = element_blank(), panel.grid.minor = element_blank()) +
ylim(c(-7 + min(chi.obs,chi.rep),max(chi.obs,chi.rep)))
+ xlim(c(-7 + min(chi.obs,chi.rep),max(chi.obs,chi.rep)))
+ xlab("Observed") + ylab("Replicated")
dev.off()

##DISPLAY POSTERIOR CHECKING PLOTS & INFORMATION
hist(liks.dif, xlab = expression(Chi["obs"]^2 - Chi["rep"]^2), main = "")
abline(v = 0, lty = 2, lwd = 2)
text(x = min(liks.dif) + range/5, y = 200, label = paste("p-value = ",p.value,sep =
""))
par(ask = TRUE)
qplot(chi.obs,chi.rep, shape = I(1)) +
geom_abline(slope = 1, intercept = 0) +
```

146

```
theme_bw() +
geom_text(aes(x = 65 + min(chi.obs,chi.rep), y = - 2 + max(chi.obs,chi.rep), label
= paste("p-value =",p.value)), size = 4.5) +
#theme(panel.grid.major = element_blank()) +
ylim(c(-7 + min(chi.obs,chi.rep),max(chi.obs,chi.rep))) +
xlim(c(-7 + min(chi.obs,chi.rep),max(chi.obs,chi.rep))) +
xlab("Observed") + ylab("Replicated")

###
pdf(file=' ') #####ADD FILE PATH#####
hist(FullModel_inf[,11], main = "Histogram of posterior draws for Sigma", xlab = "Sigma")
dev.off()
```

7

Missing Data from a Bayesian Perspective

Before beginning our treatment of advanced Bayesian methods, it is necessary to address a problem that transcends both the basic methods discussed in Part II and the advanced methods that we discuss in Part III—namely, the problem of missing data. For the purposes of this chapter, we focus first on how missing data have been conceptualized, relying heavily on the seminal work of Little and Rubin (2002). We then overview some general methods for handling missing data. Finally, we examine Bayesian approaches to the analysis of missing data. This chapter is not meant to provide a complete description of the literature on missing data theory. Important discussions of missing data can be found in Little and Rubin (2002), Enders (2010), and Schafer (1997).

7.1 A NOMENCLATURE FOR MISSING DATA

To motivate our discussion of missing data, consider as an example, responses to three items on a parent questionnaire.[1] These items ask for

---

[1] An example of a parent questionnaire might be the international optional parent survey provided by the OECD/PISA project.

the parent's age, education level, and household income. For a sample of parents, we might observe complete data for the age question, somewhat fewer data observed for the education-level question, and even more data missing for the income question. In considering now to handle the missing data, we need to first consider the mechanisms that would lead to omitted responses to these items.

In a series of seminal papers culminating in an important book, Little and Rubin (2002) considered three possible scenarios that would give rise to missing (and observed) data in this example. Following Little and Rubin (2002; see also Enders, 2010), let M be a missing data indicator, taking the value of 1 if the data are observed and 0 if the data are missing. Further, let y be the complete data, y_{obs} represent observed data and y_{miss} represent missing data. Finally, let φ be the scalar or vector-valued parameter describing the process that generates the missing data. In the first instance, the missing data on education and income might be unrelated to the age, education, or income level of the participants. In this instance, we say that the missing data are *missing completely at random* or MCAR. More formally, MCAR implies that

$$f(M|y) = f(M|\varphi) \tag{7.1}$$

which is to say that the missing data indicator is unrelated to the data, missing or observed, and only related to some unknown missing data-generating mechanism. Conditions in which the missing data might be MCAR include random coding errors, instances of missing by design, such as occurs with balanced incomplete block spiraling designs (Kaplan, 1995), or statistical matching/data fusion (see, e.g., Rässler, 2002). It has been recognized that MCAR is a fairly unrealistic assumption in most social science data.

In the second instance, missing data on, say, education, may be due to the age or income of the respondents. Similarly, missing data on income may be due to the age or education of the respondents. So, for example, a parent may not reveal his/her income level based on his/her age and/or education. In this case, we say that the missing data are *missing at random* or MAR. Again, in terms of our notation, MAR implies that

$$f(M|y) = f(M|y_{obs}, \varphi) \tag{7.2}$$

which states that the missing data mechanism is unrelated to variables that are missing, but could be related to other observed variables in the analysis. We note for now that MAR is a more realistic assumption than MCAR.

Finally, missing data on, say, income might be related to the income of the respondents and not necessarily to their age or education level. That is, individuals choose to omit their response on the income question because of their level of income, regardless of their age or education level. In this case, we say that the missing data are *not missing at random* or NMAR. More formally,

$$f(M|y) = f(M|y_{obs}, y_{miss}, \varphi) \tag{7.3}$$

meaning that the missing data are related to the variable on which there is missing data as well as, possibly, the observed data. It has been argued that NMAR is probably the most realistic scenario of why omitted responses are occurring.

7.2 AD HOC DELETION METHODS FOR HANDLING MISSING DATA

Given the formal definitions in the last section, we next examine traditional methods that have been used in the past to address the problem of missing data. In this section, we briefly review six traditional methods for addressing missing data before turning to more advanced methods, including Bayesian approaches. These are (1) listwise deletion, (2) pairwise deletion, (3) mean imputation, (4) regression imputation, (5) stochastic regression imputation, and (6) hot-deck imputation.

7.2.1 Listwise Deletion

Simply put, listwise deletion (also referred to as casewise deletion) involves omitting any respondent for which there are any missing data on any variable to be used in an analysis. Listwise deletion is used as a convenient method for handling missing data but suffers from two critical flaws. First, from the frequentist framework, listwise deletion can result in an unacceptable loss of data, hence reducing statistical power.

More importantly, perhaps, is that listwise deletion assumes that the missing data are MCAR, and as we noted, this is probably a highly unrealistic assumption in most practical settings. Put another way, the missing data mechanism presumed under listwise deletion is misspecified.

7.2.2 Pairwise Deletion

Pairwise deletion is essentially the use of listwise deletion when statistical methods require using pairs of variables in the estimation. The simplest example is the calculation of a covariance matrix among a set of variables. Using the age, education, and income example from above, we may find it of interest to calculate the covariance matrix among these three variables. In calculating the covariance between age and education, the sample would be listwise deleted, and hence the sample size for education would be used for that calculation. Similarly, for the covariance between age and income, the sample would again be listwise deleted and the sample size for income would be used—and similarly, for the education and income covariance calculation.

There are three fundamental flaws with the use of pairwise deletion. First, as with listwise deletion, pairwise deletion rests on the somewhat unrealistic assumption that the missing data are MCAR. Second, from the standpoint of the frequentist framework, pairwise deletion will result in a loss of power due to the decrease in sample size. However, and perhaps more seriously, the decrease in the sample size is not uniform across covariance calculations. In other words, the sample sizes on which the covariances are calculated are different for different elements of the covariance matrix. The result of the covariance matrix being based on different element sample sizes is that it no longer will follow a Wishart distribution and, in some cases, might not be positive definite. Thus, methods such as regression and structural equation modeling, which can use the covariance matrix as a sufficient statistic for estimation, could result in bias or estimation problems. Generally speaking, pairwise deletion should be avoided.

7.3 SINGLE IMPUTATION METHODS

The methods of listwise deletion and pairwise deletion result in a loss of data. To get around the loss of data, it might be preferable to impute values for the missing data. Two types of imputations are possible. The first, discussed next, involves imputing one single value for each missing data point. Methods discussed next are *mean imputation, regression imputation*, and *stochastic regression imputation*. This is followed by a brief discussion of multiple imputation that will set the stage for Bayesian methods. This section does not present an exhaustive review of single imputation methods.

7.3.1 Mean Imputation

One approach is *mean imputation*. Simply put, mean imputation for a given variable y_k, $(k = 1, 2, \ldots, K)$, requires that we calculate the mean $\bar{y}_k$ and insert that value for all cases that are missing on y_k.

Mean imputation suffers from two problems. First, mean imputation assumes that the missing data are MCAR, which, again, might be unrealistic. Second, and perhaps more critically, a constant $\bar{y}_k$ is imputed for all occurrences of missing data on y_k. In the situation with a large amount of missing data, mean imputation will result in a loss of variation on that variable.

7.3.2 Regression Imputation

Regression imputation represents an improvement on the previous procedures. Again, consider the case of missing data on parent age, education, and income. Regression imputation begins by specifying a regression equation to predict the missing data on each variable. Using listwise deletion to start, we can form a regression equation for the missing data on income and the missing data on education. We can write the models for parent i $(i = 1, 2, \ldots, n)$ as

$$Educ_i = \beta_0 + \beta_1(age_i) + \beta_2(income_i) + e_{i,educ} \qquad (7.4)$$

and

$$Income_i = \beta_0 + \beta_1(age_i) + \beta_2(educ_i) + e_{i,income} \qquad (7.5)$$

From here, predicted values of education and income are obtained as

$$\widehat{Educ}_i = \hat{\beta}_0 + \hat{\beta}_1(age_i) + \hat{\beta}_2(income_i) \qquad (7.6)$$

and

$$\widehat{Income}_i = \hat{\beta}_0 + \hat{\beta}_1(age_i) + \hat{\beta}_2(educ_i) \tag{7.7}$$

and these predicted values are imputed for the corresponding missing data point.

Although single regression imputation is an improvement upon mean imputation and the ad hoc deletion methods, it suffers from one major drawback. Specifically, the predicted values based on the regression in Equations 7.6 and 7.7 will, by definition, lie exactly on the regression line. This implies that, among the subset of observations for which there is missing data, the correlations among the variables of interest will be 1.0. As a result, the overall R^2 value will be overestimated. Second, as with mean imputation, it is presumed that the imputed values would be the ones observed had there been no missing data. For this to be true, the regression model would have to be correctly specified.

7.3.3 Stochastic Regression Imputation

Recall that the major problem of regression imputation is that for the subset of observations with missing values, the imputed values will lie exactly on the regression line, thus overestimating the strength of association. To address this problem, we can add a random term to Equations 7.6 and 7.7 that serve to *perturb* the imputed values from the predicted line. We would then write Equations 7.6 and 7.7 as

$$\widehat{Educ}_i = \hat{\beta}_0 + \hat{\beta}_1(age_i) + \hat{\beta}_2(income_i) + r_{i,educ} \tag{7.8}$$

and

$$\widehat{Income}_i = \hat{\beta}_0 + \hat{\beta}_1(age_i) + \hat{\beta}_2(educ_i) + r_{i,income} \tag{7.9}$$

where $r_{i,educ}$ and $r_{i,income}$ are values drawn from a normal distribution, with mean 0 and variance equal to the residual variance obtained from estimation of Equation 7.4.

A distinct advantage of stochastic regression imputation is that it preserves the variability in the data that is lost with mean imputation and regression imputation. As a result, it has been shown that stochastic regression imputation yields unbiased estimates under the somewhat more realistic assumption of MAR and performs quite similarly to multiple imputation (Enders, 2010). However, stochastic regression imputation only applies one draw from the normal distribution to be used for residual terms in Equations 7.8 and 7.9.

7.3.4 Hot-Deck Imputation

A rather different form of single imputation involves replacing the missing value on a variable from some individual by a value from a "similar" individual who, in fact, did respond to the variable. This method is referred to as *hot-deck imputation*. The method of hot-deck imputation is rather generic, with differences in methods based on how "similarity" is defined. In the simplest case, a sample of respondents would be classified across a variety of selected demographic characteristics. Then, a missing value would be replaced by a draw from the subsample of individuals who are as similar as possible on the selected demographic characteristics as the individual who omitted the response (Enders, 2010).

The method just described is not limited to categorical variables such as most background demographic characteristics. Continuous variables can also be used for hot-deck matching, and algorithms such as *nearest neighbor* matching can be employed. Following Little and Rubin (2002), the basic idea behind nearest neighbor hot-deck matching is as follows. Let $\mathbf{x}_i = (x_{i1}, x_{i2}, \ldots, x_{iK})'$ be a set of K covariates $k = 1, 2, \ldots, K$ measured on individual i, and let y_i be a variable that is missing for individual i. Then, an indicator variable $d(i, j)$ can be formed as

$$d(i, j) = \begin{cases} 0, & i, j \text{ in same cell} \\ 1, & i, j \text{ in different cells} \end{cases}$$

This approach would result in partitioning the sample into cells that can be used for conventional hot-deck matching described above. However, other metrics can be defined as well. For example, the metric of *maximum deviation* can be defined as

$$\text{Maximum deviation:} \quad d(i, j) = \max_k |x_{ik} - x_{jk}| \qquad (7.10)$$

and the *Mahalanobis* distance metric can be defined as

$$\text{Mahalanobis:} \quad d(i, j) = (\mathbf{x}_i - \mathbf{x}_j)'\mathbf{S}_{xx}^{-1}(\mathbf{x}_i - \mathbf{x}_j) \qquad (7.11)$$

where $\mathbf{S}_{xx}$ is the sample covariance matrix of $\mathbf{x}_i$.

7.3.5 Predictive Mean Matching

Regression imputation and hot-deck matching sets the groundwork for so-called *predictive mean matching* introduced by Rubin (1986). The essential idea is that a missing value is imputed by matching its predicted value based on regression imputation to the predicted values of the observed data on the basis of a predictive mean metric.

$$\text{Predictive mean:} \quad d(i, j) = [\hat{y}(\mathbf{x}_i) - \hat{y}(\mathbf{x}_j)]^2 \qquad (7.12)$$

Once a match is found, the procedure uses the actual observed value for the imputation. That is, for each regression, there is a predicted value for the missing data and also a predicted value for the observed data. The predicted value for the observed data is then matched to a predicted value of the missing data using, say, a nearest neighbor distance metric. Once the match is found, the actual observed value (rather than the predicted value) replaces the missing value. In this sense, predictive mean matching operates much like hot-deck matching.

7.4 BAYESIAN METHODS OF MULTIPLE IMPUTATION

In the previous section, we discussed single imputation models, including mean imputation, regression imputation, stochastic regression imputation, hot-deck, and predictive mean matching. In each case, a single value is imputed for the missing data point. Among the methods discussed in the previous section, stochastic regression imputation returns some of the variability in the data by imputing a missing value with some error that allows the missing data point to deviate from the regression line. Nevertheless, it is still the case that a single value is being imputed and treated as though that is the value that would have been obtained if the missing data point had, in fact, been observed. In other words, the imputed missing data point based on a single imputation method does not account for uncertainty about the missing data point itself. Thus, rather than imputing a single value, it may be theoretically better justified to draw multiple plausible missing data values. This idea forms the basis of *multiple imputation*, which fundamentally rests on Bayesian theory.

The central reason for adopting a Bayesian perspective on missing data problems is that by viewing parameters probabilistically and specifying a prior distribution on the parameters of interest, the imputation method is *Bayesianly proper* (Rubin, 1987) insofar as the imputations reflect uncertainty about the missing data as well as uncertainty about the unknown model parameters. Moreover, the Bayesian view of statistical inference allows for the incorporation of prior knowledge, which can further reduce uncertainty in model parameters. It is important to point out that although the method of stochastic regression imputation described above has a Bayesian flavor, it is not Bayesianly proper insofar as it does not account for parameter uncertainty, but rather only uncertainty in the predicted missing data values.

In this section, we discuss Bayesian approaches to multiple imputation. To begin, we first consider the *data augmentation* algorithm of Tanner and Wong (1987), which is a Bayesian approach to addressing missing data problems and is similar to Gibbs sampling (see Section 4.3). We then discuss an approach to multiple imputation using the chained equation algorithm of van Buuren (2012). From there, we consider two more modern approaches to multiple imputation. The first of these is based on the *expectation–maximization* (EM) algorithm, and the second is based on a combination of the so-called *Bayesian bootstrap* and predictive mean matching discussed earlier.

We apply each Bayesian multiple imputation method to the PISA 2009 reading example from Chapter 6 using the same set of noninformative and informative priors. For comparison purposes, the multiply imputed datasets under each method are analyzed using conventional frequentist regression and are summarized using Rubin's rules (Rubin, 1987). These examples are not a definitive comparison of the efficacy of these methods, insofar as this is not an experimental study. Experimental investigations of these procedures can be found in Rässler (2002) and Koller-Meinfelder (2009). A recent natural experiment involving data fusion (statistical matching) based on PISA 2009 data from Iceland can be found in Kaplan and McCarty (2013).

7.4.1 Data Augmentation

In this section we introduce a *Bayesianly proper* approach to handling missing data, referred to as *data augmentation* (DA) developed by Tanner and Wong (1987), and can be useful for handling missing data problems in the presence of small sample sizes.

Following Little and Rubin (2002), the Bayesian core of the DA algorithm recognizes that under the ignorable missing data assumption, the posterior distribution of the model parameters, given observed data, can be written as

$$p(\theta|y_{obs}) \propto p(y_{obs}|\theta)p(\theta) \qquad (7.13)$$

where, as before, $p(\theta)$ is the prior distribution. The DA algorithm is composed of two steps—referred to as the I(mputation) step and the P(osterior) step. The I-step begins with an initial value of θ, denoted as θ^s. Then,

$$\text{I-step:} \quad \text{Draw } y_{miss}^{(s+1)} \text{ from } p(y_{miss}|y_{obs}, \theta^s)$$

In other words, we use the current value $\theta^{(s)}$ and the observed data y_{obs} to generate a value for the missing data from the predictive distribution of the missing data $p(y_{miss}|y_{obs}, \theta^s)$. The I-step is followed by the P-step which draws a new value of θ, namely, $\theta^{(s+1)}$, from the posterior distribution of θ given the observed data y_{miss} and simulated missing data from the previous step, $y_{miss}^{(s+1)}$. Formally,

$$\text{P-step:} \quad \text{Draw } \theta^{(s+1)} \text{ from } p(\theta|y_{obs}, y_{miss}^{(s+1)})$$

As the number of iterations goes to infinity, the DA algorithm converges to a draw from the joint posterior distribution $p(\theta, y_{miss}|y_{obs})$ (Little & Rubin, 2002, p. 201).

Results of the comparative study for multiple imputation under data augmentation are given in Table 7.1. The analysis uses the R program "norm" (Shafer, 2012).

TABLE 7.1. Multiple Imputation Using Data Augmentation

Parameter	Noninformative prior		Informative prior		Frequentist	
	EAP	*SD*	EAP	*SD*	Coef	*SE*
Full model						
INTERCEPT	487.66	3.25	482.37	2.49	487.67	3.28
READING on GENDER	5.98	2.29	10.76	1.78	5.98	2.29
READING on NATIVE	–6.04	3.79	–5.74	3.00	–6.05	3.79
READING on SLANG	7.55	4.42	10.93	3.23	7.54	4.46
READING on ESCS	31.24	1.29	33.02	1.00	31.25	1.29
READING on JOYREAD	28.82	1.25	25.41	0.99	28.81	1.24
READING on DIVREAD	–4.57	1.16	–1.87	0.91	–4.58	1.17
READING on MEMOR	–19.06	1.30	–18.79	1.06	–19.05	1.29
READING on ELAB	–14.92	1.23	–14.33	1.03	–14.92	1.23
READING on CSTRAT	28.13	1.43	27.12	1.14	28.13	1.44

Note. EAP, expected a posteriori; *SD*, standard deviation; Coef, coefficient; *SE*, standard error.

7.4.2 Chained Equations

In this section we concentrate on another *Bayesianly proper* form of multiple imputation using the method of chained equations. This method recognizes that in many instances, it might be better to engage in a series of single univariate imputations along with diagnostic checking rather than an omnibus multivariate model for imputation that might be sensitive to specification issues. An overview of previous work on chained equations can be found in van Buuren (2012).

The essence of the chained equations approach is that univariate regression models consistent with the scale of the variable with missing data are used to provide predicted values of the missing data given the observed data. Thus, if a variable with missing data is continuous, then a normal model is used. If a variable is a count, then a Poisson model would be appropriate. This is a major advantage over other Bayesianly proper methods such as data augmentation that assume a common distribution for all of the variables. Once a variable of interest is "filled in," that variable, along with the variables for which there is complete data, is used in the sequence to fill in another variable. In general, the order of the sequence is determined by the amount of missing data,

TABLE 7.2. Multiple Imputation Using Chained Equations: Noninformative and Informative Priors

Parameter	Noninformative prior		Informative prior		Frequentist	
	EAP	SD	EAP	SD	Coef	SE
Full model						
INTERCEPT	487.92	3.27	482.59	2.50	487.93	3.31
READING on GENDER	6.21	2.29	10.91	1.78	6.22	2.30
READING on NATIVE	−6.56	3.85	−6.07	3.03	−6.57	3.85
READING on SLANG	7.68	4.46	10.96	3.24	7.66	4.50
READING on ESCS	31.27	1.31	33.05	1.00	31.29	1.30
READING on JOYREAD	28.67	1.24	25.36	0.99	28.67	1.23
READING on DIVREAD	−4.46	1.18	−1.82	0.92	−4.47	1.18
READING on MEMOR	−19.36	1.32	−18.98	1.07	−19.35	1.31
READING on ELAB	−15.05	1.26	−14.40	1.05	−15.04	1.26
READING on CSTRAT	28.46	1.46	27.31	1.15	28.45	1.47

Note. EAP, expected a posteriori; *SD*, standard deviation; Coef, coefficient; *SE*, standard error.

where the variable with the least amount of missing data is imputed first, and so on.

Once the sequence is completed for all variables with missing data, the posterior distribution of the regression parameters is obtained and the process is started again. Specifically, the filled-in data from the previous cycle, along with complete data, are used for the second and subsequent cycles (Enders, 2010). The Gibbs sampler (see Chapter 4) is used to generate the sequence of iterations. Finally, running the Gibbs sampler with *m* chains provides *m* imputed datasets.

Results of the comparative study for multiple imputation using chained equations are given in Table 7.2. The analysis uses the R program "mi" (Su, Gelman, Hill, & Yajima, 2011).

7.4.3 EM Bootstrap: A Hybrid Bayesian/Frequentist Method

In this section we examine an approach that combines Bayesian imputation concepts with the frequentist idea of bootstrap sampling. Essentially, bootstrapping is a data-based simulation method that relies on drawing repeated samples from the data to estimate the sample distribution of almost any statistic. The method was developed as a simplified alternative to inferences derived from statistical theory (Efron, 1979). Specifically, this section considers the implementation of the EM algorithm with bootstrapping.

Briefly, EM stands for *expectation–maximization* and is an algorithm that is widely used to obtain maximum likelihood estimates of model parameters in the context of missing data problems (Dempster, Laird, & Rubin, 1977).

The essence of the EM algorithm proceeds as follows. Using a set of starting values for the means and the covariance matrix of the data (perhaps obtained from listwise deletion), the E-step of the EM algorithm creates the sufficient statistics necessary to obtain regression equations that yield the predictions of the missing data, given the observed data and the initial set of model parameters. The next step is to use the "filled-in" data to obtain new estimates of model parameters via the M-step, which is simply the use of straightforward equations to obtain new estimates of the vector of means and the covariance matrix of the data. The algorithm then iterates back to the E-step to obtain new regression equations. The algorithm cycles between the E-step and the M-step until a convergence criterion has been met, at which point the maximum likelihood estimates have been obtained. The E-step and M-step are the likelihood counterparts of the Bayesian I-step and P-step in data augmentation.

Following Little and Rubin (2002), the basic idea behind the EM algorithm is as follows. We recognize that the missing data y_{miss} contains information relevant to estimating a parameter θ and that given an estimate of θ, we can obtain information regarding y_{miss}. Thus, a sensible approach would be to start with an initial value of θ, say $\theta^{(0)}$, estimate y_{miss} based on that value, and then with the "filled-in" data re-estimate θ via maximum likelihood, referring to this new estimate as $\theta^{(1)}$. The process then continues until the s iterations ($s = 0, 1, 2, \ldots$) converge.

From the previous description, it may appear that the EM algorithm is simply another form of imputation. However, unlike imputation methods described in Section 7.3, the "missing data" are not elements of y_{miss}. Rather, they are functions of the missing data that are part of the complete data log likelihood, $l(\theta|y)$ (Little & Rubin, 2002, p. 168).

More formally, the EM algorithm has two steps: the (E)xpectation step and the (M)aximization step. The E-step begins with an initial value of the parameter, $\theta^{(s)}$, treating it as θ, and obtains the expected complete data log likelihood

$$Q(\theta|\theta^{(s)}) = \int l(\theta|y)p(y_{\text{miss}}|y_{\text{obs}}, \theta^{(s)})dy_{\text{miss}} \tag{7.14}$$

The M-step then obtains $\theta^{(s+1)}$ via maximum likelihood estimation of expected complete data log likelihood in Equation 7.14. Dempster et al. (1977; see also Schafer, 1997) showed that $\theta^{(s+1)}$ is a better estimate than $\theta^{(s)}$ insofar as the observed data log likelihood under $\theta^{(s+1)}$ is at least as large as that obtained under $\theta^{(s)}$—that is,

$$l(\theta^{(s+1)}|y_{\text{obs}}) \geq l(\theta^{(s)}|y_{\text{obs}}) \tag{7.15}$$

because $\theta^{(s+1)}$ was chosen so that

$$Q(\theta^{(s+1)}|\theta^{(s)}) \geq Q(\theta|\theta^{(s)}) \quad \text{for all } \theta \tag{7.16}$$

The EM algorithm has been extended to handle the problem of multiple imputation without the need for computationally intensive draws from the posterior distribution, as with the data augmentation approach. The idea is to extend the EM algorithm using a bootstrap approach. This approach is labeled *EMB* (Honaker & King, 2010) and implemented in the R program "Amelia" (Honaker, King, & Blackwell, 2011), which we use in our analyses below.

Following Honaker and King (2010) and Honaker (personal communication, June 2011), the first step is to bootstrap the dataset to create *m* versions of the incomplete data, where *m* ranges typically from 3 to 5 as in other multiple imputation approaches. Bootstrap resampling involves taking a sample of size *n* with replacement from the original dataset. Here, the *m* bootstrap samples of size *n* are obtained from the dataset, where *n* is the total sample size of the file. Second, for each bootstrapped dataset, the EM algorithm is run. It is here that Honaker and King (2010) allow for the inclusion of prior distributions on the model parameters estimated via the EM algorithm. Notice that because *m* bootstrapped samples are obtained, and each EM run on these samples may contain priors, then once the EM algorithm has run, the

TABLE 7.3. Multiple Imputation Using the EM Bootstrap

Parameter	Noninformative prior		Informative prior		Frequentist	
	EAP	*SD*	EAP	*SD*	Coef.	*SE*
Full model						
INTERCEPT	488.10	3.26	482.61	2.50	488.11	3.29
READING on GENDER	6.11	2.29	10.88	1.78	6.12	2.30
READING on NATIVE	−6.25	3.89	−5.92	3.06	−6.26	3.88
READING on SLANG	7.08	4.46	10.68	3.24	7.06	4.50
READING on ESCS	31.41	1.29	33.12	1.00	31.42	1.29
READING on JOYREAD	28.95	1.25	25.52	0.99	28.95	1.24
READING on DIVREAD	−4.52	1.18	−1.83	0.92	−4.53	1.19
READING on MEMOR	−19.01	1.31	−18.76	1.07	−19.00	1.30
READING on ELAB	−15.15	1.25	−14.48	1.04	−15.14	1.24
READING on CSTRAT	28.15	1.43	27.14	1.14	28.15	1.44

Note. EAP, expected a posteriori; *SD*, standard deviation; Coef., coefficient; *SE*, standard error.

model parameters will be different. With priors, the final results are the *maximum a posteriori* (MAP) estimates, the Bayesian counterpart of the maximum likelihood estimates. Finally, missing values are imputed based on the final converged estimates for each *m* dataset. These *m* versions can then be used in subsequent analyses.

Results of the comparative study for multiple imputation under the EM bootstrap are given in Table 7.3. The analysis uses the R program "Amelia" (Honaker et al., 2011).

7.4.4 Bayesian Bootstrap Predictive Mean Matching

Multiple imputation via data augmentation is inherently a parametric method. That is, in estimating a Bayesian linear regression, the posterior distributions are obtained via Bayes' theorem which requires parametric assumptions. It may be desirable, however, to relax assumptions regarding the posterior distributions of the model parameters. To do this requires replacement of the step that draws the conditional predictive distribution of the missing data given the observed data. A hybrid of predictive mean matching (discussed in Section 7.3.5), referred to as *posterior predictive mean matching*, proceeds first by obtaining parameter draws using classical MI approaches. However, the final step then uses those values to obtain predicted values of the data followed by conventional predictive mean matching.

Posterior predictive mean matching sets the groundwork for *Bayesian bootstrap predictive mean matching* (BBPMM). The goal of BBPMM is to further relax the distributional assumptions associated with draws from the posterior distributions of the model parameters. The algorithm begins by forming a Bayesian bootstrap of the observations (Rubin, 1981). The Bayesian bootstrap (BB) is quite similar to the conventional frequentist bootstrap (Efron, 1979) except that it provides a method for simulating the posterior distribution of the parameter(s) of interest rather than the sampling distribution of parameter(s) of interest. As such, the Bayesian bootstrap is more robust to violations of distributional assumptions associated with the posterior distribution. For specific details, see Rubin (1981). Next, BBPMM obtains estimates of the regression parameters from the BB sample. This is followed by the calculation of predicted values of the observed and missing data based on the regression parameters from the BB sample. Then, predictive mean matching is performed as described earlier. As with conventional MI, these steps can be carried out $m \geq 1$ times to create m multiply imputed datasets.

Results of the comparative study for multiple imputation under the Bayesian bootstrap predictive mean matching are given in Table 7.4. The analysis uses the R program "BaBooN" (Meinfelder, 2011).

An inspection of Tables 7.1–7.4 reveals similar results across methods of imputation for both the informative and noninformative cases, but sizable differences, particularly for the noninformative cases, when compared to the frequentist results in Table 6.1. Of course, it is difficult to draw generalizations about these methods when based on real data, but the results do serve as a caution that important differences can occur, depending on whether and how missing data are handled.

7.5 SUMMARY

This chapter presented an overview of advanced methods for handling problems of missing data. Given theoretical developments discussed in Little and Rubin (2002); extended by Schafer (1997), Rässler (2002), and van Buuren (2012) among others; and summarized recently in Enders

TABLE 7.4. Multiple Imputation Using Bayesian Bootstrap Predictive Mean Matching

Parameter	Noninformative prior EAP	*SD*	Informative prior EAP	*SD*	Frequentist Coef.	*SE*
Full model						
INTERCEPT	487.71	3.32	482.44	2.52	487.72	3.36
READING on GENDER	6.27	2.30	10.96	1.78	6.27	2.30
READING on NATIVE	−6.62	3.87	−6.12	3.04	−6.63	3.87
READING on SLANG	7.79	4.55	11.03	3.27	7.77	4.59
READING on ESCS	31.34	1.31	33.09	1.00	31.35	1.30
READING on JOYREAD	28.76	1.26	25.39	1.00	28.76	1.25
READING on DIVREAD	−4.51	1.19	−1.83	0.93	−4.51	1.19
READING on MEMOR	−19.10	1.31	−18.82	1.07	−19.09	1.30
READING on ELAB	−15.12	1.27	−14.47	1.05	−15.11	1.26
READING on CSTRAT	28.12	1.44	27.10	1.15	28.12	1.45

Note. EAP, expected a posteriori; *SD*, standard deviation; Coef., coefficient; *SE*, standard error.

(2010), there is no defensible reason to resort to ad hoc methods such as listwise and pairwise deletion. The central idea of multiple imputation originated by Rubin (1987) is essentially Bayesian, and various algorithms described in this chapter, such as data augmentation and chained equations, now allow for a full Bayesian approach to addressing uncertainty in missing data and analyzing multiple imputed datasets using fully Bayesian methods.

The next two chapters present Bayesian approaches to two popular methods used in the social sciences. These include multilevel modeling and latent variable models with continuous and categorical latent variables.

7.6 SUGGESTED READINGS

Enders, C. K. (2010). *Applied missing data analysis*. New York: Guilford Press.

Little, R. J. A., & Rubin, D. B. (2002). *Statistical analysis with missing data* (2nd ed.). Hoboken, NJ: Wiley.

Rässler, S. (2002). *Statistical matching: A frequentist theory, practical applications, and alternative Bayesian approaches*. New York: Springer.

Rubin, D. B. (1987). *Multiple imputation in nonresponse surveys*. New York: Wiley.

Schafer, J. L. (1997). *Analysis of incomplete multivariate data*. New York: Chapman and Hall/CRC Press.

van Buuren, S. (2012). *Flexible imputation of missing data*. New York: Chapman and Hall.

APPENDIX 7.1
R CODE FOR CHAPTER 7

```
#--------EXAMPLE 7.1: A COMPARATIVE EXAMPLE OF MISSING DATA METHODS--------#
#Read in data file
datafile <- read.csv("U:/bayesian/Bayes regression book/reg/datafile.csv",header=T)
datafile9 <- subset(datafile, select=c(rcomb1, gender, native, slang, ESCS,
    JOYREAD, DIVREAD, MEMOR, ELAB, CSTRAT))
head(datafile9)
nrow(datafile9)

##################################################
# Norm (Data Augmentation)
##################################################
install.packages("norm")
require("norm")
library(MCMCpack)

#Transfer data into a matrix
a <- as.matrix(datafile9)

#Preliminary manipuation
s <- prelim.norm(a)

#find the MLE for a starting value
thetahat <- em.norm(s)
```

```
#set random number generator seed
rngseed(1234567)

#Run the NORM program, specifying the data object, start value, and number of steps
theta <- da.norm(s,thetahat,steps=20,showits=TRUE)

#Generated Imputed data set using theta
IMP.norm<-imp.norm(s,theta,a )
IMP.norm<-as.data.frame(IMP.norm)

#Conduct Bayesian Regression using imputed data
noninf.norm<- MCMCregress(formula=rcomb1~gender+ native+ slang+ ESCS+
        JOYREAD+ DIVREAD+ MEMOR+ ELAB+ CSTRAT, data=IMP.norm, prior.m=0, prior.p=0)

#Conduct Bayesian Regression with informative prior
inf.norm<- MCMCregress(formula=rcomb1~gender+ native+ slang+ ESCS+
        JOYREAD+ DIVREAD+ MEMOR+ ELAB+ CSTRAT, data=IMP.norm, marginal.
likelihood="Chib95",mcmc=10000
        b0=c( 477.6,15.3, 4.8, 20.4, 36.2, 21.1, 1.7, -17.8, -13.3, 25.5 ),
        B0=c( 0.0435, 0.1089, 0.0247, 0.0298, 0.3824, 0.3202,
0.4207, 0.2397, 0.2306, 0.1950 ))

#Conduct frequentist regression
freq.norm<- lm(formula=rcomb1~gender+ native+ slang+ ESCS+
        JOYREAD+ DIVREAD+ MEMOR+ ELAB+ CSTRAT, data=IMP.norm)
```

168

```
##############################################################
# Chained equations
##############################################################
library(mi)
#Impute data
IMP <- mi(datafile9, n.imp=5,n.iter=300, add.noise=FALSE,seed=12345 )

#Conduct Bayesian Regression with non informative prior
noninf<- Bayesglm.mi.ce(formula=rcomb1~gender+ native+ slang+ ESCS+
    JOYREAD+ DIVREAD+ MEMOR+ ELAB+ CSTRAT, mi.object=IMP, prior.m=0, prior.p=0)

#Conduct Bayesian Regression with informative prior
inf<- Bayesglm.mi.ce(formula=rcomb1~gender+ native+ slang+ ESCS+
    JOYREAD+ DIVREAD+ MEMOR+ ELAB+ CSTRAT, mi.object=IMP,
prior.m=c( 477.6,15.3, 4.8, 20.4, 36.2, 21.1, 1.7, -17.8, -13.3, 25.5 ),
prior.p=c( 0.0435, 0.1089, 0.0247, 0.0298, 0.3824, 0.3202,
0.4207, 0.2397, 0.2306, 0.1950 ) )

#Conduct frequentist regression
b<-lm.mi(formula=rcomb1~gender+ native+ slang+ ESCS+
    JOYREAD+ DIVREAD+ MEMOR+ ELAB+ CSTRAT, mi.object=IMP)
display(b)

##############################################################
# Amelia (EM Boostrap)
##############################################################
```

```
install.packages("Amelia")
require(Amelia)

#Set bounds on variables to be imputed. These should be determined by the actual
distributions of each variable.
bds <- matrix(c(1,-3.5,3.5, 2,1,4, 3,-3.5,3.5, 4,-3.5,3.5), nrow = 4, ncol=3,
byrow=TRUE)

#Run the AMELIA program, specifying the data object, the number of imputed data sets
desired, and the bounds for imputed variables
IMP.amelia <- amelia(x=datafile9,m=5, bounds=bds)

#Conduct Bayesian Regression using imputed data
noninf.amelia<- Bayesglm.mi.amelia(formula=rcomb1~gender+ native+ slang+ ESCS+
    JOYREAD+ DIVREAD+ MEMOR+ ELAB+ CSTRAT, mi.object=IMP.amelia, prior.m=0, prior.
p=0)

#Conduct Bayesian Regression with informative prior
inf.amelia<- Bayesglm.mi.amelia(formula=rcomb1~gender+ native+ slang+ ESCS+
    JOYREAD+ DIVREAD+ MEMOR+ ELAB+ CSTRAT, mi.object=IMP.amelia,
prior.m=c( 477.6,15.3, 4.8, 20.4, 36.2, 21.1, 1.7, -17.8, -13.3, 25.5 ),
prior.p=c( 0.0435, 0.1089, 0.0247, 0.0298, 0.3824, 0.3202,
0.4207, 0.2397, 0.2306, 0.1950 ))

#Conduct frequentist regression
freq.amelia<-freq.mi.amelia(formula=rcomb1~gender+ native+ slang+ ESCS+
    JOYREAD+ DIVREAD+ MEMOR+ ELAB+ CSTRAT, mi.object=IMP.amelia)
```

170

```
##############################################################
# BaBooN (Bayesian Predictive Mean Matching)
##############################################################
install.packages("BaBooN")
require(BaBooN)

#Run BaBooN program, specifying the data object, number of iterations desired, and
the number of imputed data sets desired.
IMP.bbpmm <- BBPMM(datafile9, nIter=5, M=5)

#Conduct Bayesian Regression using imputed data
noninf.bbpmm<- Bayesglm.mi.bbpmm(formula=rcomb1~gender+ native+ slang+ ESCS+
        JOYREAD+ DIVREAD+ MEMOR+ ELAB+ CSTRAT, mi.object=IMP.bbpmm, prior.m=0, prior.p=0)

#Conduct Bayesian Regression with informative prior
inf.bbpmm<- Bayesglm.mi.bbpmm(formula=rcomb1~gender+ native+ slang+ ESCS+
        JOYREAD+ DIVREAD+ MEMOR+ ELAB+ CSTRAT, mi.object=IMP.bbpmm,
        prior.m=c( 477.6,15.3, 4.8, 20.4, 36.2, 21.1, 1.7, -17.8, -13.3, 25.5 ),
        prior.p=c( 0.0435, 0.1089, 0.0247, 0.0298, 0.3824, 0.3202,
0.4207, 0.2397, 0.2306, 0.1950 ) )

#Conduct frequentist regression
freq.bbpmm<-freq.mi.bbpmm(formula=rcomb1~gender+ native+ slang+ ESCS+
        JOYREAD+ DIVREAD+ MEMOR+ ELAB+ CSTRAT, mi.object=IMP.bbpmm)

####### FUNCTIONS FOR COMBINING FILES ###############
```

```
# MCMCreg.mi.ce    For chained equations

MCMCreg.mi.ce <-function(formula, mi.object, prior.m, prior.p)
{
    call    <-match.call()
    library(MCMCpack)
    m       <- m(mi.object)
    result <- vector( "list", m )

    names( result ) <- as.character(paste( "Chain", seq( m ), sep = "" ))
    mi.data <- mi.completed(mi.object)

    for ( i in 1:m ) {
as.data.frame(do.call(rbind, mi.data[[i]]))
        result[[i]] <- MCMCregress(formula,data=mi.data[i]],marginal.likelihood="none"
,mcmc=10000,b0=prior.m,B0=prior.p)
    }

    coef    <- vector( "list", m )
    se      <- vector( "list", m )
    for( j in 1:m ) {
        coef[[j]]<- lapply( result, summary )[[ j ]]$statistics[ ,1]
        se[[j]] <- lapply( result, summary )[[ j ]]$statistics[ ,2]
    }

    pooled <- mi.pooled(coef, se)
    print(pooled)
}
```

```
# MCMCreg.mi.bbpmm For Bayesian bootstrap pred. mean matching

MCMCreg.mi.bbpmm <-function(formula, mi.object, prior.m, prior.p)
{
    call    <-match.call()
    library(MCMCpack)
    m       <- mi.object$M
    result <- vector( "list", m )
    names( result ) <- as.character(paste( "Chain", seq( m ), sep = "" ))
    mi.data <- mi.object$impdata

    for ( i in 1:m ) {
as.data.frame(do.call(rbind, mi.data[[i]]))
    result[[i]] <- MCMCregress(formula,data=mi.data[[i]],marginal.likelihood="none"
,mcmc=10000,b0=prior.m,B0=prior.p)
    }

    coef   <- vector( "list", m )
    se     <- vector( "list", m )
    for( j in 1:m ) {
        coef[[j]]<- lapply( result, summary )[[ j ]]$statistics[ ,1]
        se[[j]] <- lapply( result, summary )[[ j ]]$statistics[ ,2]
    }
    pooled <- mi.pooled(coef, se)
    print(pooled)
}
```

173

```
# MCMCreg.mi.amelia For the EM boostrap

MCMCreg.mi.amelia <-function(formula, mi.object, prior.m, prior.p)
{
    call    <-match.call()
    library(MCMCpack)
    m       <- mi.object$m
    result <- vector( "list", m )
    names( result ) <- as.character(paste( "Chain", seq( m ), sep = "" ))
    mi.data <- mi.object$imputations

    for ( i in 1:m ) {
as.data.frame(do.call(rbind, mi.data[[i]]))
    result[[i]] <- MCMCregress(formula,data=mi.data[[i]],marginal.likelihood="none"
,mcmc=10000,b0=prior.m,B0=prior.p)
    }
    coef   <- vector( "list", m )
    se     <- vector( "list", m )
    for( j in 1:m ) {
        coef[[j]]<- lapply( result, summary )[[ j ]]$statistics[ ,1]
        se[[j]] <- lapply( result, summary )[[ j ]]$statistics[ ,2]
    }
    pooled <- mi.pooled(coef, se)
    print(pooled)
}
```

174

```
# freq.mi.bbpmm #

freq.mi.bbpmm <-function(formula, mi.object)
{
    call    <-match.call()
    m       <- mi.object$M
    result <- vector( "list", m )
    names( result ) <- as.character(paste( "Chain", seq( m ), sep = "" ))
    mi.data <- mi.object$impdata

    for ( i in 1:m ) {
as.data.frame(do.call(rbind, mi.data[[i]]))
        result[[i]] <- lm(formula,data=mi.data[[i]])
    }
    coef    <- vector( "list", m )
    se      <- vector( "list", m )
    for( j in 1:m ) {
        coef[[j]]<- lapply( result, summary )[[ j ]]$coefficients[ ,1]
        se[[j]] <- lapply( result, summary )[[ j ]]$coefficients[ ,2]
    }
    pooled <- mi.pooled(coef, se)
    print(pooled)
}

# freq.mi.amelia#
```

175

```
freq.mi.amelia <-function(formula, mi.object)
{
    call    <-match.call()
    m       <- mi.object$m
    result <- vector( "list", m )
    names( result ) <- as.character(paste( "Chain", seq( m ), sep = "" ))
    mi.data <- mi.object$imputations

    for ( i in 1:m ) {
as.data.frame(do.call(rbind, mi.data[[i]]))
        result[[i]] <- lm(formula,data=mi.data[[i]])

    }
    coef    <- vector( "list", m )
    se      <- vector( "list", m )
    for( j in 1:m ) {
        coef[[j]]<- lapply( result, summary )[[ j ]]$coefficients[ ,1]
        se[[j]] <- lapply( result, summary )[[ j ]]$coefficients[ ,2]
    }
    pooled <- mi.pooled(coef, se)
    print(pooled)

}
```

## Part III

Advanced Bayesian Modeling Methods

8

Bayesian Multilevel Modeling

A common feature of data collection in the social sciences is that units of analysis (e.g., students or employees) are nested in higher organizational units (e.g., schools or companies, respectively). In many instances, the substantive problem concerns specifically an understanding of the role that units at both levels play in some outcome of interest. For example, the OECD/PISA study deliberately samples schools (within a country) and then takes an age-based sample of 15-year-olds within sampled schools. Such data collection plans are generically referred to as *clustered sampling designs*. Data from such clustered sampling designs are then collected at both levels for the purposes of understanding each level separately, but also to understand the inputs and processes of student- and school-level variables as they predict both school- and student-level outcomes.

It is probably no exaggeration to say that one of the most important contributions to the empirical analysis of data arising from such data collection efforts has been the development of so-called *multilevel models*. Original contributions to the theory of multilevel modeling for the social sciences can be found in Burstein (1980), Goldstein (2011), and Raudenbush and Bryk (2002), among others.

This chapter highlights the fact that multilevel models can be conceptualized as Bayesian hierarchical models. Apart from the advantages gained from being able to incorporate priors directly into a multilevel model, the Bayesian conception of multilevel modeling has another advantage—namely, it clears up a great deal of confusion in the presentation of multilevel models. Specifically, the literature on multilevel modeling attempts to make a distinction between so-called *fixed effects* and *random effects*. Gelman and Hill (2003) have recognized this issue and present five different definitions of fixed and random effects. Moreover, there are differences in the presentation of multilevel models. For example, Raudenbush and Bryk (2002) provide a pedagogically useful presentation of HLM as one of modeling different organizational levels. Others (e.g., Pinheiro & Bates, 2000) present HLM as a single-level "mixed-effects" model. Although these two presentations are mathematically identical, such differences in presentations and the varying uses of terminology can be confusing.

The advantage of the Bayesian approach to multilevel modeling is that no distinction needs to be made between fixed and random effects. That is, all parameters are assumed to be random, characterized by prior distributions that are, in turn, characterized by hyperparameters. Thus, when conceived of as a Bayesian hierarchical model, much of the confusion surrounding terminology disappears. However, the fact that the Bayesian approach to multilevel modeling clears up terminology is not sufficient to warrant its use. Rather, the advantage of the Bayesian approach to multilevel modeling lies in the incorporation of prior information on all model parameters.

In this chapter we outline the simple random effects analysis-of-variance model as a Bayesian hierarchical model. Then, we revisit the concept of exchangeability and in particular discuss conditional exchangeability as a concept that sets the stage for the slopes-and-intercept-as-outcomes model. We recognize that the topic of multilevel modeling would not be complete without a discussion of growth curve modeling. Indeed, a major benefit of the multilevel modeling perspective is the flexibility with which longitudinal data can be handled (see, e.g., Raudenbush & Bryk, 2002). However, we defer the discussion of growth curve modeling until Chapter 9 when we discuss latent variable modeling because, arguably, the latent variable perspective on growth curve modeling is, in general, more flexible.

8.1 BAYESIAN RANDOM EFFECTS ANALYSIS OF VARIANCE

Perhaps the most basic multilevel model is the random effects analysis of variance model. As a simple example, consider whether there are differences among G schools ($g = 1, 2, \ldots, G$) on the outcome of student reading performance y obtained from n students ($i = 1, 2, \ldots, n$). In this example, it is assumed that the G schools are a random sample from a population of schools.[1] The model can be written as a two-level hierarchical linear model as follows: Let

$$y_{ig} = \beta_g + r_{ij} \tag{8.1}$$

where y_{ig} is a reading performance score for student i in school g, β_g is the school random effect, and r_{ig} is a disturbance term with homoskedastic variance σ^2. The model for the school random effect can be written as

$$\beta_g = \mu + u_g \tag{8.2}$$

where μ is a grand mean and u_g is a homoskedastic error term with variance ω^2 that picks up the school effect over and above the grand mean. Inserting Equation 8.2 into Equation 8.1 yields

$$y_{ig} = \mu + u_g + r_{ig} \tag{8.3}$$

Recall that a fully Bayesian perspective requires specifying the prior distributions on all model parameters. For the model in Equation 8.3, we first specify the distribution of the reading performance outcome y_{ig} given the school effect u_g and the within school variance σ^2. Specifically,

$$y_{ig} | u_g, \sigma^2 \sim N(u_g, \sigma^2) \tag{8.4}$$

---

[1] In many large-scale studies of schooling, the schools themselves may be obtained from a complex sampling scheme. However, we will stay with the simple example of random sampling.

Given that parameters are assumed to be random in the Bayesian context, we next specify the prior distribution on the remaining model parameters. For this model, we specify conjugate priors

$$u_g | \mu, \omega^2 \sim N(0, \omega^2) \tag{8.5}$$

$$\mu \sim N(b_0, B_0) \tag{8.6}$$

$$\sigma^2 \sim \text{inverse-gamma}(v_0/2, v_0\sigma_0^2/2) \tag{8.7}$$

$$\omega^2 \sim \text{inverse-gamma}(\kappa_0/2, \kappa_0\omega_0^2/2) \tag{8.8}$$

where b_0 and B_0 are the mean and variance hyperparameters on μ that are assumed to be *fixed* and *known*.

To see how this specification fits into a Bayesian hierarchical model, note that we can arrange all of the parameters of the random effects ANOVA model into a vector θ and write the prior distribution as

$$p(\theta) = p(u_1, u_2, \ldots, u_G, \mu, \sigma^2, \omega^2) \tag{8.9}$$

where, under the assumption of exchangeability of the school effects u_g, we obtain (see, e.g., Jackman, 2009)

$$p(\theta) = \prod_{g=1}^{G} p(u_g | \mu, \omega^2) p(\mu) p(\sigma^2) p(\omega^2) \tag{8.10}$$

EXAMPLE 8.1. BAYESIAN RANDOM EFFECTS ANOVA

For this example we run a simple Bayesian random effects ANOVA on reading literacy. The analysis simply examines whether there are school differences in the average reading performance of students within schools. The analysis makes use of the R programs "MCMChregress" (A. D. Martin et al., 2010) and "coda" (Plummer et al., 2006). The R code for this example is provided in Appendix 8.1.

Convergence Diagnostics.   The trace and density plots are shown in Figure 8.1. The plots show some evidence of nonconvergence, particularly the trace plot for the variance component of the random intercept. The Geweke plots shown in Figure 8.2 indicate that the chains for the intercept and variance component for the intercept have converged.

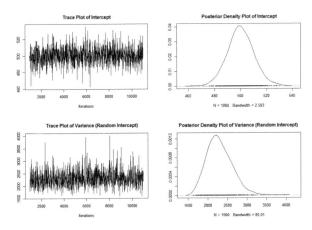

FIGURE 8.1. Trace and density plots for Bayesian random effects ANOVA.

The Heidelberger–Welch diagnostic *p*-values are each greater than .05 for the random intercept and variance component.

Results.   The results are presented in Table 8.1. The results of this simple random effects ANOVA indicate that the average reading score is 500.11. There is a 95% chance that the true average reading score lies between 470.70 and 520.60.

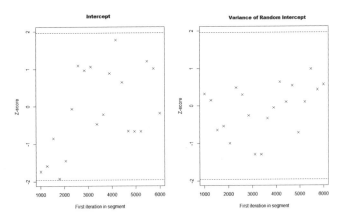

FIGURE 8.2. Geweke plots for Bayesian random effects ANOVA.

TABLE 8.1. Parameter Estimates of Example 8.1: Bayesian Random Effects ANOVA

Parameter	EAP	SD	95% PPI
Fixed effect			
Intercept	500.11	10.19	479.70, 520.60
Variance component of random intercept			
Intercept	2303.00	328.32	1758.00, 3008.00

Note. EAP, expected a posteriori; *SD*, posterior standard deviation; PPI, posterior probability interval.

8.2 REVISITING EXCHANGEABILITY

In Section 2.1 we discussed the role of exchangeability and its importance in providing a firm mathematical basis for the existence of prior distributions. To reiterate, exchangeability specifies that the joint distribution of the data, $p(y_1, y_2, \ldots, y_n)$, is invariant to permutations of the subscripts. For example, in a sequence of binary outcomes, the number of 1's and 0's matter, not their position in the vector. In other words, we can exchange the positions of the responses without changing our belief about the probability model that generated the data. Given that the order does not matter, the probability model, governed by a parameter θ, exists prior to observing the data. The fact that we can describe θ without reference to a particular dataset is, in fact, what is implied by the idea of a prior distribution.

We also briefly noted that one condition where exchangeability might not hold is when observations are clustered in higher-level units, such as our example at the beginning of the chapter that motivated the use of multilevel modeling. Here, observations are not exchangeable across schools but may be conditionally exchangeable, conditional on knowledge of the schools.

To motivate the problem of exchangeability in the context of multilevel models, consider our example of school differences in reading competency. Recall that the Bayesian perspective treats data and parameters as random. Then, assuming that we have no information to differentiate one school from another (e.g., whether the school is public or private), we can assume that exchangeability holds for both the student-level data vector y_{ig} and the school means β_g. Assuming exchangeability allows us to assign the same prior probability for the parameters β_g. In other words, lacking any information about the G schools, we find exchangeability of the β_g to be a reasonable assumption.

Now consider the situation in which we learn that some subset of the G schools are public schools and the remainder are private schools. Given this knowledge, it might not be appropriate to specify the same prior distribution for these different types of schools. Instead, we might be able to argue that *conditional* on school type, the β_g's are exchangeable; that is, we might feel comfortable assigning the same prior distribution within public and private schools. For this to be reasonable, we would need to directly add school type to our random effects ANOVA model, yielding a more general multilevel model, which is described next.

Yet another implication of exchangeability in the context of multilevel models concerns the notion of *borrowing strength* (see, e.g., Jackman, 2009, p. 307). The central idea is that inferences regarding the school means β_g come from two sources. The first source is information coming from school g itself. However, under exchangeability, another source of information arises from the remaining schools via the prior distribution on β_g. Specifically, given that the prior distribution is generated from hyperparameters μ and ω^2, and given that these parameters are unknown, in essence the data coming from school g is being used to update the priors μ and ω^2. As Jackman (2009) points out, the phenomenon of borrowing strength is (1) a consequence of hierarchical modeling and (2) possible only under the exchangeability of β_g.

8.3 BAYESIAN MULTILEVEL REGRESSION

In the simple random effects ANOVA model, exchangeability warrants the existence of prior distributions on the school means β_g. We have already noted that a condition where exchangeability might not hold is if we are in possession of some knowledge about the schools—for example, if some are public schools and others are private schools. In this case, exchangeability across the entire set of schools is not likely to hold, and instead we must invoke the assumption of *conditional exchangeability*. That is, we might be willing to accept exchangeability within school types. Our knowledge of school type, therefore, warrants the specification of a more general multilevel specification that models the school means as a function of school-level characteristics. We refer to this general model as the *multilevel regression model*, first discussed in Burstein (1980) and later developed by Raudenbush and Bryk (2002).

To contextualize the multilevel regression model, consider again an analysis of the OECD/PISA study (OECD, 2010). To anticipate the example below, suppose again that interest centers on reading proficiency among 15-year-old students in the United States. Denote y_{ig} as the reading proficiency score (READING) of student i in school g. We may wish to model READING as a function of the student's gender (GENDER), a measure of his/her joy in reading (JOYREAD), a measure of the extent to which the teacher uses memorization tasks to teach reading (MEMOR), and a measure of the student's perception of the disciplinary climate of the school (DISCLIM). We can write this model as

$$\text{READING}_{ig} = \beta_{0ig} + \beta_{1ig}(\text{GENDER}) + \beta_{2ig}(\text{JOYREAD}) \quad (8.11)$$
$$+ \beta_{3ig}(\text{MEMOR}) + \beta_{4ig}(\text{DISCLIM}) + r_{ig}$$

where $\beta_{kig}(k = 0, 1, 2, \ldots, K)$ is the intercept and regression coefficients (slopes) that are allowed to vary over the G groups. Raudenbush and Bryk (2002) refer to the model in Equation 8.11 as the "level-1" model.

Interest in multilevel regression models stems from the fact that we can model the intercept and slopes as a function of school-level predictors, which we will denote as $\mathbf{z}_g$. For the following example, the school-level predictors include a measure of teacher shortage in the school (TCSHORT) and a measure of the school size (SCHSIZE). Allowing the intercept β_{0g} to be modeled as a function of both school-level variables and allowing the slope of READING on JOYREAD to be modeled as a function of both school-level variables, we can write the model

$$\beta_{0g} = \gamma_{00} + \gamma_{01}(\text{SCHSIZE}) + \gamma_{02}(\text{TCSHORT}) + u_{0g} \quad (8.12a)$$

$$\beta_{1g} = \gamma_{10} + u_{1g} \quad (8.12b)$$

$$\beta_{2g} = \gamma_{20} + \gamma_{21}(\text{TCSHORT}) + u_{2g} \quad (8.12c)$$

$$\beta_{3g} = \gamma_{30} + u_{3g} \quad (8.12d)$$

$$\beta_{4g} = \gamma_{40} + u_{4g} \quad (8.12e)$$

where γ's are the coefficients relating β_{kg} to the school-level predictors. Note that Equations 8.12a and 8.12c represent the substantive model of interest, while Equations 8.12b, 8.12d, and 8.12e allow for unconditional and randomly varying coefficients. From Raudenbush and Bryk (2002) the model in Equation 9.14 is referred to as the "level-2" model. We assume the following distributions for y_{ig} and β_{gk},

$$y_{ig} \sim N(\mathbf{x}_{ig}\boldsymbol{\beta}_g, \sigma_g^2) \tag{8.13}$$

$$\beta_{kg} \sim N(\mathbf{z}_g\gamma_k, \omega_k^2) \tag{8.14}$$

We can substitute Equation 8.12 into Equation 8.11 to yield the full model

$$\begin{aligned}
\text{READING}_{ig} = {} & \gamma_{00} + \gamma_{01}(\text{SCHSIZE}) + \gamma_{02}(\text{TCSHORT}) \\
& + \gamma_{10}(\text{GENDER}) + \gamma_{20}(\text{JOYREAD}) \\
& + \gamma_{21}(\text{TCSHORT})(\text{JOYREAD}) \\
& + \gamma_{30}(\text{MEMOR}) + \gamma_{40}(\text{DISCLIM}) \\
& + r_{ig} + u_{0g} + u_{1g}(\text{GENDER}) + u_{2g}(\text{JOYREAD}) + u_{3g} + u_{4g}
\end{aligned} \tag{8.15}$$

In terms of a Bayesian hierarchical model, prior distributions would have to be chosen for σ_g^2, γ_g, and ω_k^2.

EXAMPLE 8.2. BAYESIAN MULTILEVEL REGRESSION MODEL[2]

This example presents a Bayesian multilevel regression analysis based on an unweighted sample of 5,000 15-year-old students in the United States who were administered PISA 2009 (OECD, 2010). The first plausible value of reading performance (READING) served as a dependent variable and was regressed on two student-level and school-level predictors. Student-level predictors included gender (GENDER) as well as three measures of student engagement and strategies in reading were included as predictors—specifically, enjoyment of reading (JOYREAD),

---

[2]This example is adapted from Kaplan and Park (2014). By permission of Taylor & Francis Group, LLC.

memorization strategies (MEMOR), and perceptions of disciplinary climate (DISCLIMA). School-level predictors included school size (SCHSIZE) and shortage in staff (TCSHORT). The level-1 model regresses the reading performance score on JOYREAD, GENDER, MEMOR, and DISCLIMA. The level-2 model allows the random intercept and the random slope of READING on JOYREAD to be regressed on SCHSIZE and TCSHORT. Informative priors were obtained from a conventional multilevel regression analysis of the PISA 2000 data in a manner similar to the regression analysis example in Chapter 6 except that weakly informative inverse-gamma priors were used for the disturbance variances.

Convergence Diagnostics.   Diagnostic plots in Figures 8.3 and 8.4 show evidence that the chains converged. The Heidelberger–Welch diagnostic *p*-values were all greater than .05.

Results.   The results are presented in Table 8.2 and indicate the positive effects of self-reported joy of reading and gender on reading performance. Poor disciplinary climate was found to have a negative

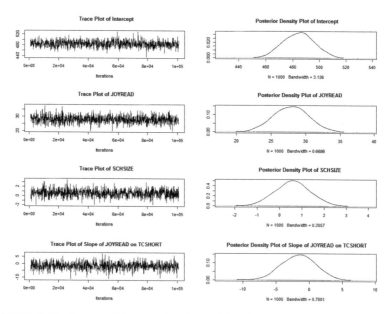

FIGURE 8.3. Trace and density plots for multilevel regression model.

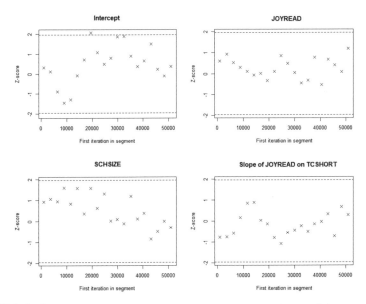

FIGURE 8.4. Geweke plots for Bayesian multilevel regression model.

TABLE 8.2. Parameter Estimates for Multilevel Regression Model

Parameter	EAP	SD	95% PPI
Fixed effects			
Intercept	484.61	11.74	463.01, 506.86
READING on JOYREAD	27.90	2.59	22.91, 33.06
READING on GENDER	14.54	4.78	5.38, 23.92
READING on MEMOR	−1.11	2.23	−5.37, 3.38
READING on DISCLIMA	−6.51	2.69	−11.85, −0.96
Intercept on SCHSIZE	0.59	0.80	−0.93, 2.15
Intercept on TCSHORT	−11.13	7.32	−25.99, 2.32
Slope of JOYREAD on TCSHORT	−1.61	2.63	−6.83, 3.33
Variance components of random effects			
Intercept	1369.11	320.14	941.62, 2136.75
JOYREAD	46.41	17.75	20.61, 88.86
GENDER	5.12	12.52	0.60, 29.92
MEMOR	3.35	4.11	0.62, 13.34
DISCLIMA	62.82	19.67	32.77, 108.07

Note. EAP, expected a posteriori; *SD*, posterior standard deviation; PPI, posterior probability interval.

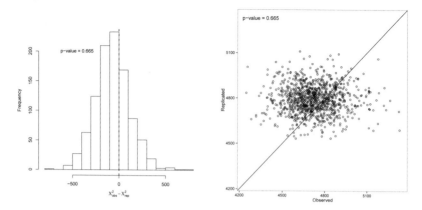

FIGURE 8.5. PPC scatterplot and histogram for HLM: Informative priors.

effect on reading performance. The 95% PPIs indicate that the effect of memorization on reading is as likely as no relationship because the null value also lies within the 95% PPI. The same holds true for the effect of school size and teacher shortage on the random intercept and the relationship of teacher shortage on the random slope.

Posterior Predictive Check for Multilevel Regression Model. The histogram and scatterplot for the posterior predictive check based on Equation 5.8 are shown in Figure 8.5. Recalling that we expect the posterior *p*-value to concentrate around .5 if the model is true, we find that this model shows slightly poor posterior predictive quality, with a resulting *p*-value of .67.

8.4 SUMMARY

Multilevel modeling has become an extremely important and powerful tool in the array of methodologies for the social sciences by virtue of the fact that many research studies in the social sciences result in data with some sort of clustering. The conventional approach to multilevel modeling is based on some variant of the mixed effects model. A pedagogically useful approach conceives of multilevel models in terms of levels, as in the work of Raudenbush and Bryk (2002) and colleagues. The Bayesian perspective of multilevel modeling is to treat the problem as one of a hierarchy of parameters treated as unknown and where our uncertainty about the parameters is described by probability distributions. This chapter attempted to maintain the discussion of multilevel models as levels but also to show that they are essentially Bayesian hierarchical models. We also point out that the assumption of exchangeability requires careful consideration in the context of Bayesian hierarchical models.

8.5 SUGGESTED READINGS

Gelman, A., Carlin, J. B., Stern, H. S., & Rubin, D. B. (2003). *Bayesian data analysis* (2nd ed.). London: Chapman and Hall.

Gelman, A., & Hill, J. (2003). *Data analysis using regression and multi-level/hierarchical models.* Cambridge, UK: Cambridge University Press.

Goldstein, H. (2011). *Multilevel statistical models* (4th ed.). Hoboken, NJ: Wiley.

Raudenbush, S. W., & Bryk, A. S. (2002). *Hierarchical linear models: Applications and data analysis methods* (2nd ed.). Thousand Oaks, CA: Sage.

APPENDIX 8.1
R CODE FOR CHAPTER 8

```
#--------------------------------------------------------
# EXAMPLE 8.1: BAYESIAN RANDOM EFFECTS ANOVA
#       Program Steps
# 1. Read in data
# 2. Call MCMChregress from MCMCpack and specify model
# 3. For random effects ANOVA regress outcome on the intercept
#    and define the intercept as random
# 4. Set starting values and priors
# 5. Summarize the values in the model object (here model_inf)
# 6. Obtain plots
#
# Remaining code shows MCMChregress for informative priors
# and code to obtain posterior predictive checks.
#--------------------------------------------------------
install.packages("MCMCpack")
install.packages("coda")
require(MCMCpack)
require(coda)

hlmdata <- read.csv(file.choose(),header=T)

model_inf <- MCMChregress(fixed=rcomb1~1, random=~1,
    group="SCHOOLID", data=hlmdata, burnin=1000, mcmc=10000, thin=10, verbose=1,
```

```
     seed=2012, beta.start=0, sigma2.start=1,
     Vb.start=1, mubeta=500, Vbeta=100,
     r=1, R=diag(100,1,1), nu=0.001, delta=0.001)

summary(model_inf$mcmc[,1])  #Posterior Mean and SD for the Fixed Effect

summary(model_inf$mcmc[,167:169]) #Posterior Mean and SD for variance components

plot(model_inf$mcmc[,c(1,167)])         #Trace Plots and Density Plots for Selected Fixed
Effects

geweke.plot(model_inf$mcmc[,c(1,167)])
geweke.diag(model_inf$mcmc[,c(1,167)])
heidel.diag(model_inf$mcmc[,c(1,167)])
raftery.diag(model_inf$mcmc[,c(1,167)])

#---------EXAMPLE 8.2: Multilevel Model: Informative Priors from PISA 2000---------#
#install.packages("MCMCpack")
require(MCMCpack)

hlmdata <- read.csv(file.choose(),header=T)

model_inf <- CMChregress(fixed=rcomb1~JOYREAD+gender+MEMOR+DISCLIMA+SCHSIZE+TCSHORT+
JOYREAD:TCSHORT
     random=~JOYREAD+gender+MEMOR+DISCLIMA,
     group="SCHOOLID",data=hlmdata, burnin=1000, mcmc=100000, thin=100,verbose=1,
```

```
          seed=2012, beta.start=0, sigma2.start=1,
          Vb.start=1, mubeta=c(484.4,27.84, 14.75,-1.17,-6.63, 0.59,-11.24, -1.45),
Vbeta=2*c(66.85,
          3.47, 11.17, 2.58, 3.57, 0.33, 26.23,3.43),
          r=5, R=diag(c(2000,50,1,1,100)), nu=0.001, delta=0.001)

summary(model_inf$mcmc[,1:8]) #Posterior Mean and SD for Selected Fixed Effects

# varaince components
ncol(model_inf$mcmc)
summary(model_inf$mcmc[,834:860])

# #Trace Plots and Density Plots for Selected Fixed Effects
plot(model_inf$mcmc[,c(1,2,6)])

#--------------------------POSTERIOR PREDICTIVE CHECK -------------------------#

library(ggplot2)
library(gridExtra)
library(coda)
require(MCMCpack)

set.seed(515)
###These grab the data from the MCMC object
df.hlm <- data.frame(as.matrix(model_inf$mcmc))
var.list <- c(".Intercept.","JOYREAD","gender","MEMOR","DISCLIMA","SCHSIZE","TCSHORT",
```

194

```
"JOYREAD.TCSHORT
var.list <- paste("beta.",var.list, sep = "")
eff.list <- c(".Intercept.","JOYREAD","gender","MEMOR","DISCLIMA")
eff.list <- sapply(eff.list,function(x) paste(x,".",x,sep = ""))
eff.list <- paste("VCV.",eff.list, sep = "")
df.hlm <- df.hlm[,c(var.list,eff.list,"sigma2")]

##function to calculate the chi-square discrepancy statistic
discrep.stat <- function(x) {

y.rep <- y.posterior[[3*x-2]] ##creates all the y.reps for simulation number x
nas <- which(is.na(y.rep)) ##remove the NA's due to missing values in the X matrix
y.rep <- y.rep[-nas]
y.rep.ev <- y.posterior[[3*x-1]] ##creates the expected values based upon the theta
draws and the X matrix

y.rep.ev <- y.rep.ev[-nas]
y.rep.var <- y.posterior[[3*x]] ##creates the variance based on the theta draws
obs <- hlmdata$rcomb1 ##grabs the observed values
obs <- obs[-nas]

val1 <- ((y.rep - y.rep.ev)^2)/y.rep.var ##y.rep chi.square
val2 <- ((obs - y.rep.ev)^2)/y.rep.var ##y.obs chi.square

return(c(sum(val1),sum(val2)))
```

195

```r
}##END function lik.ratio.chi.square

##Function to calculate the posterior y.reps
simulate.posterior <- function(x, obs = as.matrix(hlmdata), betas = as.matrix(df.hlm))
{
obs.cols <- match(c("JOYREAD","gender","MEMOR","DISCLIMA","SCHSIZE","TCSHORT"),
attr(obs,"dimnames")[[2]]
)
obs.x <- obs[,obs.cols]
obs.x <- cbind(obs.x,as.matrix(obs[,obs.cols[1]] * obs[,obs.cols[6]]))
pred.x <- cbind(1,obs.x) %*% as.numeric(betas[x,1:8])
size <- nrow(obs)
pred.x.rand <- pred.x + rnorm(size,0,sqrt(betas[x,9])) + ## random error from Intercept
rnorm(size,0,sqrt(betas[x,10])) + ## random error from JOYREAD
rnorm(size,0,sqrt(betas[x,11])) + ## random error from gender
rnorm(size,0,sqrt(betas[x,12])) + ## random error from MEMOR
rnorm(size,0,sqrt(betas[x,13])) + ## random error from DISCLIMA
rnorm(size,0,sqrt(betas[x,14])) ## overall random error
var.x = sum(betas[x,9:14])
return(list(pred.x.rand, pred.x, var.x))
}##END function simulate.posterior

##These are the lines that actually run the above functions
y.posterior <- sapply(1:1000,simulate.posterior) ##create the 1000 posterior simulations
of sample size n = 5322
posterior.check <- t(sapply(1:1000,discrep.stat)) ##create the 1000 discrepancy
```

```r
statistics for both y.rep and y.obs
chi.obs <- posterior.check[,2]
chi.rep <- posterior.check[,1]
chi.discrepancy <- posterior.check[,2] - posterior.check[,1] ##get the difference
between y.obs and y.rep
p.value <- round(length(which(chi.discrepancy < 0))/length(chi.discrepancy),3)
range <- max(chi.discrepancy) - min(chi.discrepancy) ##range
x.breaks <- c(round(median(chi.discrepancy),1),0,seq(round(range(chi.discrepancy)
[1],0),round(range(chi.discr x.breaks <- x.breaks[order(x.breaks)]

##SAVE PDF POSTERIOR CHECKING PLOTS

liks.dif <- chi.obs - chi.rep
range <- max(liks.dif) - min(liks.dif)
p.value <- round(length(which(liks.dif < 0))/length(liks.dif),3)
pdf(file=' ') ####ADD FILE PATH#####
par(ask = FALSE)
hist(liks.dif, xlab = expression(Chi["obs"]^2 - Chi["rep"]^2), main = "")
abline(v = 0, lty = 2, lwd = 2)
text(x = min(liks.dif) + range/5, y = 200, label = paste("p-value = ",p.value,sep = ""))
dev.off()
pdf(file=' ') ####ADD FILE PATH#####
qplot(chi.obs,chi.rep, shape = I(1)) +
geom_abline(slope = 1, intercept = 0) +
theme_bw() +
geom_text(aes(x = 100 + min(chi.obs,chi.rep) , y = - 2 + max(chi.obs,chi.rep), label
```

197

```
= paste("p-value =",p.value)), size = 4.5) +
theme(panel.grid.major = element_blank(), panel.grid.minor = element_blank()) +
ylim(c(-7 + min(chi.obs,chi.rep),max(chi.obs,chi.rep))) +
xlim(c(-7 + min(chi.obs,chi.rep),max(chi.obs,chi.rep))) +
xlab("Observed") + ylab("Replicated")
dev.off()


##DISPLAY POSTERIOR CHECKING PLOTS & INFORMATION
hist(liks.dif, xlab = expression(Chi["obs"]^2 - Chi["rep"]^2), main = "")
abline(v = 0, lty = 2, lwd = 2)
text(x = min(liks.dif) + range/5, y = 200, label = paste("p-value = ",p.value,sep = ""))
par(ask = TRUE)
qplot(chi.obs,chi.rep, shape = I(1)) +
geom_abline(slope = 1, intercept = 0) +
theme_bw() +
geom_text(aes(x = 100 + min(chi.obs,chi.rep) , y = - 2 + max(chi.obs,chi.rep), label
= paste("p-value =",p.value)), size = 4.5) +
#theme(panel.grid.major = element_blank()) +
ylim(c(-7 + min(chi.obs,chi.rep),max(chi.obs,chi.rep))) +
xlim(c(-7 + min(chi.obs,chi.rep),max(chi.obs,chi.rep))) +
xlab("Observed") + ylab("Replicated")


##PRINT OUT MEDIAN DIFFERENCE and P-VALUE
print(data.frame(Median.Difference = median(chi.discrepancy), p.value = p.value))
```

9

Bayesian Modeling for Continuous and Categorical Latent Variables

The history of structural equation modeling (SEM) can be roughly divided into two generations. The *first generation* of structural equation modeling began with the initial merging of confirmatory factor analysis and simultaneous equation modeling (see, e.g., Jöreskog, 1973). In addition to these founding concepts, the first generation of SEM witnessed important methodological developments in handling nonstandard conditions of the data. These developments included methods for dealing with non-normal data, missing data, and sample-size sensitivity problems (see, e.g., Kaplan, 2009). The *second generation* of SEM could be broadly characterized by another merger: this time, combining models for continuous latent variables developed in the first generation with models for categorical latent variables (see B. Muthén, 2001). The integration of continuous and categorical latent variables into a general modeling framework was due to the extension of finite mixture modeling to the SEM framework. This extension has provided an elegant theory, resulting in a marked increase in important applications. These applications include, but are not limited to, methods for handling the evaluation of interventions with noncompliance (Jo & Muthén, 2001), discrete-time mixture survival models (B. Muthén & Masyn,

Portions of this chapter are adapted from Kaplan and Depaoli (2012a, 2012b). By permission from Oxford University Press, USA, and The Guilford Press.

2005), and models for examining unique trajectories of growth in academic outcomes (Kaplan, 2003). A more comprehensive review of the history of SEM can be found in Matsueda (2012).

A parallel development to first- and second-generation SEM has been the expansion of Bayesian methods for complex statistical models, including structural equation models. Early papers include J. K. Martin and McDonald (1975), Lee (1981), and Scheines, Hoijtink, and Boomsma (1999). Recent treatments by Song and Lee (2012) and Lee (2007) provide up-to-date reviews and extensions of Bayesian SEM. The increased use of Bayesian tools for statistical modeling has come about primarily as a result of progress in computational algorithms based on Markov chain Monte Carlo (MCMC) sampling. The MCMC algorithm is implemented in software programs such as "WinBugs" (Lunn et al., 2000), various packages within the R archive (R Development Core Team, 2012), and most recently in "Mplus" (L. K. Muthén & Muthén, 1998–2012; B. Muthén & Asparouhov, 2012), which makes Bayesian estimation of complex structural equation models readily available.

This chapter introduces Bayesian SEM as an important alternative to conventional frequentist approaches to SEM. However, to fully realize the utility of the Bayesian approach to SEM, it is necessary not only to demonstrate its applicability to first-generation SEM but also to demonstrate how Bayesian methodology can be applied to models characterizing the second generation of SEM. We follow closely a recent chapter by Kaplan and Depaoli (2012b).

In this chapter we consider Bayesian estimation of the confirmatory factor analysis (CFA) model.[1] We then discuss Bayesian structural equation modeling and show its extension to Bayesian multilevel structural equation modeling. We then provide a discussion and example of Bayesian growth curve modeling. These methods consider models with continuous latent variables. We then follow with a description of models for categorical latent variables that include latent class models. We discuss Bayesian methods for categorical latent variables via the specification of the finite mixture model.

---

[1] For this chapter, it was decided to use the common term *confirmatory* when describing this procedure. However, the term *confirmatory* represents a controversy for frequentist approaches to factor analysis—particularly with respect to error rate inflation when modifying such models (see, e.g., Kaplan, 2009).

9.1 BAYESIAN ESTIMATION OF THE CFA MODEL

Following the general notation originally provided by Jöreskog (1967), we write the factor analysis model as

$$\mathbf{y} = \boldsymbol{\alpha} + \boldsymbol{\Lambda}\boldsymbol{\eta} + \boldsymbol{\epsilon} \qquad (9.1)$$

where $\mathbf{y}$ is a vector of manifest variables, $\boldsymbol{\alpha}$ is a vector of measurement intercepts, $\boldsymbol{\Lambda}$ is a factor loading matrix, $\boldsymbol{\eta}$ is a vector of latent variables, and $\boldsymbol{\epsilon}$ is a vector of uniquenesses with covariance matrix $\boldsymbol{\Psi}$, typically specified to be diagonal. Under conventional assumptions described in, for example, Kaplan (2009), we obtain the model expressed in terms of the population covariance matrix $\boldsymbol{\Sigma}$ as

$$\boldsymbol{\Sigma} = \boldsymbol{\Lambda}\boldsymbol{\Phi}\boldsymbol{\Lambda}' + \boldsymbol{\Psi} \qquad (9.2)$$

where $\boldsymbol{\Phi}$ is the covariance matrix of the common factors.

For this chapter we focus on the CFA model. Unlike the exploratory factor analysis model, the confirmatory factor model results from the a priori number and location of (typically) zero values in the factor loading matrix $\boldsymbol{\Lambda}$. In the conventional approach to factor analysis, the additional restrictions placed on $\boldsymbol{\Lambda}$ preclude rotation to simple structure (Lawley & Maxwell, 1971).

9.1.1 Conjugate Priors for CFA Model Parameters

A Bayesian approach to confirmatory factor analysis requires the specification of priors on all model parameters. To specify the prior distributions, it is notationally convenient to arrange the model parameters as sets of common conjugate distributions (see Kaplan & Depaoli, 2012b). For this model, let $\theta_{norm} = \{\boldsymbol{\alpha}, \boldsymbol{\Lambda}\}$ be the set of free model parameters that are assumed to follow a normal distribution and let $\theta_{IW} = \{\boldsymbol{\Phi}, \boldsymbol{\Psi}\}$ be the set of free model parameters that are assumed to follow an inverse-Wishart distribution. Thus,

$$\theta_{norm} \sim N(\boldsymbol{\mu}, \boldsymbol{\Omega}) \qquad (9.3)$$

where μ and Ω are the mean and variance hyperparameters, respectively, of the normal prior. The uniqueness covariance matrix $\mathbf{\Psi}$ and the covariance matrix of the common factors $\mathbf{\Phi}$ are assumed to follow an inverse-Wishart distribution. Specifically,

$$\theta_{IW} \sim IW(\mathbf{R}, \delta) \tag{9.4}$$

where $\mathbf{R}$ is a positive definite matrix and $\delta > q - 1$, where q is the number of observed variables. Different choices for $\mathbf{R}$ and δ will yield different degrees of "informativeness" for the inverse-Wishart distribution. The inverse-Wishart distribution was discussed in Chapter 3.

EXAMPLE 9.1. BAYESIAN CFA[2]

This example is based on a reanalysis of a confirmatory factor analysis described in the PISA 2009 technical report (OECD, 2010). In the report, confirmatory factor analysis was employed to construct two indices indicating teacher and student behavioral problems (TEACBEHA and STUDBEHA), using a weighted sample of students from the OECD countries. For this example, we used an unweighted sample of 165 school principals in the United States who participated in PISA 2009. The principals were administered a questionnaire asking to what extent student learning is hindered by student or teacher behavioral problems. Each item has the following four categories: not at all, very little, to some extent, and a lot.

The confirmatory factor model in this example was specified to have two factors labeled as teacher and student behavioral problems. The factor related to teacher behavioral problems contains the following seven items: teachers' low expectation of students (SC17Q01), poor student–teacher relations (SC17Q03, teachers not meeting individual students' needs (SC17Q05), teacher absenteeism (SC17Q06), staff resistance of change (SC17Q09), teachers being too strict with students (SC17Q11), and students not being encouraged to achieve their full potential (SC17Q13). The second factor relates to student behavioral problems and contains the following six items: student absenteeism (SC17Q02), disruption of classes by students (SC17Q04), students skip-

---

[2]This example is adapted from Kaplan and Park (2014). By permission of Taylor & Francis Group, LLC.

ping classes (SC17Q07), students lacking respect for teachers (SC17Q08), students using alcohol or illegal drugs (SC17Q10), and students intimidating or bullying other students (SC17Q12).

The analysis for this example used the Gibbs sampler as implemented in "rjags" with two chains, 50,000 iterations with 5,000 burn-ins, and a thinning interval of 50. Thus, summary statistics on the model parameters are based on 1,000 draws from the posterior distribution generated via the Gibbs sampler.[3]

Convergence Diagnostics.   Figure 9.1 presents the trace plots and autocorrelation plots for both the noninformative and informative cases. The plots show evidence of convergence. Figure 9.2 shows the Geweke plots for selected parameters for both the noninformative and informative cases. Here also, we find evidence for convergence. The Heidelberger–Welch diagnostic *p*-values were all greater than .05, indicating that the chains stabilized.

Results.   The results of the CFA model for the noninformative (upper panel) and informative (lower panel) cases are displayed in Table 9.1. For the noninformative case, a normal prior was chosen for the factor loadings, with a mean of zero and a variance of 10^6, and a noninformative inverse-gamma prior was chosen for the factor variances and unique variances. For the informative priors case, priors on the factor loadings were based on a previous factor analysis of the PISA 2000 data. Weakly informative inverse-gamma priors were chosen for the factor variances and unique variances. Not unexpectedly, we find that although the EAP estimates of the factor loadings are roughly the same regardless of priors, the 95% PPIs are generally narrower for the informative prior case.

Posterior Predictive Check for CFA Model.   In the context of frequentist confirmatory factor analysis, it is of interest to assess the fit of the model. This is usually accomplished by presenting a large number of goodness-of-fit indices, including the likelihood ratio chi-square, the root mean squared error of approximation, and measures of comparative

[3] We are grateful to Professor Joseph Lucke of the University of Buffalo: The State University of New York, for providing the general structure for this program.

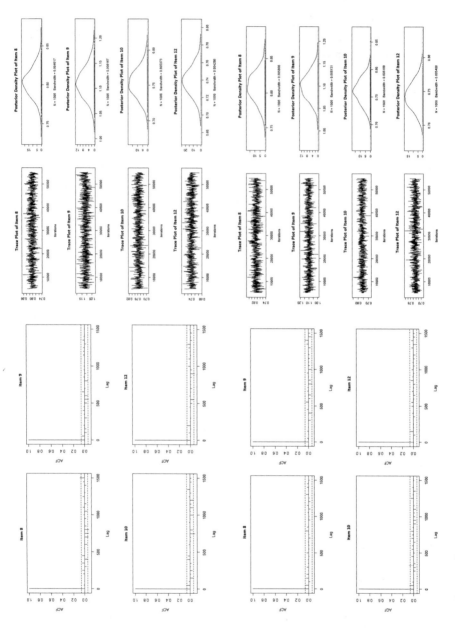

FIGURE 9.1. Autocorrelation, trace, and density plots for selected parameters: Bayesian CFA.

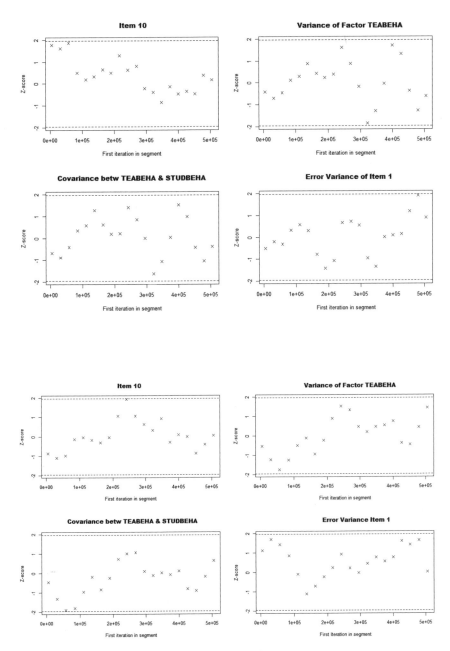

FIGURE 9.2. Geweke plots for selected parameters: Bayesian CFA, noninformative priors (top panel) and informative priors (bottom panel).

TABLE 9.1. Parameter Estimates for CFA Example 9.1: Noninformative and Informative Priors

Parameter	EAP	*SD*	95% PPI	Intercepts (EAP/*SD*)	Residuals (EAP/*SD*)
		Noninformative prior			
Loadings: TEABEHA *by*					
Item SC17Q01	1.00	0.00	1.00, 1.00	2.03 (0.06)	0.30 (0.04)
Item SC17Q03	0.98	0.12	0.77, 1.24	1.92 (0.05)	0.15 (0.02)
Item SC17Q05	0.90	0.11	0.70, 1.14	2.16 (0.05)	0.19 (0.03)
Item SC17Q06	0.67	0.11	0.46, 0.90	1.82 (0.05)	0.28 (0.03)
Item SC17Q09	0.95	0.12	0.73, 1.21	2.27 (0.05)	0.25 (0.03)
Item SC17Q11	0.49	0.10	0.31, 0.69	1.72 (0.04)	0.25 (0.03)
Item SC17Q13	0.96	0.12	0.74, 1.22	1.88 (0.05)	0.23 (0.03)
Loadings: STUDBEHA *by*					
Item SC17Q02	1.00	0.00	1.00, 1.00	2.68 (0.06)	0.33 (0.04)
Item SC17Q04	0.89	0.11	0.68, 1.14	2.05 (0.05)	0.19 (0.03)
Item SC17Q07	1.08	0.14	0.83, 1.37	2.21 (0.06)	0.31 (0.04)
Item SC17Q08	0.99	0.12	0.77, 1.25	2.13 (0.05)	0.16 (0.02)
Item SC17Q10	0.53	0.10	0.33, 0.74	2.03 (0.05)	0.31 (0.04)
Item SC17Q12	0.57	0.09	0.42, 0.76	1.99 (0.04)	0.14 (0.02)
Factor correlation:	0.69	0.05	0.58, 0.78		
		Informative prior			
Loadings: TEABEHA *by*					
Item SC17Q01	1.00	0.00	1.00, 1.00	2.03 (0.06)	0.30 (0.04)
Item SC17Q03	0.94	0.08	0.79, 1.11	1.92 (0.06)	0.16 (0.04)
Item SC17Q05	0.98	0.09	0.81, 1.15	2.16 (0.05)	0.19 (0.02)
Item SC17Q06	0.74	0.09	0.57, 0.92	1.82 (0.05)	0.27 (0.03)
Item SC17Q09	0.99	0.09	0.82, 1.18	2.26 (0.05)	0.24 (0.02)
Item SC17Q11	0.55	0.08	0.40, 0.70	1.72 (0.05)	0.25 (0.03)
Item SC17Q13	1.01	0.09	0.84, 1.20	1.88 (0.06)	0.23 (0.04)
Loadings: STUDBEHA *by*					
Item SC17Q02	1.00	0.00	1.00, 1.00	2.67 (0.05)	0.33 (0.02)
Item SC17Q04	0.92	0.09	0.75, 1.10	2.05 (0.05)	0.19 (0.03)
Item SC17Q07	1.17	0.12	0.95, 1.42	2.21 (0.05)	0.31 (0.04)
Item SC17Q08	1.03	0.09	0.85, 1.22	2.13 (0.04)	0.16 (0.03)
Item SC17Q10	0.66	0.10	0.47, 0.85	2.03 (0.04)	0.31 (0.02)
Item SC17Q12	0.65	0.08	0.51, 0.82	1.99 (0.05)	0.14 (0.03)
Factor correlation:	0.68	0.06	0.56, 0.78		

Note. EAP, expected a posteriori; *SD*, posterior standard deviation; PPI, posterior probability interval.

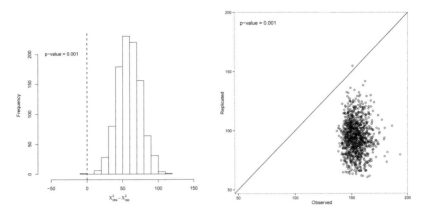

FIGURE 9.3. PPC scatterplot and histogram for CFA: Informative priors.

fit, such as the comparative fit index or the non-normed fit index, to name just two. The relative differences among these measures are discussed in Kaplan (2009). In Bayesian CFA, the goal is to assess the posterior predictive adequacy of the model. Figure 9.3 shows the histogram and scatterplot for the posterior predictive check based on the likelihood ratio chi-square given in Equation 5.9 of Chapter 5. On the basis of the posterior predictive p-value of .001 and the plots, we conclude that this model shows very poor posterior predictive quality.

9.2 BAYESIAN SEM

SEMs are specified in two parts—a measurement part that links observed variables to latent variables and a structural part that relates latent variables to each other. Following the general notation given by Jöreskog (1977), we denote the measurement model as

$$\mathbf{y} = \boldsymbol{\alpha} + \boldsymbol{\Lambda}\boldsymbol{\eta} + \mathbf{Kx} + \boldsymbol{\epsilon} \tag{9.5}$$

where $\mathbf{y}$ is a vector of manifest variables, $\boldsymbol{\alpha}$ is a vector of measurement intercepts, $\boldsymbol{\Lambda}$ is a factor loading matrix, $\boldsymbol{\eta}$ is a vector of latent variables, $\mathbf{K}$ is a matrix of regression coefficients relating the manifest variables

y to observed variables **x**, and ϵ is a vector of uniquenesses with covariance matrix Ξ, assumed to be diagonal. The structural model relating common factors to each other and possibly to a vector of manifest variables **x** is written as

$$\eta = \nu + \mathbf{B}\eta + \Gamma\mathbf{x} + \zeta \tag{9.6}$$

where ν is a vector of structural intercepts, **B** and Γ are matrices of structural coefficients, and ζ is a vector of structural disturbances with covariance matrix Ψ, which is assumed to be diagonal.

9.2.1 Conjugate Priors for SEM Parameters

As with the Bayesian CFA example above, we follow Kaplan and Depaoli (2012b) and arrange the parameters as follows. Parameters with the subscript *norm* follow a normal distribution, while those with the subscript *IW* follow an inverse-Wishart distribution. Let $\theta_{norm} = \{\alpha, \nu,$ $\Lambda, \mathbf{B}, \Gamma, \mathbf{K}\}$ be the vector of free model parameters that are assumed to follow a normal distribution, and let $\theta_{IW} = \{\Xi, \Psi\}$ be the vector of free model parameters that are assumed to follow the inverse-Wishart distribution. Formally, we write

$$\theta_{norm} \sim N(\mu, \Omega) \tag{9.7}$$

where μ and Ω are the mean and variance hyperparameters, respectively, of the normal prior. For blocks of variances and covariances in Ξ and Ψ, we assume that the prior distribution is inverse-Wishart, that is,[4]

$$\theta_{IW} \sim IW(\mathbf{R}, \delta) \tag{9.8}$$

where **R** is a positive definite matrix, and $\delta > q - 1$, where q is the number of observed variables. Different choices for **R** and δ will yield different degrees of "informativeness" for the inverse-Wishart distribution.

---

[4]Note that in the case where there is only one element in the block, the prior distribution is assumed to be inverse-gamma, that is, $\theta_{IW} \sim IG(a, b)$.

9.2.2 MCMC Sampling for Bayesian SEM

The Bayesian approach to SEM begins by considering η as missing data. Then, the observed data $\mathbf{y}$ are augmented with η in the posterior analysis. The Gibbs sampler then produces a posterior distribution $[\theta_{norm}, \theta_{IW}, \eta | \mathbf{y}]$ via the following algorithm. At the $(s + 1)$th iteration, using current values of $\eta^{(s)}$, $\theta_{norm}^{(s)}$, and $\theta_{IW}^{(s)}$,

$$1.\ \text{Sample}\quad \eta^{(s+1)}\quad \text{from}\quad p(\eta | \theta_{norm}^{(s)}, \theta_{IW}^{(s)}, \mathbf{y}) \tag{9.9a}$$

$$2.\ \text{Sample}\quad \theta_{norm}^{(s+1)}\quad \text{from}\quad p(\theta_{norm} | \theta_{IW}^{(s)}, \eta^{(s+1)}, \mathbf{y}) \tag{9.9b}$$

$$3.\ \text{Sample}\quad \theta_{IW}^{(s+1)}\quad \text{from}\quad p(\theta_{IW} | \theta_{norm}^{(s+1)}, \eta^{(s+1)}, \mathbf{y}) \tag{9.9c}$$

In words, Equations 9.9a–9.9c first require start values for $\theta_{norm}^{(0)}$ and $\theta_{IW}^{(0)}$ to begin the MCMC generation. Then, given these current start values and the data $\mathbf{y}$ at iteration s, we generate η at iteration $s + 1$. Given the latent data and observed data, we generate estimates of the measurement model and structural model parameters in Equations 9.5 and 9.6, respectively. The computational details can be found in Asparouhov and Muthén (2010).

EXAMPLE 9.2. BAYESIAN SEM

This example presents a within-school path analysis of mathematics achievement using data from 5,456 U.S. students from the PISA 2003 survey (OECD, 2004). The path diagram is depicted in Figure 9.4. The final outcome variable at the student level was the first plausible value of the PISA 2003 mathematics assessment (MATHSCOR). Mediating predictors of mathematics achievement consisted of whether students enjoyed mathematics (ENJOY) and whether students felt mathematics was important in life (IMPORTNT). Student exogenous background variables included student's perception of teacher qualities (PERTEACH), as well as both parents' educational levels (MOMEDUC and DADEDUC). This analysis focuses on noninformative priors only. A path diagram of this model is shown in Figure 9.4.

Convergence Diagnostics.   Diagnostic plots for selected parameters are shown in Figures 9.5–9.7. These plots and those for the remaining parameters show evidence of convergence. Moreover, the Heidelberger–

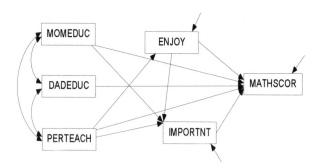

FIGURE 9.4. Path diagram for student-level model.

Welch diagnostic *p*-values are all greater than .05, indicating that the chains for this SEM model have converged.

Results.   The results are shown in Table 9.2, and all but one effect are positive, with the null value of zero lying outside the 95% PPI. The exception is the effect of ENJOY on MATHSCOR where the 95% PPI includes zero.

Posterior Predictive Check for the SEM Model.   Figure 9.8 shows the histogram and scatterplot for the posterior predictive check based

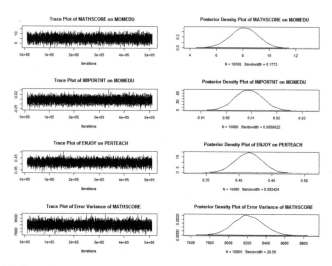

FIGURE 9.5. Trace and density plots for Bayesian single-level SEM.

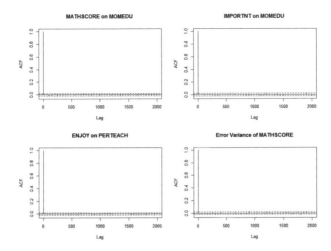

FIGURE 9.6. Autocorrelation plots for single-level Bayesian SEM.

on the likelihood ratio chi-square given in Equation 5.9 in Chapter 5. On the basis of the posterior predictive p-value of .293, we conclude that the model shows poor posterior predictive quality. Again, recall that this conclusion rests on substantive judgment and depends, in part, on the uses of the model.

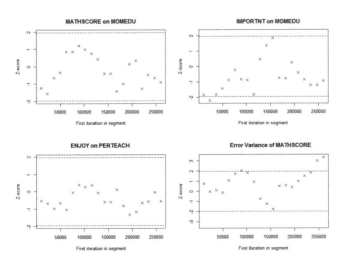

FIGURE 9.7. Geweke plots for single-level Bayesian SEM.

TABLE 9.2. Bayesian Single-Level Path Analysis Estimates: PISA 2003

Parameter	EAP	SD	95% PPI	
MATHSCOR *on*				
INTERCEPT	357.00	7.59	342.20,	372.10
MOMEDUC	8.09	1.05	6.00,	10.14
DADEDUC	7.14	1.13	4.92,	9.35
PERTEACH	9.80	1.98	5.92,	13.68
IMPORTNT	11.31	1.79	7.78,	14.84
ENJOY	1.60	1.61	−1.53,	4.73
IMPORTNT *on*				
INTERCEPT	1.27	0.05	1.18,	1.36
MOMEDUC	0.01	0.01	0.00,	0.02
PERTEACH	0.21	0.01	0.18,	0.24
ENJOY	0.48	0.01	0.47,	0.50
ENJOY *on*				
INTERCEPT	1.09	0.06	0.98,	1.21
PERTEACH	0.41	0.02	0.37,	0.45
Residual variances				
ENJOY	0.57	0.01	0.55,	0.60
IMPORTNT	0.29	0.01	0.28,	0.30
MATHSCOR	8209.00	157.70	7909.00,	8524.00

Note. EAP, expected a posteriori; *SD*, posterior standard deviation; PPI, posterior probability interval.

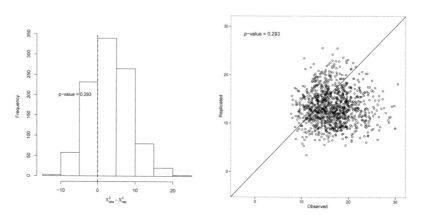

FIGURE 9.8. PPC scatterplot and histogram for SEM: Noninformative priors.

9.3 BAYESIAN MULTILEVEL SEM

Over the years, attempts have been made to integrate multilevel modeling with SEM so as to provide a general methodology that can account for issues of measurement error, mediation, and simultaneity. One of the earliest attempts to develop multilevel latent variable modeling was by Schmidt (1969), who derived a maximum likelihood estimator for a general multilevel covariance structure model but did not attempt to introduce group-level variables into the model. Fundamental contributions to multilevel models with latent variables have been made by McDonald and his colleagues (e.g., Goldstein & McDonald, 1988; McDonald & Goldstein, 1989; McDonald, 1993; B. Muthén, 1989; B. Muthén & Satorra, 1989). Later, Kaplan and Elliott (1997a), building on the work of B. Muthén (1989), derived the reduced-form specification of a multilevel path model, and this was applied to a policy analysis problem by Kaplan and Kreisman (2000). For a review, see Kaplan, Kim, and Kim (2009).

In this section, we provide the general specification and estimation of Bayesian multilevel structural equation modeling, following closely the chapter by Kaplan et al. (2009), who focused on frequentist multilevel SEM. For ease of notation and development of concepts, our discussion will focus on multilevel path analysis. By focusing on this model, we are assuming that reliable and valid measures of the variables are available. We recognize that this assumption may be unreasonable for most social and behavioral science research, however, multilevel measurement models exist that allow one to examine group heterogeneity in measurement structure. As a matter of modeling strategy, it may be very informative to examine the group heterogeneity in measurement structure prior to forming scales to be used in multilevel path analysis. However, it is possible to combine multilevel path models and measurement models into a comprehensive multilevel SEM.

The model that we will consider allows for varying intercepts and varying structural regression coefficients. Earlier work on multilevel path analysis by Kaplan and Elliott (1997a), building on the work of B. Muthén and Satorra (1989), specified a structural model for varying intercepts only. This "intercepts as outcomes" model was applied to a specific educational problem in Kaplan and Elliott (1997b) and Kaplan and Kreisman (2000).

In what follows, we write the within-school (level-1) full SEM as

$$\mathbf{y}_{ig} = \boldsymbol{\alpha}_g + \mathbf{B}_g \mathbf{y}_{ig} + \boldsymbol{\Gamma}_g \mathbf{x}_{ig} + \mathbf{r}_{ig}, \quad g = 1, 2, \ldots, G \qquad (9.10)$$

where $\mathbf{y}_{ig}$ is a p-dimensional vector of endogenous variables for student i in school g, $\mathbf{x}_{ig}$ is a q-dimensional vector of within-school exogenous variables, $\boldsymbol{\alpha}_g$ is a vector of structural intercepts that can vary across schools, $\mathbf{B}_g$ and $\boldsymbol{\Gamma}_g$ are structural coefficients that are allowed to vary across schools, and $\mathbf{r}_{ig}$ is the within-school disturbance term assumed to be normally distributed with mean zero and constant within-school variance σ_r^2.

From here, we can model the structural intercepts and slopes as a function of between-school endogenous variables $\mathbf{z}_g$ and between-school exogenous variables $\mathbf{w}_g$. Specifically, we write the level-2 model as

$$\boldsymbol{\alpha}_g = \boldsymbol{\alpha}_{00} + \boldsymbol{\alpha}_{01} \mathbf{z}_g + \boldsymbol{\alpha}_{02} \mathbf{w}_g + \boldsymbol{\epsilon}_g \qquad (9.11)$$

$$\mathbf{B}_g = \mathbf{B}_{00} + \mathbf{B}_{01} \mathbf{z}_g + \mathbf{B}_{02} \mathbf{w}_g + \boldsymbol{\zeta}_g \qquad (9.12)$$

$$\boldsymbol{\Gamma}_g = \boldsymbol{\Gamma}_{00} + \boldsymbol{\Gamma}_{01} \mathbf{z}_g + \boldsymbol{\Gamma}_{02} \mathbf{w}_g + \boldsymbol{\theta}_g \qquad (9.13)$$

Note how Equations 9.11–9.13 allow for randomly varying intercepts and two types of randomly varying slopes—namely, $\mathbf{B}_g$ are randomly varying slopes relating endogenous variables to each other, and $\boldsymbol{\Gamma}_g$ are randomly varying slopes relating endogenous variables to exogenous variables. These randomly varying structural coefficients are modeled as functions of a set of between-school predictors $\mathbf{z}_g$ and $\mathbf{w}_g$.

Of particular importance for substantive research is the fact that the full multilevel path model allows for a set of structural relationships among between-school endogenous and exogenous variables, which we can write as

$$\mathbf{z}_g = \boldsymbol{\tau} + \boldsymbol{\Delta} \mathbf{z}_g + \boldsymbol{\Omega} \mathbf{w}_g + \boldsymbol{\delta}_g \qquad (9.14)$$

where $\boldsymbol{\tau}$, $\boldsymbol{\Delta}$, and $\boldsymbol{\Omega}$ are the fixed structural effects. Finally, $\boldsymbol{\epsilon}$, $\boldsymbol{\zeta}$, $\boldsymbol{\theta}$, and $\boldsymbol{\delta}$ are disturbances terms that are assumed to be normally distributed with mean zero and covariance matrix $\mathbf{T}$ with elements

$$
\mathbf{T} = \begin{pmatrix} \sigma^2_\epsilon & & & \\ \sigma_{\zeta\epsilon} & \sigma^2_\zeta & & \\ \sigma_{\theta\epsilon} & \sigma_{\theta\zeta} & \sigma^2_\theta & \\ \sigma_{\delta\epsilon} & \sigma_{\delta\zeta} & \sigma_{\delta\theta} & \sigma^2_\delta \end{pmatrix} \tag{9.15}
$$

After a series of substitutions, we can obtain the reduced form of the level-1 model and level-2 model and express $\mathbf{y}_{ig}$ as a function of a grand mean, the main effect of within-school variables, the main effect of between-school variables, and the cross-level moderator effects of between- and within-school variables. These reduced-form effects contain the structural relations as specified in Equations 9.10–9.14.

Although this discussion has focused on multilevel SEM with manifest variables, it is relatively straightforward to specify a multilevel structural equation among latent variables.

EXAMPLE 9.3. BAYESIAN MULTILEVEL SEM

This example is based on a reanalysis of a multilevel path analysis described in Kaplan et al. (2009). In their study, a multilevel path analysis was employed to examine within- and between-school predictors of mathematics competency (MATHSCOR) using data from the PISA 2003 survey (OECD, 2004). Data were based on a sample of 5,456 U.S. students nested in 272 schools. In addition to the within-school model analyzed in Example 9.2, a school-level model was specified to predict the extent to which students are encouraged to achieve their full potential (ENCOURAG). A measure of teachers' enthusiasm for their work (ENTHUSIA) was viewed as an important mediator variable between background variables and encouragement for students to achieve their full potential. The variables used to predict encouragement via teachers' enthusiasm consisted of math teachers' use of new methodology (NEWMETHO), consensus among math teachers with regard to school expectations and teaching goals as they pertain directly to mathematics instruction (CNSENSUS), and the teaching conditions of the school (CNDITION). The teaching condition variable was computed from the shortage of the school's equipment, so higher values on this variable reflect worse teaching conditions. Finally, a random slope

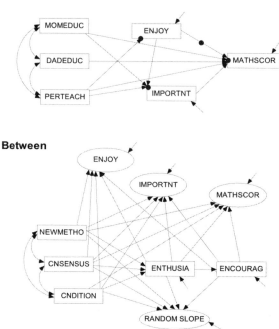

FIGURE 9.9. Multilevel SEM path diagram. From Kaplan, Kim, and Kim (2009). Reprinted by permission of Sage Publications, Inc.

relating MATHSCOR, on ENJOY is regressed on NEWMETHO, ENTHUSIA, CNSENSUS, CNDITION, and ENCOURAG. The full multilevel path diagram is depicted in Figure 9.9 where the black dots in the within-level model represent the random intercepts and random slope modeled as a function of the between-school variables.

For this example, we do not presume to have prior knowledge of any parameter in the model. This is reasonable insofar as no prior PISA assessment focused on math and few, if any, large-scale international assessments have focused on the PISA-eligible age group. Thus, all model parameters received normal prior distributions, with the mean hyperparameter set at zero and the variance hyperparameter specified as 10^{10}. All disturbance terms were set to noninformative inverse-gamma distributions with shape and scale of .001. With these settings, posterior estimates can take on a large number of possible values.

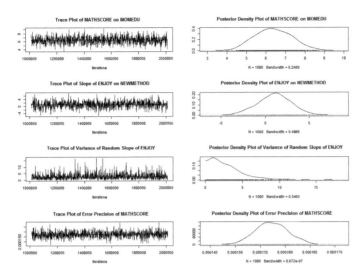

FIGURE 9.10. Trace and density plots for Bayesian multilevel SEM.

Convergence Diagnostics.   Preliminary analyses indicated that this model had a difficult time converging. Overall, this multilevel path analysis required 1,000,000 iterations, 5,000 burn-in iterations, and a thinning interval of 1,000 in order to reduce autocorrelation. Figures 9.10–9.12 present trace and density plots, autocorrelation plots, and

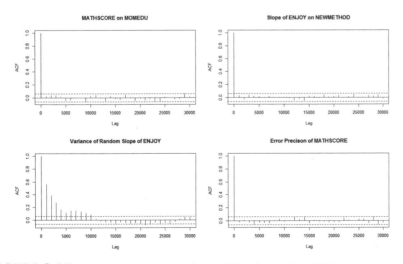

FIGURE 9.11. Autocorrelation plots for multilevel Bayesian SEM.

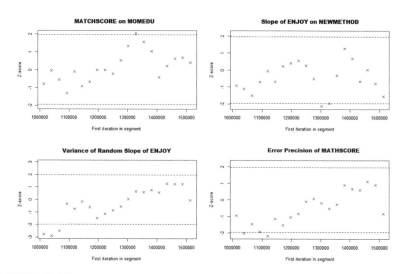

FIGURE 9.12. Geweke plots for multilevel Bayesian SEM.

Geweke plots for selected model parameters at the within and between levels. The plots indicate convergence for these and the remaining parameters in the model. An exception is the variance of the random slope between MATHSCOR and ENJOY, which shows some problems with convergence.

Results. Table 9.3 presents results for the within-level and the between-level parameters in the model. For the within-level results, we find that MOMEDUC, DADEDUC, PERTEACH, and IMPORTNT are positive predictors of MATHSCOR. Likewise, ENJOY is positively predicted by PERTEACH. Finally, MOMEDUC, PERTEACH, and ENJOY are positive predictors of IMPORTNT.

The between-level results presented here are for the random slopes in the model that relate ENJOY to MATHSCOR. For example, the results indicate that teacher enthusiasm moderates the relationship between enjoyment of mathematics and math achievement, with higher levels of teacher-reported enthusiasm associated with a stronger positive relationship between enjoyment of math and math achievement. Likewise, the math teachers' use of new methodology also demonstrates a moderating effect on the relationship between enjoyment of math and math achievement, where less usage of new methodology lowers the relation-

TABLE 9.3. Selected Bayesian Multilevel Path Analysis Estimates: PISA 2003

Parameter	EAP	*SD*	95% PPI	
MATHSCOR *on*				
MOMEDUC	6.36	0.95	4.41,	8.27
DADEDUC	5.29	1.05	3.19,	7.30
PERTEACH	12.89	1.81	9.12,	16.41
IMPORTNT	16.23	1.77	12.91,	19.71
IMPORTNT *on*				
MOMEDUC	0.01	0.01	0.00,	0.02
PERTEACH	0.21	0.02	0.18,	0.24
ENJOY	0.48	0.01	0.47,	0.50
ENJOY *on*				
PERTEACH	0.42	0.02	0.38,	0.46
SLOPE *on*				
NEWMETHO	0.98	2.01	−2.78,	5.05
ENTHUSIA	0.40	2.18	−3.74,	4.78
CNSENSUS	1.08	1.89	−2.73,	4.92
CNDITION	−1.72	1.64	−4.70,	1.46
ENCOURAG	−1.10	1.78	−4.54,	2.30
Variance components of random effects				
INTERCEPT	1713.13	365.25	1082.00,	2598.00
SLOPE of ENJOY	55.45	23.84	17.02,	110.06

Note. EAP, expected a posteriori; *SD*, posterior standard deviation; PPI, posterior probability interval.

ship between enjoyment of mathematics and math achievement. The other random slopes in the between level can be interpreted in a similar manner. Focusing on the predictors of the random slope, we find that 95% PPIs all contain zero, indicating that the EAP estimates are probably a null effect.

9.4 BAYESIAN GROWTH CURVE MODELING

Many of the questions facing social scientists concern the nature of change or development over time. For example, we may be interested in the development of science competencies over the middle school and early high school years. In addition, we may wish to study equity issues related to growth in science competency and examine the extent to which change in science competency over time is related to gender. As with conventional multilevel modeling, we may also be interested in school-level contextual effects, such as resources available for science instruction and how such resources impact change in science competency over time.

It has been long understood that growth curve modeling can be viewed as a hierarchical linear model (Raudenbush & Bryk, 2002), where level-1 represents intraindividual differences in an outcome over time and level-2 represents individual differences in change over time. In addition, a third level can be specified that allows for the study of change over time among individuals nested in organizations. In addition to the hierarchical linear modeling perspective, it has also been long known that growth curve modeling can be parameterized as a latent variable model (see, e.g., Willett & Sayer, 1994). Following the discussion in Kaplan et al. (2009), this section provides the specification of a two-level growth curve modeling within the latent variable context.

In the multilevel latent variable context, the conventional growth curve model that is used in this section can be written in the form of a factor analysis model with a structure imposed on the observed variable means. Specifically, the level-1 intraindividual model can be written as

$$\mathbf{y}_{ig} = \boldsymbol{\alpha} + \boldsymbol{\Lambda}\boldsymbol{\eta}_{ig} + \boldsymbol{\epsilon}_{ig} \tag{9.16}$$

where $\mathbf{y}$ is a vector representing the repeated science achievement measures for student i in group g. In line with the specification of mean structure analysis (Sörbom, 1974), $\boldsymbol{\alpha}$ is an initial status vector with elements fixed to zero, $\boldsymbol{\Lambda}$ is a fixed matrix containing a column of ones and a column of fixed constant time values. For example, for five equidistant time points, and the centering of the intercept at the first time point, the second column of $\boldsymbol{\Lambda}$ would be coded 0, 1, 2, 3, and 4. The centering value can be chosen to be at any time point (Willett & Sayer, 1994). Continuing, in line with the specification of a mean structure analysis and given the particular specification of $\boldsymbol{\Lambda}$, the vector $\boldsymbol{\eta}_{ig}$ contains the initial status and growth parameters. The vector $\boldsymbol{\epsilon}_{ig}$ is a diagonal matrix of measurement errors assumed to have mean zero and variance σ_ϵ^2. The model in Equation 9.16 can also be specified to handle quadratic growth as well as time varying covariates.

Consider a model examining science achievement for five time points over the middle and high school years with no time-varying variables. Further consider the simplest case where the time points are equally spaced and the first time point is designated as the initial status. From here, the standard form of a structural equation model can be specified to handle interindividual differences in the growth model and relate them to time-invariant individual characteristics, such as gender or race. This constitutes the level-2 model, and the form of this model is

$$\boldsymbol{\eta}_{ig} = \boldsymbol{v}_g + \mathbf{B}_g \boldsymbol{\eta}_{ig} + \boldsymbol{\Gamma}_g \mathbf{x}_{ig} + \boldsymbol{\zeta}_{ig} \tag{9.17}$$

where, as before, $\boldsymbol{\eta}_{ig}$ contains the initial status and growth parameters, $\mathbf{B}_g$ is a matrix of regression coefficients that can allow, say, the growth rate to be regressed on the initial status, and where this slope can vary across schools, $\boldsymbol{\Gamma}_g$ is a matrix of regression coefficients that allows growth parameters to be regressed on time-invariant predictors contained in $\mathbf{x}_{ig}$ which can also vary across schools, and $\boldsymbol{\zeta}_{ig}$ is a disturbance term with mean zero and variance σ_ζ^2.

A Bayesian framework for the growth curve model in Equations 9.16 and 9.17 simply requires placing priors on all model parameters. The choice of conjugate priors follows those that were given in Equations 9.3 and 9.4. In this context, priors would not be given to factor loadings because they are fixed parameters used to parameterize the growth curve model. Priors would need to be provided for the factor means representing the growth parameters, the factor variances and covariances, as well as the measurement error variances.

EXAMPLE 9.3. BAYESIAN GROWTH CURVE MODELING: BASELINE MODEL

For this example, we utilize data from the Longitudinal Study of American Youth to specify a simple baseline model of growth in science achievement. LSAY is a national longitudinal study of middle and high school students funded by the National Science Foundation. The goal of LSAY is to provide a description of students' attitudes toward science and mathematics, also focusing on these areas as possible career choices (Miller et al., 1992, p. 1). The items for the science achievement tests were drawn from the item pool of the 1986 National Assess-

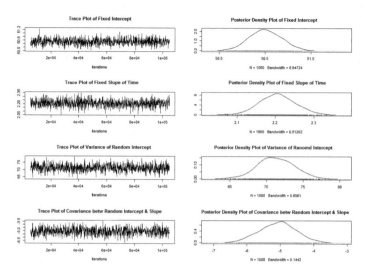

FIGURE 9.13. Trace and density plots for Bayesian growth curve modeling: Baseline model.

ment of Educational Progress tests. The sample size for this example is 3,116.

The program "rjags" was used to estimate the baseline growth curve model. Noninformative priors were specified for the random intercept and slope; specifically they were set to have a prior mean of zero and a prior precision of 10^{-6}. A total of 100,000 iterations were run, with 5,000 burn-in iterations and a thinning interval of 100. The details of the "rjags" code can be found in Appendix 9.1.

Figures 9.13–9.15 provide the diagnostic plots. Overall, the evidence suggests good convergence. The Heidelberger–Welch diagnostic p-values also indicate that the stationarity of the iterations has been achieved. The results are displayed in Table 9.4. The results indicate a positive growth rate in science over the middle school years. The 95% PPI is fairly narrow insofar as there is a 95% probability that the growth rate is between 2.12 and 2.30.

EXAMPLE 9.4. BAYESIAN GROWTH CURVE MODELING: TIME-INVARIANT PREDICTOR

For this example, we utilize the same data as in Example 9.3. However, we add the time-invariant predictor of gender (male = 1). Again, we

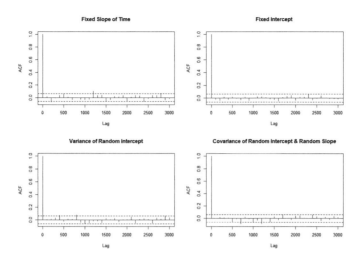

FIGURE 9.14. Autocorrelation plots for Bayesian growth curve modeling: Baseline model.

examine the case with noninformative priors only. The diagnostic plots are shown in Figures 9.16–9.18. Again, the diagnostic plots and the Heidelberger–Welch p-value show good convergence. The results are displayed in Table 9.5. The results once again show a positive increase

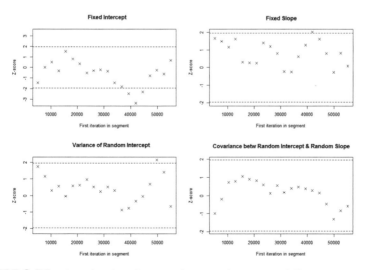

FIGURE 9.15. Geweke plots for Bayesian growth curve modeling.

TABLE 9.4. Parameter Estimates of Example 9.3

Parameter	EAP	*SD*	95% PPI
Fixed effects			
Intercept	50.51	1.18	50.17, 50.89
Time	2.21	0.05	2.12, 2.30
Variance–covariance components of random effects			
Intercept	71.32	2.46	66.45, 76.08
Time	2.37	0.20	2.01, 2.77
Covariance	–5.07	0.55	–6.15, –3.97

Note. EAP, expected a posteriori; *SD*, posterior standard deviation; PPI, posterior probability interval.

in science achievement over time. We find that males start off with higher science achievement in the seventh grade. The PPI indicates that there is a 95% chance that the male–female difference in seventh-grade science achievement is as low as 0.12 and as high as 1.45, and that the null value of zero is not within the interval. We find that females have a higher growth rate in science (–0.15); however, the 95% PPI covers the null value of zero.

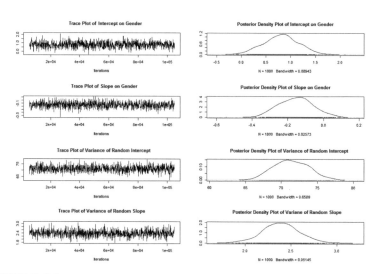

FIGURE 9.16. Trace and density plots for Bayesian growth curve modeling: With gender.

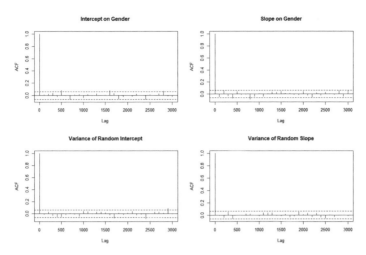

FIGURE 9.17. Autocorrelation plots for Bayesian growth curve modeling: With gender.

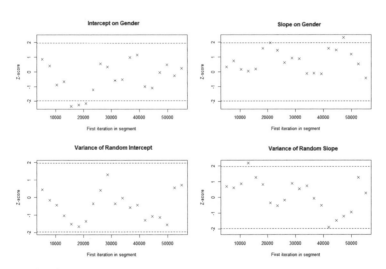

FIGURE 9.18. Geweke plots for Bayesian growth curve modeling: With gender.

TABLE 9.5. Parameter Estimates of Example 9.4

Parameter	EAP	SD	95% PPI
Fixed effects			
Intercept	50.09	0.26	49.56, 50.59
Time	2.29	0.07	2.15, 2.43
Intercept on MALE	0.81	0.36	0.12, 1.45
Slope on MALE	−0.15	0.10	−0.34, 0.04
Variance–covariance components of random effects			
Intercept	71.38	2.47	66.91, 76.34
Time	2.39	0.20	1.99, 2.80
Covariance	−5.10	0.56	−6.18, −4.00

Note. EAP, expected a posteriori; *SD*, posterior standard deviation; PPI, posterior probability interval.

9.5 BAYESIAN MODELS FOR CATEGORICAL LATENT VARIABLES

The use of continuous latent variables arguably dominates most applications of latent variable modeling. However, it is often useful to hypothesize the existence of categorical latent variables. Such categorical latent variables can be employed to explain response frequencies among dichotomous or ordered categorical manifest variables. Methods that use categorical latent variables to explain response frequencies underlying categorical manifest variables include latent class analysis and, in the longitudinal context, latent Markov modeling. However, categorical latent variables can also be used to model continuous observed variables as well, such as in the context of latent profile analysis. In all of these cases, a common estimation framework involves mixture modeling.

9.5.1 Mixture Model Specification

We begin this section by considering the general specification of models for categorical latent variables (Dempster et al., 1977) under a finite mixture modeling perspective (McLachlan & Peel, 2000; McLachlan & Krishnan, 1997). Drawing on Everitt (1984) and McLachlan and Peel (2000) let $\mathbf{y} = (\mathbf{y}_1, \mathbf{y}_2, \ldots, \mathbf{y}_n)'$ be a set of P items obtained on a random sample of size n. In our example, these items represent school principals' perceptions of student and teacher behavior measured on a four-point scale. The density of an observation $\mathbf{y}_j$ ($j = 1, 2, \ldots, n$) can be written as

$$f(\mathbf{y}_j|\mathbf{\Psi}) = \sum_{c=1}^{C} \pi_c f(\mathbf{y}_j|\boldsymbol{\theta}_c) \tag{9.18}$$

where

$$\mathbf{\Psi} = (\boldsymbol{\pi}, \mathbf{\Theta}')' \tag{9.19}$$

is a vector of unknown parameters containing the mixture class probabilities (mixing proportions) $\boldsymbol{\pi} = (\pi_1, \pi_2, \ldots, \pi_c)$ and the model parameters $\mathbf{\Theta} = (\boldsymbol{\theta}', \ldots, \boldsymbol{\theta}'_c)$. In other words, the density of the P item responses for school principal j is the sum of C densities, weighted by mixing proportions. The C densities are assumed to follow a finite mixture multivariate Bernoulli distribution with mixing proportions π_c, namely,

$$f_c(\mathbf{y}|\boldsymbol{\theta}_c) = \prod_{v=1}^{P} \theta_{vc}^{y_v}(1 - \theta_{vc})^{1-y_v} \tag{9.20}$$

where $\boldsymbol{\theta}_c = (\theta_{1c}, \theta_{2c}, \ldots, \theta_{pc})'$ and θ_{vc} is the conditional probability that $y_v = 1$ given membership in the cth mixture (latent) class.

Given n independent response vectors $(\mathbf{y}_1, \mathbf{y}_2, \ldots, \mathbf{y}_n)'$, the likelihood function can be written as

$$L = \prod_{j=1}^{n} f(\mathbf{y}_j|\mathbf{\Psi}) \tag{9.21}$$

and the observed data log-likelihood is given by

$$\log L = \sum_{j=1}^{n} \log \left\{ \sum_{c=1}^{C} \pi_c f(\mathbf{y}_j|\boldsymbol{\theta}_j) \right\} \tag{9.22}$$

Differentiating Equation 9.22 with respect to the unknown parameters yields

$$\hat{\pi}_c = \frac{1}{n} \sum_{j=1}^{n} \tau_c(\mathbf{y}_j|\hat{\boldsymbol{\theta}}_j) \tag{9.23}$$

and

$$\sum_{i=1}^{g}\sum_{j=1}^{n}\tau_c(\mathbf{y}_j|\hat{\mathbf{\Psi}}_j)\partial\log f(\mathbf{y}_j|\theta_c)/\partial\Theta = \mathbf{0} \tag{9.24}$$

where

$$\tau_c(\mathbf{y}_j|\mathbf{\Psi}) = \frac{\pi_c f(\mathbf{y}_j|\theta_c)}{\sum_{c=1}^{C}\pi_c f(\mathbf{y}_j|\Theta)} \tag{9.25}$$

is the posterior probability that $\mathbf{y}_j$ belongs to the cth mixture (latent) class.

9.5.2 Bayesian Mixture Models

The parameters of the mixture model given in the previous section can be estimated using the EM algorithm. The EM algorithm proceeds by obtaining initial starting values of π and θ_c which are then inserted into Equation 9.25 to obtain initial posterior probabilities. These initial posterior probabilities are then inserted into Equation 9.23 to obtain revised estimates of π and θ. This iterative process continues until a convergence criterion is met.

Our discussion of Bayesian mixture models follows closely that of Gelman et al. (2003; see also McLachlan & Peel, 2000). Specifically, Gelman et al. (2003) discusses how mixture models can be specified as hierarchical Bayesian models. To begin, consider again Equation 9.18. One way to see this as a hierarchical Bayesian model is to specify a set of missing data indicators z_{jc} ($j = 1, 2, \ldots, n; c = 1, 2, \ldots, C$). The missing indicators take on the values

$$z_{jc} = \begin{cases} 1, & \text{if person } j \text{ is drawn from mixture class } c \\ 0, & \text{otherwise} \end{cases} \tag{9.26}$$

Given the mixture class probabilities π, the probability model for z_{jc} is multinomial (1: $\pi_1, \pi_2, \ldots, \pi_C$). As Gelman et al. (2003) note, we can view π as the hyperparameters generating the multinomial distribution of unobserved indicators.

The above specification requires that priors be assigned to the model parameters θ and the mixture class probabilities π. Assuming that θ and π are independent, the model parameters θ represent all of the parameters underlying the mixture distributions. So, for example, if it is assumed that the distributions of the responses within each mixture class are normal, then the parameters θ may specify differing means of the mixture classes but common variance. Thus, the conjugate prior distributions on θ might be normal.

With respect to the missing data indicators z_{jc}, recall that it is assumed that the probability model is multinomial with parameters π. Thus, the natural conjugate prior for the mixture class probabilities π is the Dirichlet $(\pi_1, \pi_2, \ldots, \pi_C)$ prior. The Dirichlet prior was discussed in Chapter 3.

EXAMPLE 9.4. BAYESIAN MIXTURE CFA

Two latent classes were specified for the factor analysis given in Example 9.1.

Convergence Diagnostics. Diagnostic plots are shown in Figures 9.19–9.21. Here we find mixed evidence of convergence of the mixture model for these selected parameters. Specifically, the trace and density plots are not ideal. However, the autocorrelation plot does indicate that the chain moves to independent draws from the posterior distribution

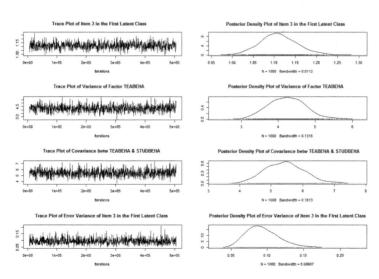

FIGURE 9.19. Trace and density plots for Bayesian mixture CFA.

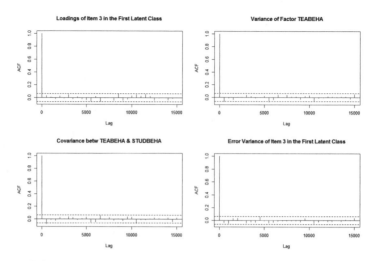

FIGURE 9.20. Autocorrelation plots for Bayesian mixture CFA.

very quickly, and Geweke plots provide evidence that the chain has converged.

Results.   The results of the Bayesian mixture CFA are shown in Table 9.6. The two latent classes are clearly distinguished by the size of the factor loadings, with latent class 2 having uniformly smaller loadings. In addition, latent class 2 makes up 60% of the sample, while latent class 1 accounts for the remaining 40%.

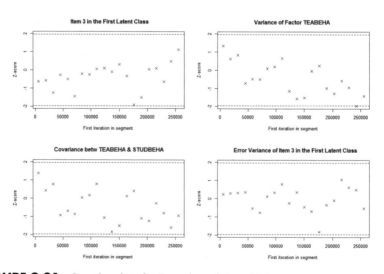

FIGURE 9.21. Geweke plots for Bayesian mixture CFA.

TABLE 9.6. Parameter Estimates of Mixture CFA

Parameter	EAP	SD	95% PPI	Error variance
		Latent class 1		
Loadings: TEABEHA *by*				
Item SC17Q01	1.00	0.00	1.00, 1.00	0.32
Item SC17Q03	1.09	0.05	1.00, 1.19	0.12
Item SC17Q05	1.18	0.05	1.09, 1.28	0.15
Item SC17Q06	1.07	0.05	0.97, 1.18	0.14
Item SC17Q09	1.28	0.06	1.17, 1.39	0.22
Item SC17Q011	1.04	0.05	0.95, 1.15	0.18
Item SC17Q013	1.07	0.05	0.97, 1.18	0.27
Loadings: STUDBEHA *by*				
Item SC17Q02	1.00	0.00	1.00, 1.00	0.00
Item SC17Q04	0.97	0.03	0.91, 1.00	0.09
Item SC17Q07	0.93	0.03	0.87, 0.99	0.28
Item SC17Q08	0.99	0.03	0.94, 1.05	0.22
Item SC17Q010	0.91	0.03	0.85, 0.97	0.27
Item SC17Q012	1.00	0.00	1.00, 1.00	0.00
		Latent class 2		
Loadings: TEABEHA *by*				
Item SC17Q01	1.00	0.00	1.00, 1.00	0.34
Item SC17Q03	0.90	0.03	0.84, 0.95	0.18
Item SC17Q05	1.02	0.03	0.96, 1.08	0.21
Item SC17Q06	0.81	0.03	0.75, 0.88	0.35
Item SC17Q09	1.05	0.03	0.98, 1.11	0.25
Item SC17Q011	0.74	0.03	0.68, 0.81	0.27
Item SC17Q013	0.87	0.03	0.81, 0.93	0.22
Loadings: STUDBEHA *by*				
Item SC17Q02	1.00	0.00	1.00, 1.00	0.24
Item SC17Q04	0.70	0.02	0.66, 0.74	0.26
Item SC17Q07	0.80	0.03	0.75, 0.86	0.39
Item SC17Q08	0.73	0.02	0.68, 0.78	0.19
Item SC17Q010	0.70	0.03	0.65, 0.75	0.34
Item SC17Q012	0.64	0.03	0.60, 0.69	0.15
		Probability in each latent class		
Latent Class 1	0.40	0.05	0.30, 0.50	
Latent Class 2	0.60	0.05	0.50, 0.70	
		Factor variance and covariance		
TEABEHA	4.26	0.51	3.36, 5.38	
STUDBEHA	7.24	0.81	5.78, 9.01	
TEABEHA with STUDBEHA	5.46	0.62	4.34, 6.84	

Note. EAP, expected a posteriori; *SD*, posterior standard deviation; PPI, posterior probability interval.

9.6 SUMMARY

This chapter examined latent variable models from a Bayesian perspective. Factor analysis, single and multilevel structural equation models, growth curve models, and models for categorical latent variables were presented, along with applications. The types of models presented in this chapter were typical, but not exhaustive, of the types of models that are generically referred to as latent variable models. We have not, for example, presented multiple group models with priors placed on factor means, nor have we examined combinations of continuous and categorical latent variables, such as general growth mixture models. Nevertheless, there is no principled reason why these models cannot be estimated from a Bayesian perspective insofar as conjugate priors are available for all the parameters that these models entail. A technical discussion of the models covered here, and extensions, can be found in Lee (2007) and Song and Lee (2012).

9.7 SUGGESTED READINGS

Kaplan, D., & Depaoli, S. (2012b). Bayesian structural equation modeling. In R. H. Hoyle (Ed.), *Handbook of structural equation modeling* (pp. 650–673). New York: Guilford Press.

Lee, S.-Y. (2007). *Structural equation modeling: A Bayesian approach*. Hoboken, NJ: Wiley.

Muthén, B., & Asparouhov, T. (2012). Bayesian SEM: A more flexible representation of substantive theory. *Psychological Methods, 17,* 313–335.

Song, X.-Y., & Lee, S.-Y. (2012). *Basic and advanced Bayesian structural equation modeling: With applications in the medical and behavioral sciences*. Hoboken, NJ: Wiley.

APPENDIX 9.1
"rjags" CODE FOR CHAPTER 9

```
#--------------------------------------------------------
# EXAMPLE 9.1 Bayesian CFA with non-informative and
# informative priors
#       Program Steps
# 1. Specify model. Note that one loading in each column of the loading matrix
#       must be set to 1.0.
# 2. Place priors on all model parameters except the fixed factor loading
# 3. End modelstring and write lines to a model.bug connection
# 4. Read in data and specify parameters and initialization values for the chain
# 5. Summarize
#
# Remaining code obtains posterior predictive plots
#--------------------------------------------------------

install.packages("rjags")
install.packages("MCMCpack")
require(rjags)
require(MCMCpack)

# Specify model
modelstring = "
model {
for (i in 1 : nData) {
```

233

```
for (j in 1 : 13) {                    # NCOL(y) = 13
  y[i,j] ~ dnorm(mu[i,j],psi[j])
}

mu[i,1]  <- w[1]+1*xi[i,1]    # Factor 1, lam[1]=1
mu[i,3]  <- w[3]+lam[3]*xi[i,1]
mu[i,5]  <- w[5]+lam[5]*xi[i,1]
mu[i,6]  <- w[6]+lam[6]*xi[i,1]
mu[i,9]  <- w[9]+lam[9]*xi[i,1]
mu[i,11] <-w[11]+lam[11]*xi[i,1]
mu[i,13] <-w[13]+lam[13]*xi[i,1]

mu[i,2]  <-w[2]+1*xi[i,2]         # Factor 2,  lam[2]=1
mu[i,4]  <- w[4]+lam[4]*xi[i,2]
mu[i,7]  <- w[7]+lam[7]*xi[i,2]
mu[i,8]  <- w[8]+lam[8]*xi[i,2]
mu[i,10] <-w[10]+lam[10]*xi[i,2]
mu[i,12] <-w[12]+lam[12]*xi[i,2]

xi[i,1:2] ~ dmnorm(u[1:2],phi[1:2,1:2])
}

# Distributions and Priors
#Priors on Intercepts and Loadings
lam[1]<-1
lam[3] ~ dnorm(0, 10^(-6))   #prior mean and prior precision
lam[5] ~ dnorm(0, 10^(-6))
```

234

```
lam[6]  ~ dnorm(0,  10^(-6))
lam[9]  ~ dnorm(0,  10^(-6))
lam[11] ~ dnorm(0,  10^(-6))
lam[13] ~ dnorm(0,  10^(-6))

lam[2] <-1
lam[4]  ~ dnorm(0,  10^(-6))
lam[7]  ~ dnorm(0,  10^(-6))
lam[8]  ~ dnorm(0,  10^(-6))
lam[10] ~ dnorm(0,  10^(-6))
lam[12] ~ dnorm(0,  10^(-6))

#prior mean and prior precision
w[1]  ~ dnorm(0,  10^(-6))
w[3]  ~ dnorm(0,  10^(-6))
w[5]  ~ dnorm(0,  10^(-6))
w[6]  ~ dnorm(0,  10^(-6))
w[9]  ~ dnorm(0,  10^(-6))
w[11] ~ dnorm(0,  10^(-6))
w[13] ~ dnorm(0,  10^(-6))

w[2]  ~ dnorm(0,  10^(-6))
w[4]  ~ dnorm(0,  10^(-6))
w[7]  ~ dnorm(0,  10^(-6))
w[8]  ~ dnorm(0,  10^(-6))
w[10] ~ dnorm(0,  10^(-6))
w[12] ~ dnorm(0,  10^(-6))
```

```
#---------------------------------------------------
#Priors on Precisions
for(j in 1:13) {
psi[j] ~ dgamma(1, 0.001) # Precision of residuals
sgm[j] <- 1/psi[j] # Error variance
}

phi[1:2,1:2] ~ dwish(R[1:2,1:2], 3) #phi is precision matrix

Sigma[1,1] <- phi[2,2]/(phi[1,1]*phi[2,2]-phi[2,1]^2) #Sigma is covariance matrix
Sigma[2,1] <- -phi[1,2]/(phi[1,1]*phi[2,2]-phi[2,1]^2)
Sigma[2,2] <- phi[1,1]/(phi[1,1]*phi[2,2]-phi[2,1]^2)
Sigma[1,2] <- Sigma[2,1]
}

"writeLines(modelstring,con="model.bug")

# READ IN DATA AND PREPARE FOR JAGS
cfadata = read.csv(file.choose(),header=TRUE) #browse to select data "cfa_imputed.csv"
(using regression imputation).
y = as.matrix(cfadata)
nData=NROW(y)

#Specify parameters
u=c(0,0)
R=matrix(c(1,0,0,1),nrow=2)
cfadata <- list(y=y, nData=nData,u=u,R=R)
```

236

```
# RUN CHAIN
# Initialize Model
parameters = c("lam","Sigma","sgm","phi","xi","w") #Specify the Parameters to Be
Estimated
adaptSteps = 5000
burnInSteps = 5000
nChains = 2
thinSteps = 500
nPerChain = 1000000

cfaModel1 = jags.model("model.bug",data=cfadata,n.chains=nChains, n.adapt=adaptSteps)

# Obtain the Posterior Sample of Factor Loadings: #
cat("Burning in the MCMC chain ...\n")
update(cfaModel1, n.iter=burnInSteps)
cat("Sampling from the final MCMC chain ... \n")
codaSamples1 = coda.samples(cfaModel1, variable.names=parameters,
n.iter=nPerChain, thin=thinSteps,seed=5555)

#Posterior Mean, posterior SD and posterior probablity interval (PPI) for the first
chain #
summary(codaSamples1[[1]])
#posterior mean of factor correlation #
mean(codaSamples1[[1]][,2]/sqrt(codaSamples1[[1]][,1]*codaSamples1[[1]][,4]))
#posterior SD of factor correlation #
sd(codaSamples1[[1]][,2]/sqrt(codaSamples1[[1]][,1]*codaSamples1[[1]][,4]))
```

237

```r
# 95% PPI of factor corr.#
quantile(codaSamples1[[1]][,2]/sqrt(codaSamples1[[1]][,1]*codaSamples1[[1]]
[,4]),c(.025,.975))
#Selected Trace plots and Density plots for loadings of items 8, 9, 10 and 12 (1st
chain). #
plot(codaSamples1[[1]][,c(12:14,16)])

#Selected Trace plots and Density plots for variance terms #
plot(codaSamples1[[1]][,c(1,2,4,22)])

#Auto-correlation plots for selected items (first chain) #
par(mfrow=c(2,2))
acf(codaSamples1[[1]][,12],main="Item 8")
acf(codaSamples1[[1]][,13],main="Item 9")
acf(codaSamples1[[1]][,14],main="Item 10")
acf(codaSamples1[[1]][,16],main="Item 12")

par(mfrow=c(2,2))
acf(codaSamples1[[1]][,1],main="Variance of Factor TEABEHA")
acf(codaSamples1[[1]][,2],main="Covariance betw TEABEHA and STUDBEHA")
acf(codaSamples1[[1]][,4],main="Variance of Factor STUDBEHA")
acf(codaSamples1[[1]][,22],main="Error Variance of Item 1")

# Diagnostics
#Geweke Diagnostic and Plot
geweke.diag(codaSamples1[[1]][,c(14,1,2,22)])
geweke.plot(codaSamples1[[1]][,c(14,1,2,22)])
```

238

```r
#Heidelberger-Welch diagnostics
heidel.diag(codaSamples1[[1]][,c(14,1,2,22)])

#Raftery.diag
raftery.diag(codaSamples1[[1]][,c(14,1,2,22)])

#------------------------POSTERIOR PREDICTIVE CHECK ---------------------------#
#install.package(ggplot2)
#install.package(gridExtra)
#install.package(lavaan)

library(ggplot2)
library(gridExtra)
library(lavaan)

##CREATE THE REPLICATED DATA
draw.reps <- function(x) {
(x <- codaSamples1[[1]][x,])
(f.draw <- mvrnorm(n = 165, mu = c(0,0), Sigma = matrix(c(x[1],x[2],x[3],x[4]),nrow
= 2, ncol = 2)))
#print(f.draw)

## create the replicated data set
y.rep <- matrix(nrow = 165, ncol = 13)
for(i in 1:13) {
if(is.na(match(i,c(1,3,5,6,9,11,13)))) { fact <- 2 } else { fact <- 1 }
```

239

```
y.rep[,i] <- x[i+34] + x[i+4]*f.draw[,fact] + rnorm(165, 0, sqrt(x[i+21]))
}##END for

## create the model implied covariance mat
obs.cov.mat <- cov(cfadata$y)
rep.cov.mat <- cov(y.rep)
lambda <- matrix(rep(0,26),nrow = 13, ncol = 2)
lambda[c(1,3,5,6,9,11,13),1] <- x[4 + c(1,3,5,6,9,11,13)]
lambda[c(2,4,7,8,10,12),2] <- x[4 + c(2,4,7,8,10,12)]
F.cov <- matrix(c(x[1],x[2],x[3],x[4]),nrow = 2, ncol = 2)
phi <- diag(x[22:34])
exp.cov.mat <- lambda %*% F.cov %*% t(lambda) + phi

## Calculate the observed and replicated X^2 values using the model implied covariance
matrix
chi.sq.obs <- nrow(cfadata$y)*(determinant(exp.cov.mat)$modulus + ## note:
determinant(x)$modulus returns log of the determinant of x
sum(diag( ##gets the trace
(obs.cov.mat) %*% solve(exp.cov.mat))
) ) -
determinant(obs.cov.mat)$modulus - 13 ### p + q = 13
)##END CHI.SQ calculation
chi.sq.rep <- nrow(y.rep)*(determinant(exp.cov.mat)$modulus + ## note:
determinant(x)$modulus returns log of the determinant of x
sum(diag( ##gets the trace
(rep.cov.mat) %*% solve(exp.cov.mat))
```

240

```
) ) -
determinant(rep.cov.mat)$modulus - 13)

return(list(y.rep,c(chi.sq.obs,chi.sq.rep)))
}##END function draw.reps

##DISCREP STAT USING LAVAAN
discrep.stat.lav <- function(x) {
lav.path <- ' chil =~ SC17Q01 + SC17Q03 + SC17Q05 + SC17Q06 + SC17Q09 + SC17Q11 +
SC17Q13
chi2 =~ SC17Q02 + SC17Q04 + SC17Q07 + SC17Q08 + SC17Q10 + SC17Q12
'
x <- data.frame(x[[1]])
names(x) <- dimnames(cfadata$y)[[2]]
rep.fit <- cfa(lav.path, data = x)
return(rep.fit@Fit@test[[1]]$stat)
}##END function discrep.stat.lav

##EASY FUNCTION TO MAKE FUNCTION CALL
get.yreps <- function(z) {
y.reps <- lapply(1:z,draw.reps)
return(y.reps)
}##END function

##BEGIN POSTERIOR CHECK
set.seed(515)
```

241

```r
y.reps <- get.yreps(1000)
chi.sq <- cbind(unlist(lapply(y.reps,function(x) return(x[[2]][1])),unlist(lapply(y.
reps,function(x)
return(x[[2]][2]))))
chi.rep <- chi.sq[,2]
chi.obs <- chi.sq[,1]

##ChiSq Using lavaan
#lav.path <- ' chi1 =~ SC17Q01 + SC17Q03 + SC17Q05 + SC17Q06 + SC17Q09 + SC17Q11 +
SC17Q13
#chi2 =~ SC17Q02 + SC17Q04 + SC17Q07 + SC17Q08 + SC17Q10 + SC17Q12
#'

#fit <- cfa(lav.path, data = data.frame(cfadata$y))
#chi.obs.lav <- fit@Fit@test[[1]]$stat
#chi.rep.lav <- unlist(lapply(y.reps,discrep.stat.lav)) ##grabs discrep stat from y.
reps, will take a minute

##SAVE PDF POSTERIOR CHECKING PLOTS
liks.dif <- chi.obs - chi.rep
range <- max(liks.dif) - min(liks.dif)
p.value <- round(length(which(liks.dif < 0))/length(liks.dif),3)
pdf(file=' ') ####ADD FILE PATH#####
par(ask = FALSE)
hist(liks.dif, xlab = expression(Chi["obs"]^2 - Chi["rep"]^2), main = "", xlim =
c(-60,150))
abline(v = 0, lty = 2, lwd = 2)
```

```r
text(x = -35, y = 200, label = paste("p-value = ",p.value,sep = ""))
dev.off()
pdf(file=' ') ####ADD MY FILE PATH#####
qplot(chi.obs,chi.rep, shape = I(1)) +
geom_abline(slope = 1, intercept = 0) +
theme_bw() +
geom_text(aes(x = 7 + min(chi.obs,chi.rep) , y = - 2 + max(chi.obs,chi.rep), label
= paste("p-value =",p.value), size = 4.5) +
theme(panel.grid.major = element_blank(), panel.grid.minor = element_blank()) +
ylim(c(-7 + min(chi.obs,chi.rep),max(chi.obs,chi.rep))) +
xlim(c(-7 + min(chi.obs,chi.rep),max(chi.obs,chi.rep))) +
xlab("Observed") + ylab("Replicated")
dev.off()

##DISPLAY POSTERIOR CHECKING PLOTS & INFORMATION

hist(liks.dif, xlab = expression(Chi["obs"]^2 - Chi["rep"]^2), main = "", xlim =
c(-60,150))
abline(v = 0, lty = 2, lwd = 2)
text(x = -35, y = 200, label = paste("p-value = ",p.value,sep = ""))
par(ask = TRUE)
qplot(chi.obs,chi.rep, shape = I(1)) +
geom_abline(slope = 1, intercept = 0) +
theme_bw() +
geom_text(aes(x = 7 + min(chi.obs,chi.rep) , y = - 2 + max(chi.obs,chi.rep), label
= paste("p-value =",p.value), size = 4.5) +
```

243

```
#theme(panel.grid.major = element_blank()) +
ylim(c(-7 + min(chi.obs,chi.rep),max(chi.obs,chi.rep))) +
xlim(c(-7 + min(chi.obs,chi.rep),max(chi.obs,chi.rep))) +
xlab("Observed") + ylab("Replicated")

###Informative Prior###
##Specify model
require(rjags)

modelstring = " model {
for (i in 1 : nData) {
for (j in 1 : 13) { # NCOL(y) = 13
y[i,j] ~ dnorm(mu[i,j],psi[j])
}

mu[i,1]  <- w[1]+1*xi[i,1]  # Factor 1,  lam[1]=1
mu[i,3]  <- w[3]+lam[3]*xi[i,1]
mu[i,5]  <- w[5]+lam[5]*xi[i,1]
mu[i,6]  <- w[6]+lam[6]*xi[i,1]
mu[i,9]  <- w[9]+lam[9]*xi[i,1]
mu[i,11] <-w[11]+lam[11]*xi[i,1]
mu[i,13] <-w[13]+lam[13]*xi[i,1]

mu[i,2]  <-w[2]+1*xi[i,2]  # Factor 2,  lam[2]=1
mu[i,4]  <- w[4]+lam[4]*xi[i,2]
mu[i,7]  <- w[7]+lam[7]*xi[i,2]
```

244

```
mu[i,8]  <- w[8]+lam[8]*xi[i,2]
mu[i,10] <-w[10]+lam[10]*xi[i,2]
mu[i,12] <-w[12]+lam[12]*xi[i,2]

xi[i,1:2] ~ dmnorm(u[1:2],phi[1:2,1:2])
}

# Distributions and Priors
#Priors on Loadings and Intercepts
lam[1]<-1
lam[3]  ~ dnorm(0.729, 1/.018)   #prior mean and prior precision
lam[5]  ~ dnorm(1.176, 1/0.028)
lam[6]  ~ dnorm(0.887, 1/0.025)
lam[9]  ~ dnorm(1.013, 1/0.029)
lam[11] ~ dnorm(0.645, 1/0.018)
lam[13] ~ dnorm(1.121, 1/0.031)

lam[2]<-1
lam[4]  ~ dnorm(0.810, 1/0.026)
lam[7]  ~ dnorm(1.359, 1/0.055)
lam[8]  ~ dnorm(0.931, 1/0.031)
lam[10] ~ dnorm(0.970, 1/0.035)
lam[12] ~ dnorm(0.942, 1/0.030)

w[1]  ~  dnorm(0, 10^(-6))
w[3]  ~  dnorm(0, 10^(-6))  #prior mean and prior precision
```

```
w[5]  ~ dnorm(0,  10^(-6))
w[6]  ~ dnorm(0,  10^(-6))
w[9]  ~ dnorm(0,  10^(-6))
w[11] ~ dnorm(0,  10^(-6))
w[13] ~ dnorm(0,  10^(-6))

w[2]  ~ dnorm(0,  10^(-6))
w[4]  ~ dnorm(0,  10^(-6))
w[7]  ~ dnorm(0,  10^(-6))
w[8]  ~ dnorm(0,  10^(-6))
w[10] ~ dnorm(0,  10^(-6))
w[12] ~ dnorm(0,  10^(-6))

#------------------------------------------------------
#Priors on Precisions
for(j in 1:13) {
psi[j] ~ dgamma(1,  0.001)  # Precision of residuals
sgm[j] <- 1/psi[j]          # Error variance
}

phi[1:2,1:2]  ~  dwish(R[1:2,1:2],  3)                       #phi is precision matrix
Sigma[1,1] <-  phi[2,2]/(phi[1,1]*phi[2,2]-phi[2,1]^2)  #Sigma is covariance matrix
Sigma[2,1] <-  -phi[1,2]/(phi[1,1]*phi[2,2]-phi[2,1]^2)
Sigma[2,2] <-  phi[1,1]/(phi[1,1]*phi[2,2]-phi[2,1]^2)
Sigma[1,2] <-  Sigma[2,1]
```

246

```r
}
"
writeLines(modelstring,con="model.bug")

# READ IN DATA AND PREPARE FOR JAGS

cfadata = read.csv(file.choose(),header=TRUE)
y = as.matrix(cfadata)
nData=NROW(y)

#Specify parameters
u=c(0,0) R=matrix(c(1,0,0,1),nrow=2)
cfadata <- list(y=y, nData=nData,u=u,R=R)

# RUN CHAIN

# Initialize Model
parameters = c("lam","Sigma","sgm","phi","xi","w") #Specify the Parameters to Be
Estimated
adaptSteps = 5000
burnInSteps = 5000
nChains = 2
thinSteps = 500
nPerChain = 1000000

cfaModel2 = jags.model("model.bug",data=cfadata,n.chains=nChains, n.adapt=adaptSteps)
```

247

```r
# Obtain the Posterior Sample of Factor Loadings:
cat("Burning in the MCMC chain ...\n")
update(cfaModel2, n.iter=burnInSteps)
cat("Sampling from the final MCMC chain ...  \n")
codaSamples2 = coda.samples(cfaModel2, variable.names=parameters,
n.iter=nPerChain, thin=thinSteps,seed=5555)
#Posterior Mean, posterior SD and posterior probablity interval (PPI) for the 1st chain
summary(codaSamples2[[1]])
#Factor correlation
mean(codaSamples2[[1]][,2]/sqrt(codaSamples2[[1]][,1]*codaSamples2[[1]][,4]))
#Posterior SD of factor correlation
sd(codaSamples2[[1]][,2]/sqrt(codaSamples2[[1]][,1]*codaSamples2[[1]][,4]))
quantile(codaSamples2[[1]][,2]/sqrt(codaSamples2[[1]][,1]*codaSamples2[[1]]
[,4]),c(.025,.975))#95%
PPI of factor corr.

# Trace and Density Plots for Selected Loadings and Variance Terms (first chain) #
plot(codaSamples2[[1]][,c(12:14,16)])
plot(codaSamples2[[1]][,c(1,2,4,22)])

#Selected Auto-Correlation Plots (first chain) #

par(mfrow=c(2,2))
acf(codaSamples2[[1]][,12],main="Item 8")
acf(codaSamples2[[1]][,13],main="Item 9")
acf(codaSamples2[[1]][,14],main="Item 10")
acf(codaSamples2[[1]][,16],main="Item 12")
```

```
par(mfrow=c(2,2))
acf(codaSamples2[[1]][,1],main="Variance of Factor TEABEHA")
acf(codaSamples2[[1]][,2],main="Covariance betw TEABEHA and STUDBEHA")
acf(codaSamples2[[1]][,4],main="Variance of Factor STUDBEHA")
acf(codaSamples2[[1]][,22],main="Error Variance of Item 1")

# Diagnostics
#Geweke Diagnostics and Plot
geweke.diag(codaSamples2[[1]][,c(14,1,2,22)])
geweke.plot(codaSamples2[[1]][,c(14,1,2,22)],frac1 = 0.1, frac2 = 0.5)

#Heidelberger-Welch diagnostics
heidel.diag(codaSamples2[[1]][,c(14,1,2,22)])

#Raftery.diag
raftery.diag(codaSamples2[[1]][,c(14,1,2,22)])

#------------------------------------------------------------
# Example 9.2 Path Analysis--Noninformative Prior
#
# Programming steps similar to Example 9.1
#------------------------------------------------------------

install.packages("MCMCpack")
install.packages("lavaan")
install.packages("rjags")
```

```
require(MCMCpack)
require(lavaan)
require(rjags)

##Specify model
modelstring = "
model {
#subject-level models
for (i in 1:nData) {
x[i,1:3]~ dmnorm(v[1:3], PI[1:3,1:3]) # obtain covariance among X's.

y[i]~dnorm(mu1[i],tau1)

mu1[i]<- a1[1] + a1[2]*momedu[i] + a1[3]*dadedu[i]+a1[4]*perteach[i]+
        a1[5]*importnt[i]+a1[6]*enjoy[i]

enjoy[i]~dnorm(mu2[i], tau2)
mu2[i]<-b1[1]+b1[2]*perteach[i]

importnt[i]~dnorm(mu3[i], tau3)
mu3[i]<-c1[1]+c1[2]*momedu[i]+c1[3]*perteach[i]+c1[4]*enjoy[i]
}##END FOR i

# Prior Specification
#Priors on regression coefficients
v[1:3] ~ dmnorm(v1[1:3], H0[1:3,1:3])
```

```
    a1[1:6] ~ dmnorm(u1[1:6],  H1[1:6,1:6])
    b1[1:2] ~ dmnorm(u2[1:2],  H2[1:2,1:2])
    c1[1:4] ~ dmnorm(u3[1:4],  H3[1:4,1:4])

    #Priors on Precisions
    tau1 <- 1/var1
    tau2 <- 1/var2
    tau3 <- 1/var3
    var1 ~ dunif(0,  10^(10))
    var2 ~ dunif(0,  10^(10))
    var3 ~ dunif(0,  10^(10))
    PI[1:3, 1:3] ~ dwish(R[1:3,1:3],  4)

} ##END Model
"

writeLines(modelstring,con="model.bug")


# READ IN DATA AND PREPARE FOR JAGS

semdata <- read.csv(file.choose(),header=TRUE) #browse to select data "sem.csv"
#colnames(semdata)
y        <- semdata$mathscor
momedu   <- semdata$momeduc
dadedu   <- semdata$dadeduc
perteach <- semdata$perteach
importnt <- semdata$importnt
```

251

```r
enjoy    <- semdata$enjoy
x <- as.matrix(cbind(momedu, dadedu, perteach)) #newly added
nData<-NROW(y)

#Specify variables
Semdata1 <- list(y=y, x=x, nData=nData, v1=rep(0,3),
      u1=rep(0,6),u2=rep(0,2),u3=rep(0,4),H0=diag(10^(-4),3,3),
      H1=diag(c(10^(-10), rep(0.1, 5)),6,6),H2=diag(c(10^(-10), 0.1),2,2),
      H3=diag(c(10^(-10), rep(0.1, 3)),4,4), R=diag(10^(-4),3,3),
      momedu=momedu, dadedu=dadedu, perteach=perteach,
      importnt= importnt, enjoy=enjoy)

# RUN CHAIN

# Initialize Model
adaptSteps = 5000
burnInSteps = 5000
nChains = 2
thinSteps = 50
nPerChain = 500000

semModel1 = jags.model("model.bug",data=Semdata1,n.chains=nChains, n.adapt=adaptSteps)

# Obtain the Posterior Sample of Factor Loadings:
parameter=c("a1","b1","c1","tau1","tau2","tau3","v","PI","var1","var2","var3")
#Specify the Parameters to Be Estimated
```

252

```r
cat("Burning in the MCMC chain ...\n")
update(semModel, n.iter=burnInSteps)
cat("Sampling from the final MCMC chain ... \n")
codaSamples1 = coda.samples(semModel, n.iter=nPerChain, variable.names=parameter,
                            thin=thinSteps,seed=5555)

summary(codaSamples1) #Posterior Mean, posterior SD and posterior probablity interval
(PPI)
                        #Note that tau1, tau2 and tau 3 are error precisions instead
of variances

plot(codaSamples1[[1]][,c(11,19,17,28)])                  #Trace plots and Density plots

par(mfrow=c(2,2))
acf(codaSamples1[[1]][,11],main="MATHSCORE on MOMEDU")           #Auto-correlation
plots
acf(codaSamples1[[1]][,19],main="IMPORTNT on MOMEDU")
acf(codaSamples1[[1]][,17],main="ENJOY on PERTEACH")
acf(codaSamples1[[1]][,28],main="Error Variance of MATHSCORE")

# Diagnostics
#Geweke Diagnostics and Plot
geweke.diag(codaSamples1[[1]][,c(11,19,17,28)])
geweke.plot(codaSamples1[[1]][,c(11,19,17,28)], frac1 = 0.1, frac2 = 0.5)

#Heidelberg-Welsh Diagnostic
heidel.diag(codaSamples1[[1]][,c(11,19,17,28)])
```

```
#Raftery.diag
raftery.diag(codaSamples1[[1]][,c(11,19,17,28)])

#-------------------------POSTERIOR PREDICTIVE CHECK----------------------#

#install.package(ggplot2)
#install.package(gridExtra)
#install.package(sem)
library(ggplot2)
library(gridExtra)
library(MASS)
library(sem)

semdf <- data.frame(momedu = semdata$momeduc, dadedu = semdata$dadeduc,
    perteach = semdata$perteach, enjoy = semdata$enjoy, importnt = semdata$importnt,
    y = semdata$mathscor)

sim.y.reps <- function(x) {

#---grab the xth draw from the posterior---#
x <- codaSamples1[[1]][x,1:27]
names(x) <- c(paste("PI",1:9,sep = ""),"mu.y","beta.ym","beta.yd","beta.yp","beta.
    yi","beta.ye","mu. "mu.i","beta.im","beta.ip","beta.ie",paste("tau",1:3,
    sep = ""),paste("v",1:3,sep=""))

# Model Implied Covariance Matrix--#
```

254

```r
#--inverse of precision matrix obtains X covariance matrix--#
sigma.xx <- solve(matrix(x[1:9],nrow = 3, ncol = 3), byrow = TRUE)

#---Beta Matrix---#
beta.enjoy <- c(0,0,0)
beta.imp <- c(x["beta.ie"],0,0)
beta.math <- c(x["beta.ye"],x["beta.yi"],0)
beta.mat <- matrix(rbind(beta.enjoy,beta.imp,beta.math),nrow = 3, ncol = 3)

#---Gamma Matrix---#
gamma.enjoy <- c(0,0,x["beta.ep"])
gamma.imp <- c(x["beta.im"],0,x["beta.ip"])
gamma.math <- c(x["beta.ym"],x["beta.yd"],x["beta.yp"])
gamma.mat <- matrix(rbind(gamma.enjoy,gamma.imp,gamma.math), nrow = 3, ncol = 3)

#---Structural to Regression conversions---#
err.vect <- c(1/x["tau2"],1/x["tau3"],1/x["tau1"]) ###--Y structural form variances--#
inv.beta <- solve(diag(3) - beta.mat) ###--I minus Beta inverse--#
PI <- inv.beta %*% gamma.mat
alpha <- inv.beta %*% c(x["mu.e"],x["mu.i"],x["mu.y"])
exp.x <- c(x["v1"],x["v2"],x["v3"]) ##--expected value of the X variables--#

exp.y <- alpha + PI %*% exp.x
sigma.yy <- PI %*% sigma.xx %*% t(PI) + inv.beta %*% diag(err.vect) %*% t(inv.beta)
sigma.xy <- sigma.xx %*% t(PI)
```

```
#---Need the replicated X variables first---#
x.rep <- mvrnorm(nrow(semdf),exp.x,sigma.xx)

#---Obtain the replicated Y variables next---#
error.mat <- inv.beta %*%
matrix(
c(rnorm(nrow(semdf),0,sqrt(err.vect[1])),
rnorm(nrow(semdf),0,sqrt(err.vect[2])),
rnorm(nrow(semdf),0,sqrt(err.vect[3]))),
nrow = 3, ncol = nrow(semdf), byrow = TRUE)
y.rep <- matrix(
c(rep(alpha[1],nrow(semdf)),
rep(alpha[2],nrow(semdf)),
rep(alpha[3],nrow(semdf))),
nrow = 3, ncol = nrow(semdf), byrow = TRUE) +
(PI %*% t(x.rep)) +
error.mat

#---Use these to double check matrix alebra, as they should give the same thing as
above---#
enjoy <- x["mu.e"] + x["beta.ep"]*x.rep[,3] + rnorm(length(semdata$perteach),0,
sqrt(1/x["tau2"]))
importnt <- x["mu.i"] + x["beta.im"]*x.rep[,1] + x["beta.ip"]*x.rep[,3] + x["beta.
ie"]*enjoy
+ rnorm(length(semdata$perteach),0,sqrt(1/x["tau3"]))
```

256

```
y <- x["mu.y"] + x["beta.ym"]*x.rep[,1] + x["beta.yd"]*x.rep[,2] + x["beta.yp"]*x.
rep[,3]
+
x["beta.yi"]*importnt + x["beta.ye"]*enjoy + rnorm(length(semdata$perteach),0,
sqrt(1/x["tau1"]))

#--Two replicates, one using matrix, one using single line equations (df1 used for
double checking)---#
rep.sem.df1 <- data.frame(momedu = x.rep[,1], dadedu = x.rep[,2], perteach = x.rep[,3],
enjoy = enjoy, importnt = importnt, y = y)
rep.sem.df <- data.frame(momedu = x.rep[,1], dadedu = x.rep[,2], perteach = x.rep[,3],
enjoy = y.rep[1,], importnt = y.rep[2,], y = y.rep[3,])

#--we have three covariance matrices, MODEL, OBSERVED, REPLICATED---#
obs.cov.mat <- cov(semdf)
rep.cov.mat <- cov(rep.sem.df)
mod.cov.mat <- rbind(cbind(sigma.xx,sigma.xy),cbind(t(sigma.xy),sigma.yy))
dimnames(mod.cov.mat) <- dimnames(obs.cov.mat)

#--optional plots to check to make sure the replicates look correct---#
#q1 <- qplot(semdf[,4], main = "enjoy (Observed)"); q2 <- qplot(semdf[,5], main =
"important
(Observed)"); q3 <- qplot(semdf[,6], main = "math score (Observed)")
#q4 <- qplot(y.rep[1,], main = "enjoy (Replicated)"); q5 <- qplot(y.rep[2,], main =
"important (Replicated)"); q6 <- qplot(y.rep[3,], main = "math score (Replicated)")
#pdf(file=' ') ####ADD FILE PATH#####
```

```
#print(grid.arrange(q1,q2,q3,q4,q5,q6, ncol = 3, nrow = 2))
#dev.off()

#q1 <- qplot(x = rep.sem.df1$y, y = rep.sem.df1$enjoy) + stat_smooth(method = "lm")
#q2 <- qplot(x = rep.sem.df$y, y = rep.sem.df$enjoy) + stat_smooth(method = "lm")
#q3 <- qplot(x = rep.sem.df1$importnt, y = rep.sem.df$importnt)
#print(grid.arrange(q1,q2, ncol = 2))

#q1 <- qplot(semdf[,1], main = "momedu (Observed)"); q2 <- qplot(semdf[,2], main =
"dadedu (Observed)"); q3 <- qplot(semdf[,3], main = "perteach (Observed)")
#q4 <- qplot(x.rep[,1], main = "momedu (Replicated)"); q5 <- qplot(x.rep[,2], main
= "dadedu (Replicated)"); q6 <- qplot(x.rep[,3], main = "perteach (Replicated)")
#pdf(file=' ') ####ADD FILE PATH#####
#print(grid.arrange(q1,q2,q3,q4,q5,q6, ncol = 3, nrow = 2))
#dev.off()

#---Optional for printing out the differing covariances matrices to visually check
their accuracy---#
#print("OBS")
#print(obs.cov.mat)
#print("REP")
#print(rep.cov.mat)
#print("MODEL")
#print(mod.cov.mat)

# End Model Implied Covariance Matrix #
```

```
#----Calculate the observed and replicated CHI-SQUARE values using the model implied
covariance matrix-----#
chi.sq.obs <- 0.5*nrow(semdf)*(determinant(mod.cov.mat)$modulus +
## note: determinant(x)$modulus returns log of the determinant of x
sum(diag( ##gets the trace
solve(mod.cov.mat) %*% (obs.cov.mat +
(c(exp.x,exp.y) - colMeans(semdf)) %*% t(c(exp.x,exp.y) - colMeans(semdf)) ##mean matrix
) )
) ) -
determinant(obs.cov.mat)$modulus - 6 ### p + q = 6?
)##END CHI.SQ calculation
chi.sq.rep <- 0.5*nrow(rep.sem.df)*(determinant(mod.cov.mat)$modulus + ## note:
determinant(x)$modul returns log of the determinant of x
sum(diag( ##gets the trace
solve(mod.cov.mat) %*% (rep.cov.mat +
(c(exp.x,exp.y) - colMeans(rep.sem.df)) %*% t(c(exp.x,exp.y) - colMeans(rep.sem.df))
##mean matrix
) )
) ) -
determinant(rep.cov.mat)$modulus - 6 ### p + q = 6?
)##END CHI.SQ calculation

return(list(rep.sem.df,c(chi.sq.obs,chi.sq.rep)))

}##END function sim.y.reps
```

```r
##RUN THE POSTERIOR FUNCTIONS
#rand.seed <- round(runif(1,1,10000),0)
#set.seed(rand.seed)
set.seed(515)
y.rep <- lapply(1:1000, sim.y.reps)
chi.sq <- cbind(unlist(lapply(y.rep,function(x) return(x[[2]][1])),unlist(lapply(y.
rep,function(x)
return(x[[2]][2]))))
chi.rep <- chi.sq[,2]
chi.obs <- chi.sq[,1]

##SAVE PDF POSTERIOR CHECKING PLOTS
liks.dif <- chi.obs - chi.rep
range <- max(liks.dif) - min(liks.dif)
p.value <- round(length(which(liks.dif < 0))/length(liks.dif),3)
pdf(file=' ') ####ADD FILE PATH#####
par(ask = FALSE)
hist(liks.dif, xlab = expression(Chi["obs"]^2 - Chi["rep"]^2), main = "")
abline(v = 0, lty = 2, lwd = 2)
text(x = min(liks.dif) + range/5, y = 200, label = paste("p-value = ",p.value,sep =
""))
dev.off()
pdf(file=' ') #ADD FILE PATH
qplot(chi.obs,chi.rep, shape = I(1)) +
geom_abline(slope = 1, intercept = 0) +
theme_bw() +
```

```r
geom_text(aes(x = -2 + min(chi.obs,chi.rep) , y = - 2 + max(chi.obs,chi.rep), label
= paste("p-value =",p.value)), size = 4.5) +
theme(panel.grid.major = element_blank(), panel.grid.minor = element_blank()) +
ylim(c(-7 + min(chi.obs,chi.rep),max(chi.obs,chi.rep))) +
xlim(c(-7 + min(chi.obs,chi.rep),max(chi.obs,chi.rep))) +
xlab("Observed") + ylab("Replicated")
dev.off()

##DISPLAY POSTERIOR CHECKING PLOTS & INFORMATION
hist(liks.dif, xlab = expression(Chi["obs"]^2 - Chi["rep"]^2), main = "")
abline(v = 0, lty = 2, lwd = 2)
text(x = min(liks.dif) + range/5, y = 200, label = paste("p-value = ",p.value,sep =
""))

par(ask = TRUE)
qplot(chi.obs,chi.rep, shape = I(1)) +
geom_abline(slope = 1, intercept = 0) +
theme_bw() +
geom_text(aes(x = -2 + min(chi.obs,chi.rep) , y = - 2 + max(chi.obs,chi.rep), label
= paste("p-value =",p.value)), size = 4.5) +
#theme(panel.grid.major = element_blank()) +
ylim(c(-7 + min(chi.obs,chi.rep),max(chi.obs,chi.rep))) +
xlim(c(-7 + min(chi.obs,chi.rep),max(chi.obs,chi.rep))) +
xlab("Observed") + ylab("Replicated")
```

```
#--------------------------------------------------------------
# Example 9.3 Multilevel Path Analysis--Noninformative Prior
#
# Programming steps the same as in Example 9.2 except that we loop
# over students i and schools g
#--------------------------------------------------------------

install.packages("rjags")
require(rjags)

##Specify model
modelstring = "
model {
#subject-level models
for (i in 1:nData)
{
for(j in (sch_order[i]):(sch_order[i]))
{
y[i]~dnorm(mu1[i],tau1)
mu1[i]<- a0[j,1] + a1[1]*momedu[i] + a1[2]*dadedu[i]+a1[3]*perteach[i]+
         a2*importnt[i]+a0[j,2]*enjoy[i]

enjoy[i]~dnorm(mu2[i], tau2)
mu2[i]<-b0[j]+b1*perteach[i]

importnt[i]~dnorm(mu3[i], tau3)
```

262

```
mu3[i]<-c0[j]+c1[1]*momedu[i]+c1[2]*perteach[i]+c2*enjoy[i]
     }
   }

# school level models
for(j in 1:G){

a0[j,1:2]~dmnorm(z[j,1:2],phi[1:2,1:2])

z[j,1]<- m[1]+ A[1]*newmetho[j] + A[2]*enthusia[j] + A[3]*cnsensus[j]
        + A[4]*cndition[j]+ A[5]*encourag[j]
z[j,2]<- m[2]+ B[1]*newmetho[j] + B[2]*enthusia[j] + B[3]*cnsensus[j]
        + B[4]*cndition[j]+ B[5]*encourag[j]

b0[j]~ dnorm(v[j],psi)
v[j]<- m[3]+ C[1]*newmetho[j] + C[2]*enthusia[j] + C[3]*cnsensus[j]
        + C[4]*cndition[j]+ C[5]*encourag[j]

c0[j]~ dnorm(w[j],xi)
w[j]<- m[4]+D[1]*newmetho[j] + D[2]*enthusia[j] + D[3]*cnsensus[j]
        + D[4]*cndition[j]+ D[5]*encourag[j]

encourag[j]~dnorm(r[j],pi)
r[j]<-m[5]+E*enthusia[j]

enthusia[j]~dnorm(p[j],delta)
```

263

```
p[j]<-m[6]+F[1]*newmetho[j]+F[2]*cnsensus[j]+ F[3]*cndition[j]

}

# Prior Specification

# Priors on regression coefficients
m[1:6]  ~ dmnorm(u1[1:6], H1[1:6,1:6])  # H1 is prior precision matrix.
A[1:5]  ~ dmnorm(u2[1:5], H2[1:5,1:5])
B[1:5]  ~ dmnorm(u3[1:5], H3[1:5,1:5])
C[1:5]  ~ dmnorm(u4[1:5], H4[1:5,1:5])
D[1:5]  ~ dmnorm(u5[1:5], H5[1:5,1:5])
E  ~ dnorm(u6,H6)
F[1:3]  ~ dmnorm(u7[1:3], H7[1:3,1:3])
a1[1:3] ~ dmnorm(u8[1:3], H8[1:3,1:3])
a2~dnorm(u9,H9)
b1  ~ dnorm(u10, H10)
c1[1:2] ~ dmnorm(u11[1:2], H11[1:2,1:2])
c2~dnorm(u12,H12)

#Priors on Precisions
tau1 ~ dgamma(0.001,0.001)
tau2 ~ dgamma(0.001,0.001)
tau3 ~ dgamma(0.001,0.001)

phi[1:2,1:2] ~ dwish(R1[1:2,1:2], 2) # Precision matrix
```

264

```
psi ~ dgamma(0.001,0.001)

xi ~ dgamma(0.001,0.001)
pi ~ dgamma(0.001,0.001)
delta ~ dgamma(0.001,0.001)
}
"

writeLines(modelstring,con="model.bug")

# READ IN DATA AND PREPARE FOR JAGS

semdata <- read.csv(file.choose(),header=TRUE) #browse to select data "PISA2003.semmodel.
csv" (using regression imputation).
#colnames(semdata)

y        <- semdata$mathscor
momedu   <- semdata$momeduc
dadedu   <- semdata$dadeduc
perteach <- semdata$perteach
importnt <- semdata$importnt
enjoy    <- semdata$enjoy
newmetho <- semdata$newmetho
enthusia <- semdata$enthusia
cnsensus <- semdata$cnsensus
cndition <- semdata$cndition
encourag <- semdata$encourag
schoolid <- semdata$schoolid
nData<-NROW(y)
```

265

```
# Calculate the order of the school that each student belongs to
# n[g] is the number of student within the g_th school  (unequal school sizes)

sch_id<-unique(schoolid)
rk<-rank(sch_id)
G<-length(sch_id) #number of schools = G
sch_order<-rep(0,nrow(semdata))
n<-rep(0,G) #initialize n for(g in 1:G)
{
  n[g]<-sum(schoolid==sch_id[g]) #n[g] is the sample size of school g
  sch_order[schoolid==sch_id[g]]=rep(rk[g],n[g])
}

# Specify parameters
semdata <- list(y=y, G=G, sch_order=sch_order,nData=nData, R1=diag(1,2,2),
         u1=rep(0,6),u2=rep(0,5),u3=rep(0,5),u4=rep(0,5),u5=rep(0,5),
         u6=rep(0,1),u7=rep(0,3), u8=rep(0,3),u9=rep(0,1),u10=rep(0,1),
         u11=rep(0,2),u12=rep(0,1),
         H1=diag(10^(-1),6,6),H2=diag(10^(-1),5,5),H3=diag(10^(-1),5,5),
         H4=diag(10^(-1),5,5),H5=diag(10^(-1),5,5),
         H6=diag(10^(-1),1,1),H7=diag(10^(-1),3,3),H8=diag(10^(-1),3,3),
         H9=diag(10^(-1),1,1),H10=diag(10^(-1),1,1),
         H11=diag(10^(-1),2,2),H12=diag(10^(-1),1,1),
         momedu=momedu, dadedu=dadedu, perteach=perteach, importnt= importnt,
         enjoy=enjoy, newmetho=newmetho, enthusia=enthusia, cnsensus=cnsensus,
         cndition=cndition, encourag=encourag)
```

266

```
# RUN CHAIN

# Initialize Model
adaptSteps = 5000
burnInSteps = 5000
nChains = 2
thinSteps = 1000
nPerChain = 1000000

semModel1 = jags.model("model.bug",data=semdata,n.chains=nChains, n.adapt=adaptSteps)

# Obtain the Posterior Sample of Factor Loadings:
parameter=c("m","A","B","C","D","E","F","a1","a2","b1","c1","c2","tau1","tau2","tau3",
            "phi","psi","xi","pi","delta") #Specify the Parameters to Be Estimated
cat("Burning in the MCMC chain ...\n")
update(semModel1, n.iter=burnInSteps)
cat("Sampling from the final MCMC chain ... \n")
codaSamples1 = coda.samples(semModel1, n.iter=nPerChain, variable.names=parameter,
                            thin=thinSteps,seed=5555)

summary(codaSamples1[[1]])        #Posterior Mean, posterior SD and posterior probablity
interval (PPI)

#Transform precision matrix of random effects to variance-covariance matrix
phi11<-codaSamples1[[1]][,40]
phi21<-codaSamples1[[1]][,41]
```

```
phi12<-codaSamples1[[1]][,42]
phi22<-codaSamples1[[1]][,43]

Sigma11 <- phi22/(phi11*phi22-phi21^2) #Sigma is covariance matrix
Sigma21 <- phi12/(phi11*phi22-phi21^2)
Sigma22 <- phi11/(phi11*phi22-phi21^2)
Sigma12 <- Sigma21

summary(Sigma11) #Posterior mean, SD and PPI of variance of random intercept
summary(Sigma22) #Posterior mean, SD and PPI of variance of random slope

plot((codaSamples1[,c(25, 6, 43, 46)]))            #Trace plots and Density plots

par(mfrow=c(2,2))
acf(codaSamples1[[1]][,25],main="MATHSCORE on MOMEDU")           #Auto-correlation
plots acf(codaSamples1[[1]][,6],main="Slope of ENJOY on NEWMETHOD")
acf(Sigma22,main="Variance of Random Slope of ENJOY")
acf(codaSamples1[[1]][,46],main="Error Precison of MATHSCORE")

require(coda)
geweke.plot(codaSamples1[[1]][,c(25, 6, 43, 46)])
geweke.diag(codaSamples1[[1]][,c(25, 6, 43, 46)])

#Heidelberger-Welch diagnostics
heidel.diag(codaSamples1[[1]][,c(25, 6, 43, 46)])
```

```
#Raftery.diag
raftery.diag(codaSamples1[[1]][,c(25, 6, 43, 46)])

#---------------------------------------------------------------
# Example 9.3 Bayesian GCM: Baseline model
#
# Programming steps similar to Example 9.3. Note
# fixing of parameters to yield slope and intercept of growth curve
#---------------------------------------------------------------
install.packages("rjags")
require(rjags)    #load the package "rjags"

###Noninformative Prior###
##Specify model
modelstring = "
model {
for (i in 1 : nData) {
for (j in 1 : 5) {          # NCOL(y) = 5
y[i,j] ~ dnorm(mu[i,j],psi[j])
}

mu[i,1] <- 1*xi[i,1]+ 0*xi[i,2]       # xi[i,1] Random Intercept, Initial Status
mu[i,2] <- 1*xi[i,1]+ 1*xi[i,2]                  # xi[i,2]: Random Slope, Growth Rate
mu[i,3] <- 1*xi[i,1]+ 2*xi[i,2]
mu[i,4] <- 1*xi[i,1]+ 3*xi[i,2]
mu[i,5] <- 1*xi[i,1]+ 4*xi[i,2]
```

269

```
xi[i,1:2] ~ dmnorm(v[1:2],phi[1:2,1:2])

}

# Distributions and Priors
#Priors on Precisions

for(j in 1:5) {
psi[j] ~ dgamma(1, 0.001)  # Error Precision
sgm[j] <- 1/psi[j]          # Error variance
}

v[1] ~ dnorm(0, 10^(-6)) #Factor mean, i.e., mean of intercept here
v[2] ~ dnorm(0, 10^(-6)) #Factor mean, i.e., mean of slope here

phi[1:2,1:2] ~ dwish(R[1:2,1:2], 5)                    #phi is precision matrix of factors
Sigma[1,1] <- phi[2,2]/(phi[1,1]*phi[2,2]-phi[2,1]^2)  #Sigma is covariance matrix of
factors
Sigma[2,1] <- -phi[1,2]/(phi[1,1]*phi[2,2]-phi[2,1]^2)
Sigma[2,2] <- phi[1,1]/(phi[1,1]*phi[2,2]-phi[2,1]^2)
Sigma[1,2] <- Sigma[2,1]

}
"

writeLines(modelstring,con="model.bug")

# READ IN DATA AND PREPARE FOR JAGS
```

```
gcmdata = read.csv(file.choose(),header=TRUE) #browse to select data "lsay_ex.csv".
y = as.matrix(gcmdata)
gender = gcmdata$gender
nData=NROW(y)

#Specify parameters
R<-matrix(c(1,0,0,1),nrow=2)
gcmdat <- list(y=y, nData=nData, R=R)

# RUN CHAIN

# Initialize Model
parameters = c("v","Sigma","sgm") #Specify the Parameters to Be Estimated
adaptSteps = 5000
burnInSteps = 5000
nChains = 2
thinSteps = 100
nPerChain = 100000

gcmModel1 = jags.model("model.bug",data=gcmdat,n.chains=nChains, n.adapt=adaptSteps)

# Obtain the Posterior Sample of Factor Loadings:

cat("Burning in the MCMC chain ...\n")
update(gcmModel1, n.iter=burnInSteps)
cat("Sampling from the final MCMC chain ...  \n")
```

```r
codaSamples1 = coda.samples(gcmModel1, variable.names=parameters,
n.iter=nPerChain, thin=thinSteps,seed=5555)

summary(codaSamples1[[1]])      #Posterior Mean, posterior SD and posterior probablity
interval (PPI) for the first chain

plot(codaSamples1[[1]][,c(10,11,1,2)])  #Selected Trace plots and Density plots

par(mfrow=c(2,2))
acf(codaSamples1[[1]][,10],  main="Fixed Slope of Time")     #Auto-correlation plots
acf(codaSamples1[[1]][,11],  main="Fixed Intercept")
acf(codaSamples1[[1]][,1],  main="Variance of Random Intercept")
acf(codaSamples1[[1]][,2],  main="Covariance of Random Intercept & Random Slope")

# Diagnostics
#Geweke Diagnostic and Plot

geweke.diag(codaSamples1[[1]])
geweke.plot(codaSamples1[[1]][,c(10,11,1,2)])

#Heidelberger-Welch diagnostics
heidel.diag(codaSamples1[[1]])

#Raftery.diag
raftery.diag(codaSamples1[[1]])
```

272

```
#--------------------------------------------------------------------
# Example 9.4 Bayesian GCM: With predictor
#
# Programming steps similar to Example 9.3. Note
# models for random intercept and random slope as functions of
# gender
#--------------------------------------------------------------------

require(rjags)   #load the package "rjags"

###Noninformative Prior####
##Specify model
modelstring = "
model {
for (i in 1 : nData) {
for (j in 1 : 5) {            # NCOL(y) = 5
y[i,j] ~ dnorm(mu[i,j],psi[j])
}

mu[i,1]  <- 1*xi[i,1]+ 0*xi[i,2]           # xi[i,1]: Random Intercept, Initial Status
mu[i,2]  <- 1*xi[i,1]+ 1*xi[i,2]                # xi[i,2]: Random Slope, Growth Rate
mu[i,3]  <- 1*xi[i,1]+ 2*xi[i,2]
mu[i,4]  <- 1*xi[i,1]+ 3*xi[i,2]
mu[i,5]  <- 1*xi[i,1]+ 4*xi[i,2]

xi[i,1]  <- alpha1+ beta1*gender[i]+ eta[i,1] #Model for random intercept
```

```
xi[i,2] <- alpha2+ beta2*gender[i]+ eta[i,2]  # Model for random slope

eta[i,1:2] ~ dmnorm(v[1:2],phi[1:2,1:2])
}

# Distributions and Priors

#Priors on Precisions
for(j in 1:5) {
psi[j] ~ dgamma(1, 0.001)  # Error Precision
sgm[j] <- 1/psi[j]         # Error variance
}

alpha1 ~ dnorm(0, 10^(-6))  #Mean of intercept
alpha2 ~ dnorm(0, 10^(-6))  #Mean of slope
beta1 ~ dnorm(0, 10^(-6))   #Intercept on gender
beta2 ~ dnorm(0, 10^(-6))   #Slope on gender

phi[1:2,1:2] ~ dwish(R[1:2,1:2], 5)                           #phi is precision matrix of
factors
Sigma[1,1] <- phi[2,2]/(phi[1,1]*phi[2,2]-phi[2,1]^2) #Sigma is covariance matrix of
factors
Sigma[2,1] <- -phi[1,2]/(phi[1,1]*phi[2,2]-phi[2,1]^2)
Sigma[2,2] <- phi[1,1]/(phi[1,1]*phi[2,2]-phi[2,1]^2)
Sigma[1,2] <- Sigma[2,1]
```

```
}
"

writeLines(modelstring,con="model.bug")

# READ IN DATA AND PREPARE FOR JAGS

gcmdata = read.csv(file.choose(),header=TRUE)  #browse to select data "lsay_ex.csv".
y = as.matrix(gcmdata[,2:6])
gender = gcmdata$gender
nData=NROW(y)

#Specify parameters
v<-c(0,0)
R<-matrix(c(1,0,0,1),nrow=2)
gcmdat <- list(y=y, gender=gender, nData=nData, v=v, R=R)

# RUN CHAIN

# Initialize Model
parameters = c("alpha1", "alpha2", "beta1","beta2","Sigma","sgm") #Specify the Parameters
to Be Estimated
adaptSteps = 5000
burnInSteps = 5000
nChains = 2
thinSteps = 100
nPerChain = 100000
```

```r
gcmModel2 = jags.model("model.bug",data=gcmdat,n.chains=nChains, n.adapt=adaptSteps)

# Obtain the Posterior Sample #

cat("Burning in the MCMC chain ...\n")
update(gcmModel2, n.iter=burnInSteps)
cat("Sampling from the final MCMC chain ... \n")
codaSamples2 = coda.samples(gcmModel2, variable.names=parameters,
n.iter=nPerChain, thin=thinSteps,seed=5555)

summary(codaSamples2[[1]])        #Posterior Mean, posterior SD and posterior probablity
interval (PPI) for the first chain

plot(codaSamples2[[1]][,c(7,8,1,4)]) #Selected Trace plots and Density plots

par(mfrow=c(2,2))
acf(codaSamples2[[1]][,7],main="Intercept on Gender")        #Auto-correlation plots
acf(codaSamples2[[1]][,8],main="Slope on Gender")
acf(codaSamples2[[1]][,1],main="Variance of Random Intercept")
acf(codaSamples2[[1]][,4],main="Variance of Random Slope")

# Diagnostics
#Geweke Diagnostic and Plot
require(coda)

geweke.diag(codaSamples2[[1]])
```

```r
geweke.plot(codaSamples2[[1]][,c(7,8,1,4)])

#Heidelberger-Welch diagnostics
heidel.diag(codaSamples2[[1]])

#Raftery.diag
raftery.diag(codaSamples2[[1]])

#-----------------------------------------------------------
# Example 9.5 Bayesian Mixture Factor Analysis
#
# Programming stepts are similar to Example 9.1. Note
# the discrete categorical distribution "dcat" used to specify a
# categorical distribution with K categories (here 2). Note also
# that the parameter pi of the categorical distribution is given
# a Dirichelet distribution with hyperparameter alpha.
#-----------------------------------------------------------

require(rjags) #load the package "rjags"

# Noninformative Prior
# Specify model
modelstring = "
model {
for (i in 1 : nData) {
```

```
for (j in 1 : 13) {          # NCOL(y) = 13
y[i,j] ~ dnorm(mu[i,j],psi[L[i],j])
}

mu[i,1]  <- 1*xi[i,1] # Factor 1,  lam[1]=1
mu[i,3]  <- lam[L[i],3]*xi[i,1]
mu[i,5]  <- lam[L[i],5]*xi[i,1]
mu[i,6]  <- lam[L[i],6]*xi[i,1]
mu[i,9]  <- lam[L[i],9]*xi[i,1]
mu[i,11] <-lam[L[i],11]*xi[i,1]
mu[i,13] <-lam[L[i],13]*xi[i,1]

mu[i,2]  <-1*xi[i,2]          # Factor 2,  lam[2]=1
mu[i,4]  <- lam[L[i],4]*xi[i,2]
mu[i,7]  <- lam[L[i],7]*xi[i,2]
mu[i,8]  <- lam[L[i],8]*xi[i,2]
mu[i,10] <-lam[L[i],10]*xi[i,2]
mu[i,12] <-lam[L[i],12]*xi[i,2]

L[i]~dcat(pi[1:K])   # Define a categorical distribution

xi[i,1:2]  ~ dmnorm(u[1:2],phi[1:2,1:2])
}

# Distributions and Priors
```

```
#Priors on Loadings
lam[1]<-1

lam[3]  ~  dnorm(0,  10^(-6))    #prior mean and prior precision
lam[5]  ~  dnorm(0,  10^(-6))
lam[6]  ~  dnorm(0,  10^(-6))
lam[9]  ~  dnorm(0,  10^(-6))
lam[11] ~  dnorm(0,  10^(-6))
lam[13] ~  dnorm(0,  10^(-6))

lam[2]<-1
lam[4]  ~  dnorm(0,  10^(-6))
lam[7]  ~  dnorm(0,  10^(-6))
lam[8]  ~  dnorm(0,  10^(-6))
lam[10] ~  dnorm(0,  10^(-6))
lam[12] ~  dnorm(0,  10^(-6))

# Priors on Precisions
for(j in 1:13) {
psi[j] ~ dgamma(1, 0.001) # Error variances
sgm[j] <- 1/psi[j]
}

phi[1:2,1:2] ~ dwish(R[1:2,1:2], 5) # Precision matrix

Sigma[1,1] <- phi[2,2]/(phi[1,1]*phi[2,2]-phi[2,1]^2) #Sigma is covariance matrix
Sigma[2,1] <- -phi[1,2]/(phi[1,1]*phi[2,2]-phi[2,1]^2)
Sigma[2,2] <- phi[1,1]/(phi[1,1]*phi[2,2]-phi[2,1]^2)
Sigma[1,2] <- Sigma[2,1]
```

```
# Priors on mixture probability
pi[1:K] ~ ddirch(alpha[])
for (j in 1:K) {alpha[j]<-1}
}
"

writeLines(modelstring,con="model.bug")

# READ IN DATA AND PREPARE FOR JAGS

cfadata = read.csv(file.choose(),header=TRUE) #browse to select data "cfa_imputed.csv"
(using regression imputation).
y = as.matrix(cfadata)
nData=NROW(y)

#Specify parameters
u=c(0,0)
R=matrix(c(1,0,0,1),nrow=2)
K=2;
cfd <- list(y=y, nData=nData, u=u, R=R, K=K)

# RUN CHAIN

# Initialize Model
parameters = c("lam","sgm","Sigma","pi") #Specify the Parameters to Be Estimated
adaptSteps = 5000
burnInSteps = 5000
```

```
nChains = 2
thinSteps = 500
nPerChain = 500000

cfaModel1 = jags.model("model.bug",data=cfd,n.chains=nChains, n.adapt=adaptSteps)

# Obtain the Posterior Samples #

cat("Burning in the MCMC chain ...\n")
update(cfaModel1, n.iter=burnInSteps)
cat("Sampling from the final MCMC chain ... \n")
codaSamples1 = coda.samples(cfaModel1, variable.names=parameters,
n.iter=nPerChain, thin=thinSteps,seed=5555)

summary(codaSamples1)    #Posterior Mean, posterior SD and posterior probablity interval
(PPI)

plot(codaSamples1[[1]][,c(9,1,2,37)])                    #Trace plots and Density plots
par(mfrow=c(2,2))
acf(codaSamples1[[1]][,9],main="Loadings of Item 3 in the First Latent Class")
#Auto-correlation plots
acf(codaSamples1[[1]][,1],main="Variance of Factor TEABEHA")
acf(codaSamples1[[1]][,2],main="Covariance betw TEABEHA & STUDBEHA")
acf(codaSamples1[[1]][,37],main="Error Variance of Item 3 in the First Latent Class")
```

281

```
# Diagnostics
# Geweke Diagnostics and Plot
require(coda)
geweke.diag(codaSamples1[[1]][,c(9,1,2,37)])
geweke.plot(codaSamples1[[1]][,c(9,1,2,37)])

# Heidelberger-Welch diagnostics
heidel.diag(codaSamples1[[1]][,c(9,1,2,37)])

# Raftery.diag
raftery.diag(codaSamples1[[1]][,c(9,1,2,37)])
```

282

10

Philosophical Debates in Bayesian Statistical Inference

The purpose of this book is to provide an accessible introduction to Bayesian statistical inference focused on common methods used in the social sciences, with examples drawn from education research. In the Preface I noted that Bayesian statistics represents a powerful alternative to frequentist (classical) statistics and is therefore controversial. Although this book did not seek to highlight the philosophical differences between these schools, a discussion of the key differences is important, and it seems that this is a good place to summarize those distinctions. Much has been written about the pros and cons of Bayesian and frequentist inference, and almost every book on Bayesian inference provides some introduction to the problem. The reason for pointing out these differences is that even though the results of a Bayesian analysis and frequentist analysis of the same data may provide "similar-looking" results, they are, in fact, different at a very fundamental level. Thus, "buying into" the Bayesian framework must come with a willingness to forego the paradigm of frequentist statistics that has so dominated research practice in the social sciences.

At its most fundamental level, the controversy lies in the differing perspectives regarding the nature of probability and the implications for statistical practice that arise from those perspectives. To reiterate, the frequentist framework views probability as synonymous with long-run frequency, and the infinitely repeating coin toss represents the canonical example of the frequentist view. All of frequentist statistical practice derives from the notion of probability as long-run frequency. Indeed frequentist statistical inference relies on asymptotic assumptions that derive from viewing probability as long-run frequency.

In contrast, the Bayesian viewpoint regarding probability is, perhaps, most succinctly expressed by de Finetti (1974) who stated, "Probability does not exist" (p. x). This simple quote by de Finetti concisely summarizes the main philosophical framework of Bayesian statistics—namely, that probability does not have an objective status, but rather represents the quantification of our experience of uncertainty. As discussed by de Finetti, the notion of probability as something external to the individual, possessing an objective status "out there," is superstition—no different from postulating the existence of "Cosmic Ether, Absolute Space and Time, . . . , or Fairies and Witches" (p. x). For de Finetti, probability is to be considered only in relation to our subjective experience of uncertainty, and, more strongly, for de Finetti, uncertainty is all that matters. Again, he states:

> The only relevant thing is uncertainty—the extent of our known knowledge and ignorance. The actual fact that events considered are, in some sense, determined, or known by other people, and so on, is of no consequence. (1974, p. xi)

The only requirement then is that our beliefs be coherent and consistent, and have a reasonable relationship to any observable data that might be collected.

Although Bayesians generally accept the notion that probability has an *epistemic* status and serves as a means of encoding our uncertain knowledge of the world around us, they have not reached universal consensus as to how, or even whether, subjective beliefs should enter into scientific investigations. Thus, we need to consider closely the distinction between *noninformative* prior probabilities and *informative* prior probabilities, and their respective roles in knowledge creation.

In this closing chapter I first summarize the essential differences between the frequentist and Bayesian frameworks that have been alluded to throughout this book. I then move to the essential debates within the Bayesian school. Specifically, I discuss the issue of subjective Bayesian analysis, focusing on ideas set forth by de Finetti, Savage, and Lindley. This is followed by a discussion of objective Bayesian statistics, with specific attention paid to the use of so-called *reference priors* as a means of attaining objectivity in Bayesian analyses. The chapter closes with an appeal to use—what I refer to as "evidence-based subjective Bayes," which represents an attempt to move toward the careful warranting of priors on the basis of empirical data.

10.1 A SUMMARY OF THE BAYESIAN VERSUS FREQUENTIST SCHOOLS OF STATISTICS

A nice summary of the distinctions between Bayesian and frequentist statistical inference can be found in Wagenmakers et al. (2008). Here, I select from their paper some of the more fundamental differences, followed by a discussion of the fundamental advantages of the Bayesian approach.

10.1.1 Conditioning on Data

An important distinction between the Bayesian and frequentist schools of statistics concerns the role that the observed data play in parameter estimation. Specifically, frequentist inference is based on a set of preexperimental/observational assumptions about the behavior of an estimator under (infinite) repeated sampling of the same experiment or observation under exactly the same conditions. These assumptions are embedded in conventional practice around concerns regarding sample sizes required for the results of statistical methods to be trustworthy. Rules of thumb have been provided for a variety of different procedures commonly used in the social sciences. These rules of thumb have been developed under frequentist procedures examining the behavior of estimators, and particularly their standard errors, under different sample size conditions and under a null hypothesis of a true model for an infinite sample size. Thus, in the frequentist practice of statistics, we warrant our conclusions about the validity of our findings from preexperimental/observational assumptions about the asymptotic behavior of an estimator.

The validity of inferences drawn from Bayesian analyses does not rely on claims regarding the asymptotic behavior of an estimator before any data are collected. Rather, Bayesian inference is based entirely on the posterior distribution of the parameters conditioning on the data in hand via Bayes' theorem, namely,

$$p(\theta|y) \propto L(\theta|y) \times p(\theta)$$

Notice that there is no appeal to pre-data asymptotics to support inferences about θ.

10.1.2 Inferences Based on Data Actually Observed

Similar to the problem of conditioning on data, frequentist inference rests on data that have not been observed. As pointed out by many others (see, e.g., Jeffreys, 1961, and more recently, Gigerenzer et al., 2004; Gigerenzer, 1993; and Wagenmakers et al., 2008), the frequentist p-value is properly interpreted as the probability of observing data at least as extreme as the data that were actually observed under the assumption that the null hypothesis is true. As Jeffreys (1961) stated,

> *What the use of the P value implies, therefore, is that a hypothesis that may be true may be rejected because it has not predicted observable results that have not occurred.* This seems a remarkable procedure. (p. 385, emphasis in original)

Moreover, as observed by Kadane (2011), considering that inferences are being drawn based on data that have not yet been observed, this is a violation of the likelihood principle. Again, by contrast, the Bayesian school concerns itself with inferences based on the data in hand, not on inferences to data that have never been observed.

Furthermore, as discussed at length in Chapter 5, the goal of hypothesis testing in the Bayesian framework is not to make statements in support or refutation of a null hypothesis, but rather to fully summarize the distribution of the parameters of interest and to examine the predictive quality of a proposed model. Posterior predictive checking provides a way of determining whether a model can predict data that actually have occurred.

10.1.3 Quantifying Evidence

Returning to the use of the frequentist p-value, recall that the frequentist framework uses the p-value as a means of quantifying evidence against a null hypothesis. Well-known guidelines have been formulated over the decades for establishing evidence against the null hypothesis, with the ubiquitous $p < .05$ having become the accepted standard in the social sciences. As Wagenmakers et al. (2008) point out, the problem with this approach is that if the p-value is a measure of evidence, then it should be applied equally across all sample sizes. This is referred to as the *p-value postulate*. That is, a study that achieved a p-value of, say, .05, based on a sample size of 10, constitutes just as much evidence against the null hypothesis as a study based on a sample size of 100. However, applied researchers in the social sciences have not reached agreement regarding this claim.[1] Indeed, there are those who believe that a significant p-value (say, .05) based on 10 observations provides stronger evidence against the null hypothesis than when it is based on 100 observations. Still others believe just the opposite.

The inconsistency regarding the p-value postulate stems from how "evidence" is defined. Specifically, a Bayesian perspective rejects the p-value postulate because the orientation of Bayesian hypothesis testing is to assign probabilities to proposed hypotheses. Taking two hypotheses, we assign posterior probabilities to these hypotheses and accept the hypothesis with the higher posterior probability. An equivalent summary of this approach is based on Bayes factors discussed in Chapter 5 (see also Jeffreys, 1961; Kass & Raftery, 1995).

10.1.4 Summarizing the Bayesian Advantage

The major distinctions that were outlined in the previous section are not exhaustive (see Wagenmakers et al., 2008, for a complete discussion). However, these distinctions do highlight important differences between the frequentist and Bayesian schools of statistical inference. The position taken throughout this book is that Bayesian statistical inference is superior to frequentist statistical inference along a number of dimen-

---

[1] However, as pointed out by Wagenmakers et al. (2008), Fisher himself held that the p-value postulate was correct.

sions. Again, borrowing from Wagenmakers et al. (2008), we find that the major advantages of Bayesian statistical inference over frequentist statistical inference are as follows.

Coherence

The rules of probability, as manifested in Bayes' theorem, cohere in such a way as to be internally consistent, providing only one method for obtaining an answer. The rules of probability along with Bayes' theorem are coherent because they align with axioms of rational decision making.

Handling Non-Nested Models

Bayesian hypothesis testing focuses on the marginal probability of the data given the kth model, that is,

$$p(y|M_k)$$

where $k = 1, 2, \ldots, K$. These marginal probabilities can be directly compared via Bayes factors which make no distinction between nested and non-nested models. This is particularly important in such methods as Bayesian SEM in which the frequentist-based likelihood ratio chi-square test requires that models be nested, whereas investigators may be interested in comparing quite different non-nested models.

Flexibility in Handling Complex Data Structures

Bayesian hierarchical models offer a flexible approach to the analysis of clustered samples. Although such methods are routinely and easily handled under the frequentist framework (see, e.g., Raudenbush & Bryk, 2002), the Bayesian perspective also clarifies the language of multilevel models. Specifically, extensive confusion surrounding the meaning of "fixed" versus "random" effects or "fixed" versus "random" coefficients is clarified under the Bayesian framework; all parameters are, by definition, unknown, with the resulting uncertainty encoded by prior probability distributions.

Marginalization

Bayesian inference conveniently allows the analyst to focus on the parameters of interest while integrating out parameters that are not of interest—the so-called *nuisance* parameter. In the example given by Wagenmakers et al. (2008), if interest centers on estimating the mean of the normal distribution μ, then σ might be considered a nuisance parameter. Thus, we are interested in summarizing the posterior distribution

$$p(\mu|y) = \int p(\mu, \sigma|y)d\sigma = \int p(\mu|\sigma, y)p(\sigma)d\sigma$$

Notice that this integration requires that σ be assigned a prior distribution, which would likely be assigned a non-informative prior (Wagenmakers et al., 2008).

Validity

Gigerenzer et al. (2004) have argued that Bayesian statistics provides inferences that the analyst actually cares about. Namely, researchers wish, and often report, results with respect to their hypotheses of interest. In other words, the analyst wishes to make statements about the probability of their particular hypothesis of interest. However, the Neyman–Pearson framework with its requirement of setting the probability of a Type I error ahead of collecting data, and the Fisherian framework of interpreting the *p*-value as the strength of evidence *against* the null hypothesis, both preclude this wish. However, the analyst's wish can come true using a Bayesian framework because it provides probability assessments of the scientific hypothesis actually under consideration.

Incorporating Prior Knowledge

Perhaps the singular advantage of the Bayesian school of statistics is that it provides a way to directly incorporate prior knowledge into a study. The frequentist school treats each study as if it is the first of its kind and as if no prior information is available on the topic at hand. However, even a casual consideration of standard frequentist practice reveals that a complete absence of prior information is patently untrue.

Perhaps the most obvious example within frequentist practice is the choice of variables to be included in a model. This choice is almost certainly made on the basis of prior information; but given that there are likely alternative interpretations of that prior information, the uncertainty in the choice is not made explicit. The Bayesian school, in stark contrast, incorporates prior knowledge into an analysis that is open to scrutiny by the scientific community and provides an immediate assessment of the analyst's view of the degree of uncertainty entering into his/her parameters and models.

Subjectivity

In a similar vein, the kind of prior knowledge that can be entered into a Bayesian framework can be "subjective" or "objective." This issue was discussed in the context of subjective and objective priors in Chapter 2. In the next section, we discuss the philosophical distinctions between the subjectivist school and the objectivist school of Bayesian statistics. Suffice to say that regardless of one's view on this matter, the fact is that Bayesian inference opens the black box of uncertainty by making explicit the manner in which priors are elicited and incorporated into the specification of statistical models.

10.2 SUBJECTIVE BAYES

An important discussion of the distinction between subjective and objective Bayesian statistics can be found in Press (2003). As mentioned earlier, subjective Bayesian practice attempts to bring prior knowledge directly into an analysis. This prior knowledge represents the analyst's (or others') degree of belief, which we prefer to consider as one's "degree of uncertainty." An analyst's degree of uncertainty is encoded directly into the specification of the prior distribution, and in particular on the degree of precision around the parameters of interest. For Press (2003), adopting subjective Bayesian practice has both advantages and disadvantages, which we summarize here. The advantages include:

1. Subjective priors are proper in the sense that they integrate (sum) to 1.0. This is in contrast to certain objective priors

such as the improper uniform distribution on the interval $[-\infty, +\infty]$.

2. The influence of a subjective prior on the posterior distribution is as if there were additional replications of data.

3. Almost by definition, a subjective prior is the only way that the analyst's background knowledge can be brought to bear on an analysis.

4. Objective and frequentist methods rely on fairly large sample sizes. Using subjective priors may be the only way that in the absence of large sample sizes a reliable analysis can be obtained.

Press (2003) cites the following disadvantages of using subjective priors:

1. It is not always easy to encode prior knowledge into probability distributions, indexed by the hyperparameters of prior distributions. This is particularly true for complex multiparameter models, such as structural equation models.

2. Subjective priors are not always appropriate in public policy or clinical situations. This is because other researchers as well as policy or clinical stakeholders may hold different priors.

3. Prior distributions may be analytically intractable unless they are conjugate priors. However, with the advent of flexible software programs, this is no longer a major concern.

10.3 OBJECTIVE BAYES

Having enumerated the advantages and disadvantages of the subjective Bayesian viewpoint, we turn our attention to the objective Bayesian viewpoint. Before beginning, however, it is important to point out that even within the framework of objective Bayesian statistics, there is disagreement about use of the term *objective* and the related term *noninformative*, particularly with respect to whether objective priors formally represent ignorance. Kass and Wasserman (1996) discuss this issue by noting two interpretations of objective priors. The first interpretation is that objective priors do, indeed, formally represent ignorance. However, given that there are a large number of objective priors to choose from, it is hard to justify that one objective prior is more "noninformative," in the sense of representing ignorance, than another. The second interpretation is more pragmatic: Objective priors are chosen with respect to how they perform in a particular situation under the specific aspects of the problem. Along the same lines, Berger (2006) points out at least four different philosophical positions on objective Bayes:

1. The major goal of statistics (indeed science) is to find a completely *coherent* objective Bayesian methodology for learning from data. This is exemplified by the attitudes of Jeffreys (1961) and Jaynes (1968).

2. Objective Bayesian analysis is the *best* method of objectively synthesizing and communicating the uncertainties that arise in a specific scenario, but is not necessarily coherent in a more general sense.

3. Objective Bayesian analysis is a convention we should adopt in scenarios in which a subjective analysis is not tenable.

4. Objective Bayesian analysis is simply a collection of ad hoc but useful methodologies for learning from data. (p. 386, emphasis in original)

Of these four viewpoints, Berger (2006) argues that viewpoint 4 is not debatable, as it is in line with the discussion of Kass and Wasserman (1996); viewpoint 1 is not attainable in practice; viewpoint 2 is attainable and should be put into practice as often as possible; but viewpoint 3 may be the best that can be accomplished in practice.

An important viewpoint regarding the notion of objectivity in the Bayesian context comes from Jaynes (1968). For Jaynes, the "personalistic" school of probability espoused by Savage (1954) is to be reserved for

the field of psychology and has no place in applied statistics. Or, to state this more constructively, objectivity requires that a statistical analysis should make use, not of anybody's personal opinions, but rather the specific factual data on which those opinions are based. (p. 228)

Both Jaynes (1968) and, later, Berger (2006) attack the practical problem of objective Bayes via the use of noninformative priors. But here, too, controversy surrounds use of the term *noninformative*. Specifically, a number of choices of prior distributions can be considered "noninformative," and these fall within the class of so-called *reference priors*—a term originally coined by Bernardo (1979) to reflect the goal of finding objective priors through a set of formal rules. The Jeffreys' prior discussed in Chapter 2 constitutes one of a number of reference priors that can be used for an objective Bayesian analysis. Others, not considered in this book, include the maximum entropy prior (Jaynes, 1968), the Berger–Bernardo method (Bernardo, 1979), and Zellner's method (Zellner, 1977), to name only three. An important summary of reference priors can be found in Kass and Wasserman (1996).

As with the discussion of subjective priors above, Press (2003) weighs the advantages and disadvantages of objective priors. In terms of advantages, Press (2003) notes:

1. Objective priors can be used as benchmarks against which choices of other priors can be compared.

2. Objective priors reflect the view that little information is available about the process that generated the data.

3. There are cases in which a Bayesian analysis with an objective prior provides results equivalent to those based on a frequentist analysis—though there are philosophical differences in interpretation that I allude to later in the chapter.

4. Objective priors are sensible public policy priors insofar as they allow for policy analysis without incorporating the prior knowledge of the analyst.

In terms of disadvantages, Press (2003) notes:

1. Objective priors can lead to improper results when the domain of the parameters lies on the real number line.

2. Parameters with objective priors are often independent of one another, whereas in most multiparameter statistical models, parameters are correlated. The problem of correlated model parameters is of extreme importance for methods such as

structural equation modeling (see, e.g., Kaplan & Wenger, 1993).

3. Expressing complete ignorance about a parameter via an objective prior leads to incorrect inferences about the functions of the parameter.

In a critique of objective priors Kadane (2011) states, among other things:

> The purpose of an algorithmic prior is to escape from the responsibility to give an opinion and justify it. At the same time, it cuts off a useful discussion about what is reasonable to believe about the parameters. Without such a discussion, appreciation of the posterior distribution of the parameters is likely to be less full, and important scientific information may be neglected. (p. 445)

10.4 FINAL THOUGHTS: A CALL FOR EVIDENCE-BASED SUBJECTIVE BAYES

Our discussion highlighted the distinctions between the subjectivist and objectivist positions within the Bayesian school. The subjectivist school, advocated by de Finetti, Savage, and others, allows for personal opinion to be elicited and incorporated into a Bayesian analysis. In the extreme, the subjectivist school would place no restriction on the source, reliability, or validity of the elicited opinion. The objectivist school, advocated by Jeffreys, Jaynes, Berger, Bernardo, and others, views personal opinion as in the realm of psychology, with no place in a statistical analysis. In their extreme form, the objectivist school would require formal rules for choosing reference priors. The difficulty with these positions lies with the everyday usage of terms such as *subjective* and *belief*. Without careful definitions of these terms, their everyday usage might be misunderstood among those who might otherwise consider adopting the Bayesian perspective. In science, we demand "objectivity," and we also require very careful, unambiguous definitions of the terms we use. Everyday usage of terms such as *belief* might appear to place Bayesian statistics on less than rigorous ground.

Within the Bayesian paradigm, however, the idea of "belief" is related to that of rational action under uncertainty. Within the field of Bayesian decision theory, a very complete set of axioms have been developed that relate belief to coherent action. These axioms of personal belief—or perhaps, as noted above, we should say "personal degrees of uncertainty"—and their relationship to coherent rational action are described in Bernardo and Smith (2000; see also Fishburn, 1986), but a discussion of those axioms is beyond the scope of this book.

"Subjectivism" within the Bayesian framework runs the gamut from the elicitation of personal beliefs to making use of the best available historical data available to inform priors. As Press (2003) points out, the use of "such 'best available' information can be incorporated into a *prior distribution*" (p. xxii, quotes and emphasis in original). Press goes on to say that "A Bayesian analysis using such a prior distribution is called *subjective* Bayesian analysis" (p. xxii, emphasis in original). I argue along the lines of Jaynes (1968)—namely, that the requirements of objective science demand reference to "specific, factual data on which those opinions are based" (p. 228). This view is also consistent with Leamer's (1978) hierarchy of confidence on which priors should be ordered. We may refer to this view as an *evidence-based* form of subjective Bayes. My choice of the term *evidence-based* reflects the goal of warranting the specification of priors against factual historical data when it exists, but acknowledges (1) the subjectivity that lies in the choice of historical data, (2) the encoding of historical data into hyperparameters of the prior distribution, and (3) the choice among competing models to be used to analyze the data.

The idea behind an *evidence-based* orientation toward subjective Bayes recognizes that there are very few, if any, situations in which a study is undertaken without reference to previous data. In Chapter 8, for example, we estimated a Bayesian hierarchical model using data from PISA 2009, wherein the priors were based on results from a similar model using data from PISA 2000. In this case, PISA is arguably a highly reliable and technically sophisticated international assessment of comparable schools and students over time. This specific example notwithstanding, the quality of the prior research can be made explicit by comparing the results of a Bayesian analysis that incorporates different priors—including reference priors as a baseline. The Bayesian toolkit has many methods for adjudicating among competing models, with the focus on what is arguably the hallmark of science—namely, prediction. Indeed, the importance of the predictive point of view for science generally and Bayesian statistics specifically has been discussed by Press

(2003) who argued for the importance of the predictive distribution (discussed in Chapter 5) as a means of comparing theories. More recently, Gelman and Shalizi (2013) argued that posterior predictive checking via the posterior predictive distribution places Bayesian practice squarely in the realm of the falsificationist philosophy of Popper (1934/1959).[2]

The question being begged is "What if factual historical data are not available?" I agree with Berger (2006) that reference priors should be used "in scenarios in which a subjective analysis is not tenable (p. 386)," although we believe that such scenarios are probably rare. The goal, nevertheless, is to shift the practice of Bayesian statistics away from the elicitation of personal opinion (expert or otherwise) which could, in principle, bias results toward a specific outcome and instead move Bayesian practice toward the warranted use of prior objective empirical data for the specification of priors. The specification of any prior should be explicitly warranted against observable, empirical data and should be available for critique by the relevant scholarly community.[3]

To conclude, we view the Bayesian school of statistical inference as entirely superior to the frequentist school as a means of creating and updating new knowledge in the social sciences. We argue that an evidence-based focus that ties the specification of priors to objective empirical data provides stronger warrants for conclusions drawn from a Bayesian analysis. In addition, we adhere to the importance of predictive criteria as a means of testing and choosing among Bayesian models. As always, the full benefit of the Bayesian approach to research in the social sciences will be realized when it is more widely adopted and yields reliable predictions that advance knowledge.

---

[2] The Gelman and Shalizi (2013) article goes much further and develops a critique against the inductive strain of Bayesian practice that focuses on learning about general patterns from particular instances. It is beyond the scope of this section to summarize their important article.

[3] If experts are consulted to elicit a prior, they should be required to provide objective empirical data to support their opinions, and their sources should also be made available for critique.

References

Asparouhov, T., & Muthén, B. (2010). *Bayesian analysis using Mplus: Technical implementation*. Unpublished manuscript.

Bauwens, L., Lubrano, M., & Richard, J.-F. (2003). *Bayesian inference in dynamic econometric models*. Oxford, UK: Oxford University Press.

Berger, J. (2006). The case for objective Bayesian analysis. *Bayesian Analysis, 3,* 385–402.

Bernardo, J. M. (1979). Reference posterior distributions for Bayesian inference (with discussion). *Journal of the Royal Statistical Society, Series B, 41,* 113–147.

Bernardo, J. M., & Smith, A. F. M. (2000). *Bayesian theory*. New York: Wiley.

Box, G., & Tiao, G. (1973). *Bayesian inference in statistical analysis*. New York: Addison-Wesley.

Brooks, S. P., & Gelman, A. (1998). General methods for monitoring convergence of iterative simulations. *Journal of Computational and Graphical Statistics, 7,* 434–455.

Burstein, L. (1980). The analysis of multilevel data in educational research and evaluation. *Review of Research in Education, 8,* 158–233.

Clogg, C. C. (1995). Latent class models. In G. Arminger, C. C. Clogg, & M. E. Sobel (Eds.), *Handbook of statistical modeling in the social and behavioral sciences* (pp. 81–110). San Francisco: Jossey-Bass.

Cohen, J. (1994). The earth is round (p < .05). *American Psychologist, 49,* 997–1003.

Dawid, A. P. (1982). The well-calibrated Bayesian. *Journal of the American Statistical Association, 77,* 605–610.

de Finetti, B. (1974). *Theory of probability* (Vols. 1 and 2). New York: Wiley.

Dempster, A. P., Laird, N. M., & Rubin, D. B. (1977). Maximum likelihood from incomplete data via the em algorithm (with discussion). *Journal of the Royal Statistical Society, Series B, 39,* 1–38.

Edwards, A. W. F. (1992). *Likelihood*. Baltimore: Johns Hopkins University Press.

Efron, B. (1979). Bootstrap methods: Another look at the jacknife. *Annals of Statistics, 7,* 1–26.

Enders, C. K. (2010). *Applied missing data analysis.* New York: Guilford Press.

Evans, M., Hastings, N. A. J., & Peacock, J. B. (2000). *Statistical distributions* (3rd ed.). New York: Wiley.

Everitt, B. S. (1984). *An introduction to latent variable models.* New York: Chapman and Hall.

Everitt, B. S., & Hothorn, T. (2012). *Mva: An introduction to applied multivariate analysis with r* [Computer software manual]. Available from *http://CRAN.R-project.org/package=MVA* (R package version 1.0-3).

Fishburn, P. C. (1986). The axioms of subjective probability. *Statistical Science, 1,* 335–345.

Fox, J. (2008). *Applied regression analysis and generalized linear models* (2nd ed.). Newbury Park, CA: Sage.

Gelman, A. (1996). Inference and monitoring convergence. In W. R. Gilks, S. Richardson, & D. J. Spiegelhalter (Eds.), *Markov chain Monte Carlo in practice* (pp. 131–143). New York: Chapman and Hall.

Gelman, A. (2013). Two simple examples for understanding posterior p-values whose distributions are far from uniform. *Electronic Journal of Statistics, 7,* 2595–2602.

Gelman, A., Carlin, J. B., Stern, H. S., & Rubin, D. B. (2003). *Bayesian data analysis* (2nd ed.). London: Chapman and Hall.

Gelman, A., & Hill, J. (2003). *Data analysis using regression and multilevel/hierarchical models.* Cambridge, UK: Cambridge University Press.

Gelman, A., & Rubin, D. B. (1992a). Inference from iterative simulation using multiple sequences. *Statistical Science, 7,* 457–511.

Gelman, A., & Rubin, D. B. (1992b). A single series from the Gibbs sampler provides a false sense of security. In J. M. Bernardo, J. O. Berger, A. P. Dawid, & A. F. M. Smith (Eds.), *Bayesian statistics 4* (pp. 625–631). Oxford, UK: Oxford University Press.

Gelman, A., & Shalizi, C. R. (2013). Philosophy and the practice of Bayesian statistics. *British Journal of Mathematical and Statistical Psychology, 66,* 8–38.

Geman, S., & Geman, D. (1984). Stochastic relaxation, Gibbs distributions and the Bayesian restoration of images. *IEEE Transactions on Pattern Analysis and Machine Intelligence, 6,* 721–741.

Geweke, J. (1992). Evaluating the accuracy of sampling-based approaches to calculating posterior moments. In J. M. Bernardo, J. O. Berger, A. P. Dawid, & A. F. M. Smith (Eds.), *Bayesian statistics 4* (pp. 169–193). Oxford, UK: Oxford University Press.

Gigerenzer, G. (1993). The superego, ego, and the id in statistical reasoning. In G. Keren & C. Lewis (Eds.), *A handbook for data analysis in the behavioral sciences: Methodological issues* (pp. 311–339). Hillsdale, NJ: Erlbaum.

Gigerenzer, G., Krauss, S., & Vitouch, O. (2004). The null ritual: What you always wanted to know about significance testing but were afraid to ask. In D. Kaplan (Ed.), *The Sage handbook of quantitative methodology for the social sciences* (pp. 391–408). Thousand Oaks, CA: Sage.

Gilks, W. R., Richardson, S., & Spiegelhalter, D. J. (1996a). Introducing Markov chain Monte Carlo. In W. R. Gilks, S. Richardson, & D. J. Spiegelhalter (Eds.), *Markov chain Monte Carlo in practice* (pp. 1–19). London: Chapman and Hall.

Gilks, W. R., Richardson, S., & Spiegelhalter, D. J. (Eds.). (1996b). *Markov chain Monte Carlo in practice*. London: Chapman and Hall.

Gill, J. (2002). *Bayesian methods: A social and behavioral sciences approach*. London: Chapman and Hall/CRC Press.

Goldstein, H. (2011). *Multilevel statistical models* (4th ed.). Hoboken, NJ: Wiley.

Goldstein, H., & McDonald, R. P. (1988). A general model for the analysis of multilevel data. *Psychometrika, 53,* 455–467.

Harlow, L. L., Mulaik, S. A., & Steiger, J. H. (1997). *What if there were no significance tests?* Mahwah, NJ: Erlbaum.

Heidelberger, P., & Welch, P. (1983). Simulation run length control in the presence of an initial transient. *Operations Research, 31,* 1109–1144.

Hoeting, J. A., Madigan, D., Raftery, A. E., & Volinsky, C. T. (1999). Bayesian model averaging: A tutorial. *Statistical Science, 14,* 382–417.

Hoeting, J. A., Raftery, A. E., & Madigan, D. (1996). A method for simultaneous variable selection and outlier identification in linear regression. *Computational Statistics and Data Analysis, 22,* 251–270.

Honaker, J., & King, G. (2010). What to do about missing values in time-series cross-section data. *American Journal of Political Science, 54,* 561–581.

Honaker, J., King, G., & Blackwell, M. (2011). Amelia II: A program for missing data. *Journal of Statistical Software, 45*(7), 1–47. Available at *www.jstatsoft.org/v45/i07.*

Howson, C., & Urbach, P. (2006). *Scientific reasoning: The Bayesian approach*. Chicago: Open Court.

Jackman, S. (2009). *Bayesian analysis for the social sciences*. Hoboken, NJ: Wiley.

Jackman, S. (2012). *pscl: Classes and methods for R developed in the political science computational laboratory* [Computer software manual]. Available from *http://pscl.stanford.edu.*

Jaynes, E. T. (1968). Prior probabilities. *IEEE Transactions of System Science and Cybernetics, 3,* 227–241.

Jeffreys, H. (1961). *Theory of probability* (3rd ed.). New York: Oxford University Press.

Jo, B., & Muthén, B. (2001). Modeling of intervention effects with non-compliance: A latent variable modeling approach for randomized trials.

In G. A. Marcoulides & R. E. Schumacker (Eds.), *New developments and techniques in structural equation modeling* (pp. 57–87). Mahwah, NJ: Erlbaum.

Jöreskog, K. G. (1967). Some contributions to maximum likelihood factor analysis. *Psychometrika, 32,* 443–482.

Jöreskog, K. G. (1973). A general method for estimating a linear structural equation system. In A. S. Goldberger & O. D. Duncan (Eds.), *Structural equation models in the social sciences* (pp. 85–112). New York: Academic Press.

Jöreskog, K. G. (1977). Structural equation models in the social sciences: Specification, estimation and testing. In P. R. Krishnaiah (Ed.), *Applications of statistics* (pp. 265–287). Amsterdam: North-Holland.

Kadane, J. B. (2011). *Principles of uncertainty.* Boca Raton, FL: Chapman and Hall/CRC Press.

Kaplan, D. (1995). The impact of BIB spiraling-induced missing data patterns on goodness-of-fit tests in factor analysis. *Journal of Educational and Behavioral Statistics, 20,* 69–82.

Kaplan, D. (2003). Methodological advances in the analysis of individual growth with relevance to education policy. *Peabody Journal of Education, 77,* 189–215.

Kaplan, D. (2009). *Structural equation modeling: Foundations and extensions* (2nd ed.). Newbury Park, CA: Sage.

Kaplan, D., & Depaoli, S. (2012a). Bayesian statistical methods. In T. D. Little (Ed.), *Oxford handbook of quantitative methods* (pp. 407–437). Oxford, UK: Oxford University Press.

Kaplan, D., & Depaoli, S. (2012b). Bayesian structural equation modeling. In R. H. Hoyle (Ed.), *Handbook of structural equation modeling* (pp. 650–673). New York: Guilford Press.

Kaplan, D., & Elliott, P. R. (1997a). A model-based approach to validating education indicators using multilevel structural equation modeling. *Journal of Educational and Behavioral Statistics, 22,* 323–348.

Kaplan, D., & Elliott, P. R. (1997b). A didactic example of multilevel structural equation modeling applicable to the study of organizations. *Structural Equation Modeling: A Multidisciplinary Quarterly, 4,* 1–24.

Kaplan, D., Kim, J.-S., & Kim, S.-Y. (2009). Multilevel latent variable modeling: Current research and recent developments. In R. E. Millsap & A. Maydeu-Olivares (Eds.), *The SAGE handbook of quantitative methods in psychology* (pp. 592–612). Newbury Park, CA: Sage.

Kaplan, D., & Kreisman, M. B. (2000). On the validation of indicators of mathematics education using TIMSS: An application of multilevel covariance structure modeling. *International Journal of Educational Policy, Research, and Practice, 1,* 217–242.

Kaplan, D., & McCarty, A. T. (2013). Data fusion with international large scale assessments: A case study using the OECD PISA and TALIS surveys. *Large-Scale Assessments in Education, 1:6.* Available at *www.large scaleassessmentsineducation.com/content/1/1/6.*

Kaplan, D., & Park, S. (2014). Analyzing international large-scale assessment data within a Bayesian framework. In L. Rutkowski, M. von Davier, & D. Rutkowski (Eds.), *Handbook of internal large-scale assessment: Background, technical issues, and methods of data analysis* (pp. 547–581). Boca Raton, FL: CRC Press.

Kaplan, D., & Wenger, R. N. (1993). Asymptotic independence and separability in covariance structure models: Implications for specification error, power, and model modification. *Multivariate Behavioral Research, 28,* 483–498.

Kass, R. E., & Raftery, A. E. (1995). Bayes factors. *Journal of the American Statistical Association, 90,* 773–795.

Kass, R. E., & Wasserman, L. (1996). The selection of prior distributions by formal rules. *Journal of the American Statistical Association, 91,* 1343–1370.

Kim, J.-S., & Bolt, D. M. (2007). Estimating item response theory models using Markov chain Monte Carlo methods. *Educational Measurement: Issues and Practice, 26,* 38–51.

Koller-Meinfelder, F. (2009). *Analysis of incomplete survey data—multiple imputation via Bayesian bootstrap predictive mean matching.* PhD thesis, University of Bamburg.

Kolmogorov, A. N. (1956). *Foundations of the theory of probability* (2nd ed.). New York: Chelsea.

Lancaster, T. (2004). *An introduction to modern Bayesian econometrics.* Malden, MA: Blackwell.

Laplace, P.-S. (1774/1951). *Essai philosophique sur les probabilités.* New York: Dover.

Lawley, D. N., & Maxwell, A. E. (1971). *Factor analysis as a statistical method.* London: Butterworth.

Leamer, E. E. (1978). *Specification searches: Ad hoc inference with nonexperimental data.* New York: Wiley.

Leamer, E. E. (1983). Model choice and specification analysis. In Z. Griliches & M. Intriligator (Eds.), *Handbook of econometrics* (Vol. 1, pp. 285–330). Amsterdam: North-Holland.

Lee, S.-Y. (1981). A Bayesian approach to confirmatory factor analysis. *Psychometrika, 46,* 153–160.

Lee, S.-Y. (2007). *Structural equation modeling: A Bayesian approach.* Hoboken, NJ: Wiley.

Ligges, U., & Mächler, M. (2003). Scatterplot3d—an R package for visualizing multivariate data. *Journal of Statistical Software, 8*(11), 1–20. Available at *www.jstatsoft.org.*

Lindley, D. V. (2007). *Understanding uncertainty.* Hoboken, NJ: Wiley.

Little, R. J. A., & Rubin, D. B. (2002). *Statistical analysis with missing data* (2nd. ed.). Hoboken, NJ: Wiley.

Lunn, D., Thomas, A., Best, N., & Spiegelhalter, D. (2000). Winbugs—a Bayesian modelling framework: Concepts, structure, and extensibility. *Statistics and Computing, 10,* 325–337.

Lynch, S. M. (2007). *Introduction to applied Bayesian statistics and estimation for social scientists.* New York: Springer.

Madigan, D., & Raftery, A. E. (1994). Model selection and accounting for model uncertainty in graphical models using Occam's window. *Journal of the American Statistical Association, 89,* 1535–1546.

Madigan, D., & York, J. (1995). Bayesian graphical models for discrete data. *International Statistical Review, 63,* 215–232.

Martin, A. D., Quinn, K. M., & Park, J. H. (2010, May 10). *Markov chain Monte Carlo (MCMC) package.* Available at *http://mcmcpack.wustl.edu.*

Martin, J. K., & McDonald, R. P. (1975). Bayesian estimation in unrestricted factor analysis: A treatment for Heywood cases. *Psychometrika, 40,* 505–517.

Matsueda, R. L. (2012). Key advances in the history of structural equation modeling. In R. H. Hoyle (Ed.), *Handbook of structural equation modeling* (pp. 17–43). New York: Guilford Press.

McCullagh, P., & Nelder, J. A. (1989). *Generalized linear models* (2nd ed., 17–42). Chapman and Hall/CRC Press.

McDonald, R. P. (1993). A general model for two-level data with responses missing at random. *Psychometrika, 58,* 575–585.

McDonald, R. P., & Goldstein, H. (1989). Balanced versus unbalanced designs for linear structural relations in two-level data. *British Journal of Mathematical and Statistical Psychology, 42,* 215–232.

McLachlan, G., & Krishnan, T. (1997). *The em algorithm and extensions.* New York: Wiley.

McLachlan, G., & Peel, D. (2000). *Finite mixture models.* New York: Wiley.

Meinfelder, F. (2011). *BaBooN: Bayesian bootstrap predictive mean matching—multiple and single imputation for discrete data* [Computer software manual]. Available from *http://CRAN.R-project.org/package=BaBooN* (R package version 2.14.0).

Mengersen, K. L., Robery, C. P., & Guihenneuc-Jouyax, C. (1999). MCMC convergence diagnostics: A review. *Bayesian Statistics, 6,* 415–440.

Metropolis, N., Rosenbluth, A. W., Rosenbluth, M. N., Teller, A. H., & Teller, E. (1953). Equations of state calculations by fast computing machines. *Journal of Chemical Physics, 21,* 1087–1091.

Miller, J. D., Hoffer, T., Sucher, R. W., Brown, K. G., & Nelson, C. (1992). *LSAY codebook: Student, parent, and teacher data for 1992 cohort two for longitudinal years one through four (1987–1991).* DeKalb, IL: Northern Illinois University.

Muthén, B. (1989). Latent variable modeling in heterogenous populations. *Psychometrika, 54,* 557–585.

Muthén, B. (2001). Second-generation structural equation modeling with a combination of categorical and continuous latent variables: New opportunities for latent class/latent growth modeling. In A. Sayer & L. Collins (Eds.), *New methods for the analysis of change* (pp. 291–322). Washington, DC: American Psychological Association.

Muthén, B., & Asparouhov, T. (2012). Bayesian SEM: A more flexible representation of substantive theory. *Psychological Methods, 17,* 313–335.

Muthén, B., & Masyn, K. (2005). Mixture discrete-time survival analysis. *Journal of Educational and Behavioral Statistics, 30,* 27–58.

Muthén, B., & Satorra, A. (1989). Multilevel aspects of varying parameters in structural models. In R. D. Bock (Ed.), *Multilevel analysis of educational data.* San Diego: Academic Press.

Muthén, L. K., & Muthén, B. (1998–2012). *Mplus users guide* (7th ed.). Los Angeles: Author.

Organisation for Economic Co-operation and Development. (2004). *The PISA 2003 assessment framework: Mathematics, reading, science, and problem solving knowledge and skills.* Paris: Author.

Organisation for Economic Co-operation and Development. (2010). *PISA 2009 results* (Vols. I–VI). Paris: Author.

Organisation for Economic Co-operation and Development. (2012). *PISA 2009. Technical report.* Paris: Author.

Pinheiro, J. C., & Bates, D. M. (2000). *Mixed-effects models in S and S-PLUS.* New York: Springer.

Plummer, M. (2003). JAGS: A program for analysis of Bayesian graphical models using Gibbs sampling. In K. Hornik, F. Leisch, & A. Zeileis (Eds.), *Proceedings of the 3rd international workshop on distributed statistical computing (dsc 2003).* Vienna, Austria.

Plummer, M. (2011). rjags: *Bayesian graphical models using MCMC* [Computer software manual]. Available from *http://CRAN.R-project.org/package=rjags* (R package version 3-5).

Plummer, M., Best, N., Cowles, K., & Vines, K. (2006). CODA: Convergence diagnosis and output analysis for MCMC. *R News, 6,* 7–11. Available from *http://CRAN.R-project.org/doc/Rnews.*

Popper, K. (1934/1959). *The logic of scientific discovery.* New York: Routledge.

Press, S. J. (2003). *Subjective and objective Bayesian statistics: Principles, models, and applications* (2nd ed.). Hoboken, NJ: Wiley.

R Development Core Team. (2012). *R: A language and environment for statistical computing* [Computer software manual]. Vienna, Austria. Available from *http://www.R-project.org.*

Raftery, A. E. (1995). Bayesian model selection in social research (with discussion). In P. V. Marsden (Ed.), *Sociological methodology* (Vol. 25, pp. 111–196). New York: Blackwell.

Raftery, A. E., Hoeting, J., Volinsky, C., Painter, I., & Yeung, K. Y. (2009, September 18). *Bayesian model averaging (BMA), version 3.12.* Available at *www2.research.att.com/~volinsky/bma.html.*

Raftery, A. E., & Lewis, S. M. (1992). How many iterations in the Gibbs sampler? In J. M. Bernardo, J. O. Berger, A. P. Dawid, & A. F. M. Smith

(Eds.), *Bayesian statistics 4* (pp. 763–773). Oxford, UK: Oxford University Press.

Raftery, A. E., & Lewis, S. M. (1996). Implementing MCMC. In W. R. Gilks, S. Richardson, & D. J. Spiegelhalter (Eds.), *Markov chain Monte Carlo in practice* (pp. 115–130). New York: Chapman and Hall.

Raftery, A. E., Madigan, D., & Hoeting, J. A. (1997). Bayesian model averaging for linear regression models. *Journal of the American Statistical Association, 92,* 179–191.

Ramsey, F. P. (1926). Truth and probability. In *The foundations of mathematics and other logical essays.* New York: Humanities Press.

Rässler, S. (2002). *Statistical matching: A frequentist theory, practical applications, and alternative Bayesian approaches.* New York: Springer.

Raudenbush, S. W., & Bryk, A. S. (2002). *Hierarchical linear models: Applications and data analysis methods* (2nd ed.). Thousand Oaks, CA: Sage.

Rényi, A. (1970). *Probability theory.* New York: Elsevier.

Royall, R. (1997). *Statistical evidence: A likelihood paradigm.* New York: Chapman and Hall.

Rubin, D. B. (1981). The Bayesian bootstrap. *Annals of Statistics, 9,* 130–134.

Rubin, D. B. (1986). Statistical matching using file concatenation with adjusted weights and multiple imputation. *Journal of Business and Economic Statistics, 4,* 87–95.

Rubin, D. B. (1987). *Multiple imputation in nonresponse surveys.* New York: Wiley.

Savage, L. J. (1954). *The foundations of statistics.* New York: Wiley.

Schafer, J. L. (1997). *Analysis of incomplete multivariate data.* New York: Chapman and Hall/CRC Press.

Scheines, R., Hoijtink, H., & Boomsma, A. (1999). Bayesian estimation and testing of structural equation models. *Psychometrika, 64,* 37–52.

Schmidt, W. H. (1969). *Covariance structure analysis of the multivariate random effects model.* Unpublished doctoral dissertation, University of Chicago.

Schwarz, G. E. (1978). Estimating the dimension of a model. *Annals of Statistics, 6,* 461–464.

Shafer, J. L. (2012). *norm: Analysis of multivariate normal datasets with missing values* [Computer software manual]. Available from *http://CRAN. R-project.org/package=norm* (R package version 1.0-9.4, ported to R by Alvaro A. Novo).

Silvey, S. D. (1975). *Statistical inference.* Boca Raton, FL: CRC Press.

Sinharay, S. (2004). Experiences with Markov chain Monte Carlo convergence assessment in two psychometric examples. *Journal of Educational and Behavioral Statistics, 29,* 461–488.

Smith, B. J. (2005, March 23). *Bayesian Output Analysis program (BOA), version 1.1.5.* Available at *www.public-health.uiowa.edu/boa.*

Song, X.-Y., & Lee, S.-Y. (2012). *Basic and advanced Bayesian structural equation modeling: With applications in the medical and behavioral sciences*. Hoboken, NJ: Wiley.

Sörbom, D. (1974). A general method for studying differences in factor means and factor structure between groups. *British Journal of Mathematical and Statistical Psychology, 27,* 229–239.

Spiegelhalter, D. J., Best, N. G., Carlin, B. P., & van der Linde, A. (2002). Bayesian measures of model complexity and fit (with discussion). *Journal of the Royal Statistical Society, Series B (Statistical Methodology), 64,* 583–639.

Spiegelhalter, D., Thomas, A., Best, N., & Lunn, D. (2003). *WinBUGS version 1.4 user manual* [Computer software manual]. Available from *www.mrc-bsu.cam.ac.uk/bugs.*

Stigler, S. M. (1988). *The history of statistics*. Cambridge, MA: Harvard University Press.

Su, Y.-S., Gelman, A., Hill, J., & Yajima, M. (2011). Multiple imputation with diagnostics (mi) in R: Opening windows into the black box. *Journal of Statistical Software, 45*(2), 1–31. Available at *www.jstatsoft.org/v45/i02.*

Suppes, P. (1986). Comment on Fishburn, 1986. *Statistical Science, 1,* 347–350.

Tanner, M. H., & Wong, W. A. (1987). The calculation of posterior distributions by data augmentation (with discussion). *Journal of the American Statistical Association, 82,* 528–550.

Tierney, L., & Kadane, J. B. (1986). Accurate approximations for posterior moments and marginal densities. *Journal of the American Statistical Association, 81,* 82–86.

van Buuren, S. (2012). *Flexible imputation of missing data*. New York: Chapman and Hall.

Wagenmakers, E., Lee, M., Lodewyckx, T., & Iverson, G. (2008). Bayesian versus frequentist inference. In H. Hoijtink, I. Klugkist, & P. A. Boelen (Eds.), *Bayesian evaluation of informative hypotheses* (pp. 181–207). New York: Springer.

Willett, J. B., & Sayer, A. G. (1994). Using covariance structure analysis to detect correlates and predictors of individual change over time. *Psychological Bulletin, 116,* 363–381.

Zellner, A. (1977). Maximal data information prior distributions. In A. Aykac & C. Brumat (Eds.), *New developments in the applications of Bayesian methods* (pp. 201–215). Amsterdam: North-Holland.

Author Index

Subject Index

About the Author

David Kaplan, PhD, is Professor of Quantitative Methods in the Department of Educational Psychology at the University of Wisconsin–Madison and holds affiliate appointments in the Department of Population Health Sciences and the Center for Demography and Ecology. Dr. Kaplan's program of research focuses on the development of Bayesian statistical methods for education research. His work on these topics is directed toward application to quasi-experimental and large-scale cross-sectional and longitudinal survey designs. He is most actively involved in the Program for International Student Assessment, sponsored by the Organisation for Economic Co-operation and Development—he served on its Technical Advisory Group from 2005 to 2009 and currently serves as Chair of its Questionnaire Expert Group. Dr. Kaplan also is a member of the Questionnaire Standing Committee of the U.S. National Assessment of Educational Progress, is a Fellow of the American Psychological Association (Division 5), and was a Jeanne Griffith Fellow at the National Center for Education Statistics.